Survival Guide for Early Career Researchers

Dominika Kwasnicka • Alden Yuanhong Lai
Editors

Survival Guide for Early Career Researchers

 Springer

Editors
Dominika Kwasnicka
SWPS University of Social Sciences
and Humanities
Wrocław, Poland

NHMRC CRE in Digital Technology
to Transform Chronic Disease Outcomes
Melbourne, VIC, Australia

School of Population and Global Health
University of Melbourne
Melbourne, VIC, Australia

Alden Yuanhong Lai
School of Global Public Health
and Stern School of Business
New York University
New York, NY, USA

ISBN 978-3-031-10756-6   ISBN 978-3-031-10754-2 (eBook)
https://doi.org/10.1007/978-3-031-10754-2

© The Editor(s) (if applicable) and The Author(s), under exclusive license to Springer Nature Switzerland AG 2022
This work is subject to copyright. All rights are solely and exclusively licensed by the Publisher, whether the whole or part of the material is concerned, specifically the rights of translation, reprinting, reuse of illustrations, recitation, broadcasting, reproduction on microfilms or in any other physical way, and transmission or information storage and retrieval, electronic adaptation, computer software, or by similar or dissimilar methodology now known or hereafter developed.
The use of general descriptive names, registered names, trademarks, service marks, etc. in this publication does not imply, even in the absence of a specific statement, that such names are exempt from the relevant protective laws and regulations and therefore free for general use.
The publisher, the authors, and the editors are safe to assume that the advice and information in this book are believed to be true and accurate at the date of publication. Neither the publisher nor the authors or the editors give a warranty, expressed or implied, with respect to the material contained herein or for any errors or omissions that may have been made. The publisher remains neutral with regard to jurisdictional claims in published maps and institutional affiliations.

This Springer imprint is published by the registered company Springer Nature Switzerland AG
The registered company address is: Gewerbestrasse 11, 6330 Cham, Switzerland

We would like to dedicate this book to our mentors and peers – past, current and future ones. Thank you for making the effort to guide and support us through our research careers.

Foreword by Barr Taylor

Survival Guide for Early Career Researchers is an incredible resource to help early career researchers (ECRs) not only survive but also thrive as they navigate the many issues and opportunities on their way to becoming independent scientists within or outside of academia.

The chapters cover many of the essential skills, for example, applying for grants and writing articles, and address many issues that are often overlooked in one's career. For instance, over the past several years, I have led a series titled *Superstar Psychologists in Technology* that featured ECRs who have taken leadership positions in industry. When asked, "what would you like to have had more training in?", a common answer was "project and team management" – issues nicely covered in this book. Another common response was "dealing with the media and presenting ideas" – also areas wonderfully described in several other chapters. Rejection is a fundamental aspect of an academic career, and I loved that the editors also included a chapter on how to deal with it.

ECRs are often reluctant to promote their work and advocate for their careers; however, both skills are central to academic success, and I applaud the editors for including chapters that address these issues. Like the author notes in Chap. 8, support from colleagues through networking can bolster these important skills, and other chapters discuss innovative ways to do so.

Every ECR also faces the challenge of undertaking multiple competing efforts and the strain put on family, friends and self. I applaud the editors for including a chapter that stresses the importance of self-care and maintaining a healthy work-life balance and another that focuses on rest and recovery following periods of intense work. These issues can be more challenging than writing a grant and often they are much more important.

ECRs are often so immersed in their work that they may not consider how their findings will be implemented, and one of the chapters nicely covers how to do science with implementation in mind.

Currently, we have a crisis which is the underrepresentation of women in science. Another chapter deals with the unique challenges women in science face and provides strategies for building one's career. Institutions must do better at supporting women in science, and ECRs need to be careful not to blame themselves for a problem that is built into many academic environments. The discussions on the nearly universal *Imposter Syndrome*, how to overcome it and how to advocate for oneself are such important issues for ECRs to consider, and I am glad that authors also covered them.

Over my career, I have had the fortune to mentor many ECRs, and I wish this resource had been available for them along the way. I would have recommended they read through it carefully once and continue to turn back to it often as their journey continues. Furthermore, those of us who are mentors and supervisors should read it as well because the ideas and issues discussed can help us do our job better. Thank you, Dom and Alden and the authors, for providing this wonderful resource.

Professor (emeritus) of Psychiatry, Barr Taylor
Stanford Medical Center, Stanford University,
Research Professor and Director of the Center for m2Health
Palo Alto University, Palo Alto, CA, USA

Foreword by Rita McMorrow

As I started my journey as an early career researcher, the world of research was unfamiliar to me as a clinician. I was encouraged by a fellow academic general practitioner to take on a leadership role to develop a program for early career primary care researchers. Here, I learned the value of peer-support, as my peers generously shared their own experiences of navigating academia and new challenges. I recognise not all early career researchers have access to suitable peer support, this book provides a game plan for almost all scenarios early career researchers will face. I have faced many of the scenarios discussed in the chapters of this book, and while I picked up tips along the way, this book brings together the shared wisdom of early career researchers from around the world.

Being both a clinician during a pandemic and an early career researcher, finding the right balance has been challenging for me. It was refreshing to read that the journey to find balance is common amongst my peers. Practical suggestions for creating balance include evaluating my values (Chap. 6) and knowing my 'why' (Chap. 19), before considering the added value of new projects (Chap. 5) and new grants (Chap. 11). This book highlighted parts of research that I want to explore further, including open science and even creating my first #BetterPoster. Having started my early research career during the pandemic, I am looking forward to applying the advice of openness and enjoyment to my next (hopefully in-person) networking opportunity. The chapter on dealing with article rejection has already helped me apply a more critical viewpoint to peer-reviews of my work.

While this book can be read from start to finish, it can also be picked up when support is needed, like an encyclopedia for early career researchers. Have an upcoming media interview? Maybe you are considering a role at a not-for-profit? Want to maximise your research impact? There are chapters for each with sound advice and further reading. Each chapter author shares their personal experiences as an early career researcher, with the guiding principle of peer-support spread across each chapter, like a shared conversation over coffee. The authors' vulnerability, when sharing their challenges, provides welcome support to the early career researcher, just as my peers did when I started my research journey.

General Practitioner, PhD Candidate and Research Fellow,   Rita McMorrow
The Department of General Practice
The University of Melbourne, Melbourne, VIC, Australia

Contents

1 Introduction: A Practical Guide on How to Survive and Thrive as an Early Career Researcher 1
Dominika Kwasnicka and Alden Yuanhong Lai

Part I It's All About You!

2 Setting Up for a Thriving Career: Assessing Your Scholarly Identity and Institutional Environment 13
Alden Yuanhong Lai

3 Developing and Maintaining Healthy Work–Life Balance for Early Career Researchers 27
Lauren A. Fowler

4 Work Hard, Snore Hard: Recovery from Work for Early Career Researchers 41
Eka Gatari, Bram Fleuren, and Alden Yuanhong Lai

5 Achieving Balance Between Research, Teaching, and Service at Work 53
Jorinde E. Spook and Sanne Raghoebar

6 Climbing the Invisible Ladder: Advancing Your Career as a Woman in Science 63
Laura Desveaux

Part II Research Skills and Competencies

7 Managing Research Projects 75
Anne van Dongen

8 Networking and Collaborating in Academia: Increasing Your Scientific Impact and Having Fun in the Process 89
Elaine Toomey

9　Accelerating Your Research Career with Open Science 99
　　Emma Norris

10　Being Agile: Honing New Skills and Fostering Curiosity
　　for Increased Scientific Impact 109
　　Olga Perski

11　To Come, to See, to Conquer: Practical Pointers in Applying
　　for Funding and Securing Your Initial Grants................... 119
　　Daan Westra and Bram Fleuren

Part III Research Dissemination

12　Being an Effective Writer..................................... 133
　　Sarah Krull Abe

13　Dealing with Rejection: Critical Thinking, Constructive
　　Feedback, and Criticism in the Peer-Review Process 143
　　Kim M. Caudwell

14　Presenting and Speaking About Your Work...................... 155
　　Silja-Riin Voolma

15　Engaging with the Press and Media 169
　　Nikki Stamp

16　Make Your Science Go Viral: How to Maximize the Impact
　　of Your Research 179
　　Mike Morrison and Kelsey Merlo

Part IV Research Outside of Academia

17　Exploring the Horizon: Navigating Research Careers
　　Outside of Academia... 195
　　Rachel Carey

18　An Alternative Career Path: Research and Evaluation
　　in the Health Service and Not-for-Profit Sectors 207
　　Jenny Olson

19　Asking Why and Saying Yes: How to Make Career
　　Decisions Strategically 219
　　Amy Hai Yan Chan

20　How to Engage the Public in Research 229
　　Rebecca Pedruzzi and Anne McKenzie

21	**Thinking Like an Implementation Scientist and Applying Your Research in Practice**	241
	Andrea K. Graham	
22	**Final Thoughts: A Fulfilling Scholarly Career**.................	253
	Dominika Kwasnicka and Alden Yuanhong Lai	

Index... 259

About the Editors and Contributors

Editors

Dominika Kwasnicka, MA, MSc, PhD, is a senior research fellow at the University of Melbourne, Australia, and SWPS University, Poland. She is the director of Open Digital Health and head editor of *Practical Health Psychology*. Her goal is to make the research world a fair and inclusive space where diversity, creativity and innovation thrive.

Alden Yuanhong Lai, PhD, MPH, is assistant professor at New York University and executive advisor to the Wellbeing for Planet Earth Foundation. He studies how to improve the jobs and working environments of healthcare workers, and seeks to apply his research on employee wellbeing to his own academic life.

Contributors

Sarah Krull Abe, PhD, MScPH, is a section head in the Division of Prevention at the National Cancer Center Japan and holds a PhD in international health. Her research focus is cancer, nutrition and social epidemiology. She enjoys pursuing fieldwork on the health benefits of green tea.

Rachel Carey, PhD, is chief scientist at Zinc, where she supports start-up founders to create new, scalable and evidence-based innovations. Rachel is a behavioural scientist with a particular interest in ways to connect scientific research with product innovation, in order to mobilise change towards better health and healthcare.

Kim M. Caudwell, PhD, is Lecturer in Psychology at Charles Darwin University, and course coordinator for the honours programme within the discipline of psychology. His research focus is health psychology, where he looks at the social cognitive and motivational factors that influence various pro-health and health risk behaviours.

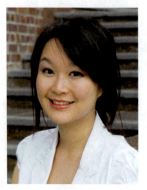

Amy Hai Yan Chan, PhD, is a senior clinical research fellow at the University of Auckland, NZ, and holds an honorary post at UCL and Asthma UK Centre of Applied Research. She is passionate about exploring factors that influence medication adherence, with interests in behavioural medicine and big data.

About the Editors and Contributors

Laura Desveaux, PhD, PT, is the scientific director of the Institute for Better Health at Trillium Health Partners and the lead for the Learning Health System Portfolio. She is also the founder and executive director of Women Who Lead. Her career and research focus on closing the gap between current performance and what science and experience tell us is possible.

Bram Fleuren, PhD, is Assistant Professor of Work and Organisational Psychology at Maastricht University, the Netherlands. His research focuses on sustainable employability, which encompasses the dynamic relationships between work and human functioning, work-induced fatigue and recovery, occupational health and well-being, inclusion, and psychometrics.

Lauren A. Fowler, PhD, is an instructor of psychiatry at Washington University in St. Louis. Her research focuses on understanding the multi-level influences (e.g., social, cognitive, organisational and policy) on health behaviours to promote health equity among historically marginalised groups, including individuals with diverse sexual orientations and gender identities.

Eka Gatari, MPsi, Psikolog, is a lecturer and member of the Leadership, Decent Work, and Diversity research group at Universitas Indonesia. She is also a PhD student at Maastricht University, funded by Indonesia's Ministry of Education, Culture, Research, and Technology. She mainly studies recovery from work and fatigue accumulation.

Andrea K. Graham, PhD, is an assistant professor in the Center for Behavioral Intervention Technologies in the Feinberg School of Medicine at Northwestern University, with an affiliation in the Center for Human-Computer Interaction + Design. Her programme of research focuses on the design, optimisation and implementation of digital health interventions.

Kelsey Merlo, PhD, is Assistant Professor of Psychology at the University of South Florida and a member of the Sunshine Education Research Center. She researches health and well-being issues within organisations.

Anne McKenzie (Telethon Kids Institute) has worked as a consumer advocate for three decades. She has worked alongside communities to increase the community voice in research, developing engagement programmes and training workshops, and facilitating priority setting projects. Anne has received several national awards for her advocacy work in research.

Mike Morrison, PhD, is a research psychologist and user experience designer at Researchable, a start-up aiming to provide quick, evidence-based answers to any question. The originator of the #betterposter movement, Mike's lifelong quest is to help bring UX design principles to science to speed up discovery.

About the Editors and Contributors xix

Jenny Olson, PhD, is a postdoctoral researcher at Penn State. She has expertise in health psychology and behavioural science, and her research focuses on the health behaviours of older adults with chronic conditions. She is passionate about reducing health disparities.

Emma Norris, PhD, is a lecturer at Brunel University London (UK) and co-chair of the European Health Psychology Society's Open Science Special Interest Group. She researches behaviour change and health psychology, exploring evidence synthesis of behaviour change interventions and development of interventions to improve health and increase open science in researchers.

Rebecca Pedruzzi, PhD, is a behavioural scientist at Telethon Kids Institute in Perth, Western Australia. Her research aims to understand the socio-ecological underpinnings of good health for pregnant women and families. Working with diverse Australian communities, Rebecca applies these insights to real-world programmes for improved and equitable health outcomes.

Olga Perski, PhD, is a senior research fellow in the Department of Behavioural Science and Health at University College London (UK). Her work is interdisciplinary in scope, drawing on theory and methods from behavioural science and human-computer interaction to develop, optimise and evaluate digital interventions for smoking cessation and alcohol reduction.

Sanne Raghoebar, PhD, is a postdoctoral researcher at both the Consumption and Healthy Lifestyles Group and the Education and Learning Sciences Group at Wageningen University and Research, the Netherlands. Her research mainly focuses on understanding the socio-ecological influences on our eating behaviour to stimulate healthy and sustainable dietary decisions.

Jorinde E. Spook, PhD, is an assistant professor at the University of Twente, the Netherlands. Her main, multidisciplinary research focuses on early mobilisation interventions for (paediatric) intensive care patients by means of gamified therapy.

Nikki Stamp, MB, FRACS, is a cardiothoracic surgeon, author and TV presenter. She is part of a number of research projects and is a PhD candidate, studying women's heart disease. She is also a teacher of medical students and surgical trainees. She writes books and hates bad health advice.

Elaine Toomey, PhD, is a lecturer at the University of Limerick (Ireland) and a Health Research Board Fellow. Her work seeks to maximise the impact of interdisciplinary health research for all end users through conducting methodological research, focusing on the implementation of research into health policy and practice, and using behavioural science.

Anne van Dongen, PhD, is an assistant professor and lecturer at the University of Twente, the Netherlands. Their multidisciplinary research focuses on development, evaluation, and implementation of (digital) behaviour change interventions and equity in healthcare, through collaboration and open science.

Silja-Riin Voolma, PhD, is the founder and CEO of Behavioral Design Global, a research and consulting agency supporting industry and government organisations in designing human-centred digital health experiences informed by intersectional approaches to behavioural science and design.

Daan Westra, PhD, is Assistant Professor of Healthcare Management at Maastricht University's (the Netherlands) Care and Public Health Research Institute (CAPHRI). His research focuses on collaboration and inter-organisational networks of health and social care providers. With it, he seeks to improve healthcare delivery by bridging theory and practice.

Chapter 1
Introduction: A Practical Guide on How to Survive and Thrive as an Early Career Researcher

Dominika Kwasnicka and Alden Yuanhong Lai

Abstract Many people complete an undergraduate degree and think 'Great, I don't have to go to uni ever again!' But there are some, like us, who are interested in a career in research – we stay on at universities or research institutions to pursue graduate degrees, postdoctoral training, and eventually our first faculty research positions. We call ourselves Early Career Researchers or ECRs for short. The name implies we are still early in our careers, still training to become independent scientists, and we are not yet expected to 'know it all' compared to our senior colleagues (in theory at least). We are encouraged to experiment with our research topics and approaches, and we often experience successes and failures along the way. Our institutions may also prioritise our status as trainees allowing more flexibility around teaching or service requirements. In short, we often have a huge sandbox to play in, while we seek to establish our independent research portfolios.

Being an ECR, however, can be quite daunting as we transition from relatively structured coursework to a much more independent work schedule. We quickly realise the need to develop a range of skills such as project management, networking, and media engagement. The challenges of building and managing a research team as the lead investigator start to surface. We may be thrown into work situations that are novel to us (e.g., talking to the media, giving an industry talk). Yet, these skills are not usually taught in formal coursework to graduate students, and we may lack the means to systematically learn them in our current positions. *The Survival Guide for Early Career Researchers* aims to fill this gap.

D. Kwasnicka (✉)
SWPS University of Social Sciences and Humanities, Wrocław, Poland

NHMRC CRE in Digital Technology to Transform Chronic Disease Outcomes, Melbourne, VIC, Australia

School of Population and Global Health, University of Melbourne, Melbourne, VIC, Australia

A. Y. Lai
School of Global Public Health and Stern School of Business, New York University, New York, NY, USA

© The Author(s), under exclusive license to Springer Nature Switzerland AG 2022
D. Kwasnicka, A. Y. Lai (eds.), *Survival Guide for Early Career Researchers*, https://doi.org/10.1007/978-3-031-10754-2_1

Keywords Academia · Early Career Researchers · Research Skills · Competencies
· Research Dissemination · Science Communication · Impact · Strategy

The academic world can be difficult to navigate. So, we asked a group of our peers who have been successful in their own early research careers to provide some guidance and tips for succeeding as an ECR. We asked them to lead you through different aspects of the research career. Academia, much like any industry, has its upsides and downsides. Our aim was to provide you with candid, relatable, and actionable content that helps you think through how you will survive and thrive in the research world.

Each chapter starts with a personal story. Your peers will take you on a journey through their own experiences, such as when they dealt with particular issues or successfully developed unique skills. We are certain that many of these personal stories will resonate with you (as they did with us), given the norms of research that seem universal across countries and institutions. After sharing their personal stories, your peers will share key content to help you foster professional and personal effectiveness. This content is based on evidence from the psychological, sociological, and management sciences. Each chapter also includes actionable recommendations that you can implement in your own life. This book includes elements of story-telling and scientific thinking, and is divided into four parts.

Part I: It's All About You!

In order to be successful, you need to put yourself first and prioritise your needs – both personal and professional. We open this book with chapters that address the most important aspect of being an ECR – putting yourself in the centre and prioritising your own values and well-being. In the first part, we discuss balancing aspects of work and life, including your scholarly identity (Chap. 2), work–life balance (Chap. 3), and rest and recovery (Chap. 4). We also address the three pillars of academia: research, teaching, and service (Chap. 5), and the issue of gender equity (Chap. 6).

In Chap. 2, Alden Lai discusses the need to assess your scholarly identity and your institutional environment so that you can maximise the fit between what you need and what your workplace offers. He points out that assessing your scholarly identity requires continuous reflection about what we work on, who we work with, and the groups we belong to. In this chapter, Alden outlines what he calls 'the fundamental elements of scholarly institutional environments', namely research, funding, teaching, mentoring, service, and professional development activities. He encourages us to assess how each of these elements interacts and shapes the norms of the institution we belong to and how they impact our scholarly identity. This chapter aims to clarify how to better align our values with the institutional expectations to enjoy your work, be good at it, and thrive.

When you are early in your academic career, your research can sometimes overtake your life. For instance, you may spend much more time on your PhD than what is expected of you or what is good for your health and well-being. In Chap. 3, Lauren Fowler guides you through the crucial topic of developing and maintaining a healthy work–life balance. As Lauren points out, ECRs are often navigating demanding timelines, unconventional work schedules, and intense pressure to reach research and career milestones (e.g., competitive funding applications). This chapter provides an overview of how to achieve a healthy work–life balance for your career success and for your personal well-being. Lauren also shares a brief exercise to help you to compare how you currently divide your time between work, social, and personal commitments, and how you might ideally distribute your time. She outlines actionable strategies to help you to find what works best for you to achieve your desired work–life balance.

On the similar topic, in Chap. 4, Eka (Tari) Gatari, Bram Fleuren, and Alden Lai discuss the importance of 'resting' – taking the time to recover from work. They encourage you to 'work hard and snore hard', emphasising the importance of intentionally taking rest breaks and resting effectively. They point out that prolonged periods of intense work with limited rest periods can lead to long-term negative effects, such as fatigue and burnout. Most of us can benefit from learning to work more effectively, rather than continually working more hours. In this chapter, you will learn about the need to relax, to create mental distance from work, to be in charge of your time when off work, and to become good at things that are beyond work. These four types of experiences help you to recover from all the hard work you do, which is crucial for all ECRs. Based on research in occupational health psychology, the authors provide several practical tips on how to recover well and work in a sustainable way.

In Chap. 5, Jorinde Spook and Sanne Raghoebar guide you through the related topic of achieving balance in your research, teaching, and service. They refer to these as the 'three pillars of academia'. As an ECR, you are often presented with opportunities to engage in additional research, teaching, or to provide service to your institution or a scientific community. Your employment contract may specify how much time you are expected to devote to each of these pillars. However, these additional opportunities can disrupt the balance between these pillars. In this chapter, Jorinde and Sanne will help you to navigate through situations where you may need to decide if you really want to (or should) take on additional research, teaching, or service. They provide guidance on the decision-making process, and how to best size the opportunities and avoid over-commitment. Your time is limited, and there will be occasions where you need to assertively decide which tasks to take on and which ones to say 'no' to. This chapter gives you some good pointers on how to artfully navigate those situations when demands or requests outstrip your resources.

The next chapter, written by Laura Desveaux, addresses the topic of advancing your career as a woman in science, or as Laura phrases it 'climbing the invisible ladder'. Laura is the founder and Executive Director of *Women Who Lead*, an organisation dedicated to supporting the career advancement and leadership development of women in the health sector. This chapter is relevant to anyone working in research, regardless of your gender identity. Laura elaborates on the topic of gender equity in academia and why supporting women in science should be a universal priority. She addresses the unique challenges that women in science face today. She also answers the question of what is driving poor representation and retention of women in science, and what we can do to fix it. In this chapter, Laura lays out a series of strategies for overcoming imposter syndrome, increasing your visibility, curating a team of mentors and sponsors, and building your bespoke career strategy. If you have ever doubted that we will reach gender equity in science – read on!

Part II: Research Skills and Competencies

In this part, we discuss developing practical research skills and competencies that are essential for modern-day ECRs. The skills and competencies that we cover include: managing research projects (Chap. 7), networking and collaborating (Chap. 8), making your science open (Chap. 9), being agile in your research (Chap. 10), and effectively applying for research funding (Chap. 11). This list of topics is not exhaustive. The skills and competencies presented are simply the top ones that our peers told us they would like guidance on.

Most ECRs are project managers; however, we rarely receive any formal training on how to successfully manage teams and research projects. In Chap. 7, Anne van Dongen highlights that project management is an essential skill that helps you to plan what you want to achieve. She discusses the resources and supports you need, and how to minimise risks during the project management process. Anne gives us useful tips for effective time management, using planning tools, and managing the research project process. In this chapter, she describes in a very engaging way how to best deal with project administration, data management, and risk assessment, including practical examples and worksheets that you can use to manage your own project. She also discusses how to manage your project team members, prepare for and chair meetings, and set up communication plans. Finally, and most importantly, Anne concludes with the need to manage your own mental health while making the most of your research project – the most useful tip for your project success!

In Chap. 8, Elaine Toomey discusses networking and collaborating, as she phrases it: 'to increase your scientific impact and (importantly!) have fun in the process'. Some of us are natural 'networkers' and have no hesitancy in approaching others at conferences or scholarly events. Many of us, however, may find it quite stressful. If you are not certain about how to go about networking, or even if it is worth your time and effort, read on! Elaine outlines several benefits of networking along with some common challenges. We learn that building a supportive network can help us to develop our careers and bring joy to our work life. Our networks are also crucial in expanding the reach and impact of our research to different audiences. In addition to explaining her core principles for building networks, Elaine strives to help you reflect on your own core principles and priorities when it comes to networking, and to support you to develop or further enhance your networks and collaborations.

Science moves at an extraordinary speed in modern times, and the Internet helps us to network and collaborate with academics around the world. Sometimes, we work with colleagues whom we have never met face-to-face. Another skill that we would like you to prioritise and develop as a modern-day scientist is making your science open, that is, making your work transparent, accessible, and reproducible. In Chap. 9, Emma Norris writes about accelerating your research career with Open Science and the benefits of adopting this practice in your work. She points out that we could all benefit from our research being more transparent and accessible. ECRs are perfectly positioned to learn about Open Science, to make their science open, and to act as advocates for the Open Science movement. The chapter provides you with a range of tools and practices designed to make the research process, data, analyses, and outputs more reproducible, understandable, and accessible by following the principles of open sharing. These practices include study pre-registration, publishing pre-print articles, and making your work freely available via Open Access publishing. This chapter also highlights some global initiatives to increase the transparency of conducting science. Importantly, it discusses how Open Science can benefit and accelerate your career and gives you some great tips on how to get started.

In the next Chapter, Olga Perski writes about the related issue of being agile as a researcher (Chap. 10). Olga frames 'academic agility' as the art of honing new skills and fostering curiosity for increased scientific impact. Because ECRs work in an ever-evolving research landscape, staying agile is a crucial skill that we need to develop to thrive in our careers. Olga opens the chapter with her own story about working as an ECR during the COVID-19 pandemic – and what this has taught her about being agile. In this personal and informative account, she shares with us: (1) how to adopt an agile mindset, (2) why is it important to be agile, and (3) what the key barriers to being agile are. She also shares practical recommendations on how to overcome these barriers. Olga suggests that being agile means not being afraid of trying new things, teaching yourself new skills, thinking outside the box, and challenging the status quo. She emphasises the importance of staying curious and learning from things that did not work out as planned. We hope that after reading this chapter, you will feel inspired to pivot to a more agile mindset.

The final skill we present to you in this part of the book is applying for funding and securing your initial grants. If your PhD and/or postdoctoral position covers both your salary and your research costs, you may not feel obliged or motivated to apply for additional funding. However, in the spirit of staying agile and learning new skills and for those of us who are expected to apply for funding, Chap. 11 becomes essential as it includes practical pointers to get started. In this chapter, Daan Westra and Bram Fleuren reflect on their multiple attempts at acquiring funding as ECRs, sharing lessons that they have learnt as they experienced rejections and successes. This chapter encourages you to consider the relevant funding opportunities you may want to apply for (e.g., anything from small travel grants to substantial programs that may fund your salary and research costs for several years). Successfully applying for grants is a skill that will definitely accelerate your academic career!

Part III: Research Dissemination

Learning how to disseminate your research is as important as learning how to conduct research. In this part, we cover specific skills relevant to science dissemination. You will read about how you can share your science to reach different audiences. This part covers effective writing (Chap. 12), dealing with article rejection (Chap. 13), presenting and speaking about your work (Chap. 14), engaging with the press and media (Chap. 15), and using social media channels effectively (Chap. 16). You can be the best scientist in the world, but to make an impact you need to learn the art of science communication and dissemination.

In Chap. 12, Sarah Abe discusses what it means to be an effective writer. She suggests that versatility is expected from ECRs, and encourages us to produce all sorts of academic written outputs, including manuscripts, reviews, grant proposals, white papers, and blogs. She emphasises how we should pay attention to our audience and platform, and to tailor our writing style accordingly. In this chapter, Sarah shares two personal strategies for effective writing: open, trusting communication with her supervisor, and a well-organised writing plan and timeline. She also provides other tips for staying organised: devoting space and allocating time, and frequent advisor meetings. She also shares the tools she personally uses, including old-school flashcards or post-its to organise her thoughts. Her key pointers are to: identify excellent pieces of writing so that you can generate a template for your writing, participate in writing workshops, and peer review journal manuscripts. Peer-reviewed articles are considered key academic outputs, but other written communications can further enhance your CV and allow you to disseminate your work.

In the world of writing academic articles, one of the most disheartening aspects is article rejection. Unfortunately, most of the articles we submit to journals are not just accepted straightaway. We regularly need to deal with rejection, or respond to invitations to revise and resubmit our articles, whether minor or major changes are required. We may agree with the suggestions of reviewers, try to argue our points, or decide to take the article to another journal. In Chap. 13, Kim Caudwell outlines how to deal with article rejection. He introduces readers to what it is like to have a manuscript rejected, what it is like to receive a 'revise and resubmit', and what to do from this point onwards. Kim defines dealing with rejection in terms of critical thinking, which he sees as an essential element in developing as a scientific writer and emergent contributor to the peer review process. In this chapter, he discusses the ways in which feedback can make an effective or ineffective contribution to the process of academic writing. With his optimistic tone, Kim suggests that 'criticism is an unavoidable yet manageable part of the research process'. He discusses the personal and institutional influences on academic writing and peer reviewing, and how to forge a thriving academic career, despite the rejection we face from time to time.

Another important aspect of communicating our academic work is presenting and speaking about it. In Chap. 14, Silja-Riin Voolma covers how to effectively engage with your audience when presenting your research at conferences and other events. She highlights three key aspects of connecting with your audience, namely: empathy, interpersonal resonance, and storytelling. To achieve these key aspects, Silja outlines the importance of mind–body connection, celebrating your audience, and having loads of practice. She encourages us to take on opportunities to present our work to diverse audiences, including academics, industry professionals, and general public. She confides her pre-presentation ritual that helps her to relax and calm down before she presents (it's a good one and you should definitely read about it!). Other useful suggestions in this chapter include imagining your audience as the main protagonists in your story, making the narrative relatable, and guiding your audience through the sequence of events. Silja also reminds us to make sure our audience has something to take away – be it a take home message, a call to action, or even some freebie give aways! She emphasises that presenting and publicly speaking about your work can provide you with further professional and personal opportunities that will benefit your career. We loved how Silja writes about her presentations, and we hope to hear her speak publicly soon.

In Chap. 15, Nikki Stamp guides us through the steps of engaging with the press and media. We asked Nikki to share her tactics for dealing effectively with press, because apart from being an ECR, she is also a cardiothoracic surgeon, author, and TV presenter. She has been involved with a variety of media in recent years and is passionate about effective science communication and the promotion of sound scientific advice. In this chapter, Nikki highlights how the media can be utilised to benefit your academic work and shares tips on how to make sure your message is clear. Her key suggestions include being prepared and getting a list of questions before your interview, and practicing to ensure that your message is succinct and understandable to a broad audience, since it usually involves avoiding jargon and complex scientific terms. Nikki also shares important practical tips for engaging with media – having good lighting and sound, being in a quiet environment, and having your pants on (well, she didn't mention the pants…). Our favourite advice from Nikki is her encouragement to enjoy yourself while engaging with press and visualising how your message is going to change the world.

The next chapter by Mike Morrison and Kelsey Merlo (Chap. 16) is on making your science go viral. Mike is the author of a widely watched cartoon about redesigning scientific posters, posted on YouTube under the hashtag #betterposter. This cartoon went viral and successfully challenged the norms of how we present information through academic posters at scientific conferences. If you haven't seen it, we strongly encourage you to check it out (just google #betterposter). In this chapter, Mike and Kelsey outline a path that you can take to reach more people with your science. In line with the chapter on Open Science (Chap. 9), Mike and Kelsey encourage you to post your scientific outputs on public Open Access repositories to boost your impact. They also challenge us to learn how to monitor our audience to see how many people are engaging with our work. In this chapter, we will also learn how to 'organically' attract people to our videos and articles. In particular, how you can maximise your scientific impact by using emotion and communicating what you personally find most meaningful about your research. According to Mike and Kelsey, 'meaning is attractive'!

Part IV: Research Outside of Academia

Our final part will take you outside of the academic world. While most ECRs work in academia, many take on research positions outside that world. In this part, we included chapters on navigating research careers in industry (Chap. 17) and the health services and not-for-profit sectors (Chap. 18), and making strategic career decisions (Chap. 19). We also emphasise how and why we should involve the public in the research process (Chap. 20) and how to effectively implement science in practice (Chap. 21). When you work as an ECR, you may be sceptical about working outside an academic institution; however, our peers have found working in the industry, healthcare, and not-for-profit sector very rewarding. We conclude the part with a summary of the themes throughout this book and key practical suggestions for a fulfilling scholarly career (Chap. 22).

In Chap. 17, Rachel Carey 'explores the horizon' of non-academic research careers and tells us how she successfully transitioned from her PhD to working with start-ups. Given the breadth of research opportunities that exist beyond academia, Rachel contends that there is no singular, linear path to a successful research career. Researchers work across a range of settings, including corporations, consultancies, charities, local authorities, health services, and start-ups. This chapter paints a picture of what a non-academic research career can look like, including the opportunities and challenges you may face while embarking on this path. The reasons that researchers might choose to pursue careers outside of academia are outlined, as well as the steps you can take to finding these opportunities. Focusing on new start-ups, Rachel discusses the ways in which early-stage innovation can foster collaboration and creativity, and how this can consequently advance scientific knowledge. She also shares reflections and recommendations for working in industry, including the need for greater permeability between research settings, and visibility of the opportunities and impact that are driven by applied research.

In a similar vein, in Chap. 18, Jen Olson outlines how she took on an alternative career path with a research and evaluation role in the health services and not-for-profit sector. Jen points out that funding bodies are transitioning towards outcomes-based funding models, with increasing pressure on funding recipients to demonstrate the impact of the programs and services they provide. Therefore, the demand for individuals with research and evaluation skills is growing in this sector. The skills required for these roles overlap with the those that we develop in our PhD programs. Additionally, researchers in the not-for-profit sector need to stay flexible, have a pragmatic approach, and demonstrate skills in advocacy, negotiation, and communication. Jen shares that depending on where you work, you may still be presented with opportunities to contribute to knowledge translation, academic manuscripts, or grant applications. Lastly, although the salaries in the not-for-profit may be less competitive than in academia, Jen confesses that work–life balance may be more attainable.

As ECRs, we are presented with many possibilities and opportunities that could take us down very different career paths. In Chap. 19, Amy Hai Yan Chan advises on how to make career decisions strategically. When deciding what career path to take – whether it be working in academia, industry, or not-for-profit, we need to assess the pros and cons of each option. We need to make a decision that is strategic, suitable for us at the given time, and aligned with our overall career aspirations and values. In this chapter, Amy discusses the importance of not losing sight of your 'why' – your personal reason for doing research. She addresses how to weigh your opportunities; and why it may be worth saying 'yes' more often than 'no'. She emphasises that being strategic often means simply being kind – to yourself and to others. This chapter provides good inspiration for you to reflect on your career strategy – where are you now and where you want to be in the next 5, 10, or 30 years.

The final topics that we include in this book are related to engaging the public in research and science implementation. In Chap. 20, Rebecca (Bec) Pedruzzi and Anne McKenzie emphasise the importance of public involvement in research, and the challenges you may face when doing so. They answer the question 'Why should we involve the public in our research?', elaborating on the principles of stakeholder and community engagement, and giving suggestions on how to best plan your engagement activities. Bec and Anne aim to make public involvement less daunting for ECRs, hoping it will become a standard component of our research one day. Most of us aim to improve people's lives and to facilitate scientific discovery. Designing studies in collaboration with the public and involving them in every stage of our research can ensure that our science is useful and applicable in the real world. If you are not systematically involving the public in your research yet, consider doing so, and read this Chapter for some practical pointers on how to do it effectively!

In Chap. 21, Andrea Graham aims to equip ECRs with an understanding of implementation science so they can successfully translate their research into practice. Implementation science is defined as the study of methods to facilitate the integration of evidence-based practices into routine practice to improve health services. Not all of our work can be implemented in the health sector; though we encourage you to read through regardless, and learn how science translates into practical applications. Andrea emphasises that when implementing programs, strategies, and tools in applied settings, we need to build and sustain research–practice partnerships, test implementation strategies and monitor adaptations, measure implementation outcomes, and sustain an intervention in practice. She gives personal examples and lessons she has learnt to demonstrate these aspects of implementation science. If you aim for your research to be more applied, this is a great chapter to read.

In the final chapter (Chap. 22), we bring together the themes of this book and summarise take-home messages to help you achieve a fulfilling scholarly career. These include making sure you are aware of your goals and aspirations, building your support team, having a career strategy and developing relevant skills, and remembering that your research should have impact. The main practical recommendations include taking care of yourself, staying open-minded, always learning, and being practical, dynamic, and adaptable. You will come across challenges that, at first, may seem difficult to overcome. Making sure you have resources and supports that you need can make you stronger and help you survive and thrive in your research career. Having this book beside you, may also come in handy!

Part I
It's All About You!

Chapter 2
Setting Up for a Thriving Career: Assessing Your Scholarly Identity and Institutional Environment

Alden Yuanhong Lai

Abstract What does it mean to be thriving in our early careers as researchers? In this chapter, I discuss the need to assess our scholarly identity and our institutional environment so that we can maximize the fit between them to craft a thriving career for ourselves. I also discuss how assessing our scholarly identities requires continuous reflection on what we do at work, as well as the communities and places that we belong to, and the ways we most want to spend our time. I consider the fundamental elements of scholarly institutional environments – research, funding, teaching, mentoring, service, and professional development activities – and look at how they shape the norms of an institution and define the extent to which we can assert our scholarly identity. This chapter aims to clarify how we can better align what our institutions expect with what we individually value as early career researchers so that we can sustainably enjoy our work and be good at it, and thus thrive.

Keywords Scholarly Identity · Institutional Environment · Research · Funding · Teaching · Mentoring · Service · Professional Development

Introduction

When I was a PhD student, I often found myself in the throes of a scholarly identity crisis, and I sometimes still feel that even now as an early career researcher. As a graduate student with layered interests, I did not always know where I belonged in the academic landscape of disciplines, schools, and departments. I received my PhD from a school of public health and from its health policy and management department. Thus, in terms of credentials, I am a public health person. However, as a PhD

A. Y. Lai (✉)
School of Global Public Health and Stern School of Business (affiliated), New York University, New York, NY, USA

student, I was also fascinated by organization science and spent a significant amount of time at the business school. I convinced several business faculty members to serve on my dissertation committee, became a teaching assistant for Master of Business Administration courses, and at some point, provided support to the business school's taskforce on curricular design and evaluation. The business school did not have a PhD program during my time, and people would sometimes jokingly refer to me as the "adopted child." I had essentially crafted my own doctoral experience to accommodate my multiple identities and interests.

When it came time to look for jobs, I wished I could continue this unique experience of belonging to and spending substantial amounts of time in two schools. While this is possible for established scholars who have received recognition in more than one field, as in the case of joint faculty appointments, it is not common for junior scholars at the beginning of their career journey. My academic job search actually required me to package myself as a scholar who belongs in a specific school, and this led me to do two essential things. First, I needed to critically understand who I am as a scholar (i.e., my scholarly identity) and how I want to spend my work time. Gaining clarity on this aspect of my identity was important for me to be true to myself. Second, I needed to identify the kind of institutional environment that would most plausibly allow me to thrive. In other words, I needed to proactively look for the best fit between me as a person and the institution where I could envision building my career.

What followed was a consideration of my training, interests, strengths, and possible career trajectories, as well as an assessment of the job market and different institutional norms and values. I knew that I wanted to pursue research on the health workforce with a strong focus on organizational behavior and qualitative methodologies. However, I also knew that my profile would make it relatively challenging to be a Principal Investigator on large federal grants, at least those from the National Institutes of Health (the leading funding agency for health-related research in the United States), which tends to prioritize large-scale interventional and applied studies. My research interests, by contrast, focus more on the critical advancing of theory in health care management. I eventually centered my job applications on schools of public health because I felt that I could leverage my strong background and experience in the health care industry. But systemic differences exist even among them. For example, some schools require early career researchers to cover a proportion of their own salaries through external grants after a grace period of 2–3 years (i.e., the "soft money" model), some provide full salary coverage (i.e., the "hard money" model), and some expect you to provide salary coverage if you receive grants (i.e., a hybrid model). Additionally, some schools provide sizeable "start-up" funds as part of the job offer and others do not.

This chapter reflects my beliefs that by critically assessing our scholarly identity(ies) and the institutions we are based in or aim to join in the future, we can maximize the chances of having a scholarly career that is thriving as well as sustainable. This chapter does not focus on how to approach an academic job search. Instead, it encompasses my understanding and experiences, as well as those of my peers and mentors, of certain institutional elements that are not always discussed during doctoral training, the job search process, or professional development programs. It is my hope that this writing will allow others to develop a deeper understanding of the relationship between who they are and where they are, and a framework for ascertaining what institutions will allow them to build the professional career they envision.

What Is Considered a Thriving Career?

What does it mean to have a thriving career? I draw from the work of Benson and Scales (2009) in developmental psychology, which describes thriving as a dynamic interplay between a person who is "intrinsically animated and energized by his/her specialness, and the developmental contexts (people, places) that know, affirm, celebrate, encourage, and guide its expression" (p. 85). Your specialness as an early career researcher refers to the unique combination of skills, interests, and identities with which you can contribute to your field. This definition highlights that while our specialness lands us work, the work itself then nourishes our specialness. Our work contexts include the administrators, colleagues, students, and staff we work with, as well as the research and industry landscapes we work in. People and places not only shower us with opportunities and supports that can materialize our specialness, but also boundaries and expectations that can continuously elicit our specialness in valued ways (Benson & Scales, 2009). In this chapter, I thus focus on both scholarly identity and institutional environment because it is the dynamic interplay *between* them that allows us to thrive. I also highlight three additional perspectives on what fosters a thriving early career in research: timing, overcoming fear, and remaining open to learning.

Thriving Is About Timing

Because thriving is a developmental process, we should understand that what we do in the early stage(s) of our career can place our professional development on entirely different paths. It is important to consider the "right" amount of resources (time, energy, finances) for specific objectives. In other words, it is important to be strategic (Boice, 2000). For example, an early career researcher needs to decide between focusing their early years on research that is considered "high-risk, high-reward" or on a research agenda that is more diversified. A senior and respected colleague of mine once shared how assistant professors might consider optimizing the 6 years typically granted before they are promoted to associate professors: the initial 2 years to conclude dissertation research and establish new pipelines, the middle 2 years to collect and analyze data for these pipelines, and the remaining 2 years to produce scholarly output. My colleague's main point is that timing matters, especially for the middle phase to occur in time to produce the output needed for an academic promotion. Collecting and analyzing "high-risk, high-reward" data is admirable, but it is unlikely to lead to a promotion if it occurs at the end of the "tenure clock" (see explanation below), and there is no immediate output.

Thriving Is About Not Allowing Fear to Take Over

There is a Buddhist teaching on how fear is an ultimate driver of people's actions (Nhat Hanh, 1998). According to this view, many of us do things fundamentally because of fear – we fear not getting enough funding to produce research; we fear not getting good scores in teaching evaluations; we fear not getting recognized in the field, if we do not publish enough; and we fear that our years of training will go to waste if we do not receive tenure. While there is a place for fear (e.g., not going too close to the edge of the cliff for fear of falling), it is often dysfunctional. In athletes, for example, fear of failure is associated with worry, stress, and anxiety (Gustafsson et al., 2017). What is alarming is that sometimes we do not even realize our work behaviors and motivation are driven by fear – we simply get used to it.

But if fear is indeed an ultimate driver of our actions, how do we let go of it, especially as early career researchers who have yet to establish ourselves or get a permanent academic position in our institutions? I found myself being able to let go of this fear when I asked myself what I ultimately love to do. I realized I could still do what I love in other places, and even in nonacademic jobs. First, I value being able to discover knowledge, conduct interdisciplinary research, translate research into practice, and educate others. Second, while these values often align with academic work, I discovered *experientially* that I could still live these values when working with partners outside academia. I emphasize "experientially" here because it was not sufficient for me to expect or imagine that there would be other suitable jobs for me. Instead, it was through sustained interactions with external colleagues and industrial partners that I understood there are people and organizations *outside* the university that espouse my work values or are amenable to co-shaping a work environment that espouses them. It may thus be helpful for early career researchers to diversify their portfolios, or initiate collaborations with industrial partners, in ways that generate first-hand insight into the different types of nonacademic roles they could occupy (also see Chap. 17). One way to initiate collaborations with industrial partners is to rely on your mentors' existing networks or projects and see if they can meaningfully include or connect you with their contacts.

Thriving Is About Learning

Some academic institutions adopt the tenure system, where researchers are given 7–12 years to gain permanent employment. The premise of granting tenure to a researcher is that once he/she is deemed worthy as a contributor to their field, guaranteed permanent employment will allow the researcher to engage in "riskier" but potentially more impactful scholarship. Receiving tenure is one of the most prestigious achievements of an academic, but the path to tenure is highly stress-inducing for many. Early career researchers can be placed in a "tenure-track" position, and the period during which one becomes eligible and evaluated for tenure is often referred to as the "tenure clock." Nagpal (2013) once wrote about treating the tenure clock as a seven-year postdoctoral fellowship. The author shared this assertion: "Tenure-track? What's that? Hey, I'm signing up for a 7-year postdoc to hang out with some of the smartest, coolest folks on the planet! It's going to be a blast. And which other company gives you 7-year job security? This is the awesomest (sic) job ever!"

I read Nagpal's article multiple times. First, it reminded me of the importance of humility. Most of us will agree that completing a PhD or doctoral degree hardly qualifies a person as an expert. More accurately, a PhD allows us to better grasp what we know, do not yet know, and should know in our respective areas of research. Treating the tenure process as an extended postdoctoral fellowship psychologically liberates us to ask questions or fail in ways that may be perceived as novice-like. Second, the article reminded me that thriving in our careers is about learning, and not simply about performing. Feeling that we are learning something and making progress in our chosen field contributes to our *eudaimonic wellbeing* – a psychological state concerned with the development of mastery and self-realization (Ryan & Deci, 2001). Fostering a sense of eudaimonic wellbeing is an essential part of a thriving early research career.

Assessing Your Scholarly Identity

Having discussed what a thriving career entails, I now turn briefly to the assessment of our scholarly identity(ies). This is a highly personal and subjective process. Some of us can tightly define our scholarly identities, so much so that we can use the same script in introducing ourselves in various settings. On the other hand, some of us define our identities in broader terms and may find ourselves constantly having to tailor our biographies to the audience and platform of interest. Of course, our scholarly identities can transition over time and are often shaped through the input of others. For example, a colleague once shared that she was able to better assess and articulate her scholarly identity after attending a conference networking event where people came up to her and said, "Oh, so you're a [insert topic and/or method] researcher!" Having not thought of those descriptors for herself, she found it illuminating to hear how others in the field perceived her profile and her research.

A fundamental way to think about our scholarly identities is to focus on what we do and where we belong (see Pratt & Ashforth, 2003). Where we belong can be broadly defined – it can be our employing institutions, the departments in which we are appointed, the community of scholars in our field, or project groups. Some of these membership types may be more salient or meaningful to us than others. A critical assessment of scholarly identities includes understanding the activities you wish to pursue (i.e., what you do) and the communities you wish to be a member of (i.e., where you belong). At the most basic level, this assessment entails knowing the kind of research that appeals to you (e.g., theoretical, applied, qualitative, quantitative, and/or mixed methods research). It can also be about the types of professional development activities you wish to engage in, the types of courses you like to teach, or the types of committees you find enticing.

Next, we can think about the communities we identify with and where we imagine ourselves belonging. For example, in my field of health care management, my colleagues come from various disciplines, including psychology, sociology, economics, management, public health, and public administration, yet we all identify as being part of the health care management community. A good benchmark in identifying the community whose membership is of value to you is feeling that "I have (truly) found my people" when you interact with them. It involves finding colleagues where your research interests, perspectives, and approaches resonate with those of others and vice versa.

Performing a critical assessment of our scholarly identity(ies) is not an overnight process. Neither is it a straightforward one. It may take time, change over time, and require spontaneous input from others before we gain sufficient clarity. However, it is a worthwhile activity because it is the first step in identifying what we need to build a thriving career. One suggestion is to review how senior colleagues whom you admire have articulated their identities. Check their biographies and pay attention to the key words they use to describe their content expertise, their epistemological approaches, and their scientific impact. Such information is also beneficial as you prepare for academic job applications, as search committee members are then able to better situate your profile among the wider scholarly community.

Assessing Your Institutional Environment

Once you have a clearer idea of your scholarly identity, it is crucial to assess the environment of the institution, whether your current institution or an ideal one, so that you can set yourself up for a thriving research career. In this section, I list several elements to consider when assessing the resources, norms, and values of an academic institution. You will want to collect information on each of these aspects, and there are multiple ways to do that: review an institution's guidelines or handbook for employees; review the profiles of colleagues who have been successful there; pay attention to what the leadership emphasizes in internal communications; talk with mentors and peers who know the institution. One caveat here is that this is a US-centric perspective, where scholars have a mix of research, teaching, and service responsibilities to navigate.

Types of Higher Education Institutions

Higher education institutions (liberal arts colleges, research-intensive universities, private universities, public universities, etc.) come with different norms about how research performance is weighted. Most, if not all, institutions state that they value excellence in research, teaching, and service, but it is important to know the criteria for evaluation on paper *and* in practice. For example, in some research-intensive institutions, an individual's research accomplishments may be subject to intense scrutiny, while their teaching evaluations may not be discussed in detail as long as their scores meet a threshold. On the other hand, liberal arts colleges are expected to pay a lot of attention to teaching evaluations and pedagogical accomplishments. Separately, public universities may have to adhere to certain state regulations in ways that private universities may not have to consider. Knowing these institutional types and norms provides some basic understanding on what is typically allowed or accepted for researchers. The type of higher education institution provides general clues on the kind of environment that you are (or will be) embedded in.

Research and Funding Activities

Universities, schools, and departments have specific expectations about research output and funding outcomes. Detailed questions can help you ascertain how these expectations fit with your goals. Are there only certain journals that count toward your productivity? Is there an expected number of publications per year, and what is considered exemplary? Do peer-reviewed commentaries or perspective pieces count? What about books, book chapters, or periodicals that are oriented toward the public or industry? What about authorship – what is considered a good mix in terms of first-authored, sole-authored, and/or last-authored papers (if applicable to your field)? Does the institution recognize contributions made toward group-authored papers or projects, even if one is not listed as the first, second, or last author? What about your scientific impact – does the institution rely heavily on citation metrics? In terms of funding, is there an expectation to bring in $x\%$ of your salary after y number of years, and does the institution favor a "soft money," "hard money," or hybrid model?

These institutional values on research and funding can inform how early career researchers should prioritize their time. Recall that a thriving career is one that involves timing and trajectories – of course we all sometimes engage in activities that are less valued by our institution, but it is important to weigh these choices in the context of proactively shaping a career path that will yield the best outcome for you in the long term. I refer to the "best outcome" meaning a career in which you produce research output commensurate with your institution's values, *as well as* engage in activities that you find meaningful. Thriving means sustainably enjoying your work and being good at it (see Abma et al., 2016).

Some institutions are engaging in new practices to redefine their ways of evaluating research output. These practices are promising in that they allow our scholarly identities to be recognized in multiple ways beyond the traditional paradigm for performance evaluation. For example, an academic department in a US public university has started to pay more attention to its faculty members' individual contributions to group-authored papers or projects as a *process*, rather than looking only at their authorship position in journal articles as an output. Specifically, this department solicits input from a researcher's collaborators (usually the Principal Investigators of projects that he/she is a part of) on *how* they contributed to the success or execution of a study. Of course, each institution is unique in what it values and how it ascertains the contributions of its members. Thus, being aware of evaluation practices will help you better determine the fit between your scholarly identity and the institutional environment. Building awareness of these practices requires conversing with mentors and colleagues in and outside the department, as well as paying attention to the profiles of colleagues who are seen as successful in a specific institution.

The research and funding activities of institutions shape the kind of scholars and communities you can expect to encounter in that context. In my experience, because researchers in "soft money" institutions are highly dependent on external grants, they often initiate collaborations to maximize the likelihood of securing grants. The institutional environment thus involves researchers who are constantly bouncing ideas, searching for collaborators, cowriting proposals, recycling ideas from unfunded projects, and coproducing research. In these contexts, there are also colleagues who are solely dedicated to research administration (e.g., a financial person who helps you finalize budgets, or a legal person who helps you review contracts with external research vendors). The advantage of such an institutional environment is that you belong to a research enterprise that is not only geared toward efficiency in securing funding, but also likely to have a strong track record of helping early career researchers become successful in securing funding. Resources are therefore typically available for you to become a productive member of the enterprise, including internal seed grants, grant-writing workshops, or a formal designation of research mentors. Such institutions may even have a career template that they recommend to all early career researchers, such as receiving an internal seed grant in the first year and submitting a nationally competitive grant in the third year. The disadvantage of such an institutional environment is that the strong norm for collaborations may lead you to spend a disproportionate amount of time being a part of others' projects, which may not be fully aligned with the type of scholarship you would like to pursue as an individual.

Teaching and Mentoring Activities

Institutions have varying expectations about what percentage of a faculty member's time should be spent on teaching and mentoring. In research-intensive universities, early career researchers are typically given "protected time" to establish their research portfolios. This often takes the form of a guaranteed period (e.g., first 2 years of the job) during which newly hired junior researchers do not have teaching responsibilities. Positions that are teaching intensive, however, do not usually come with these practices. Other things to consider when clarifying your institution's norms on teaching include whether you are expected to both design new courses and teach existing courses, whether the effort required to design new courses is accounted separately, what your standard teaching load would be once the protected time ends, and what happens to your teaching load if you receive research grants. Some institutions require researchers to have a minimum amount of teaching responsibilities regardless of their funding status, whereas some allow researchers to solely engage in research for as long as their funding allows. Although research and teaching typically form the bulk of scholarly effort, how these efforts are viewed is dependent on institutional norms. For example, a "hard money" institution may have a standard teaching load that researchers can reduce with funding, whereas a "soft money" institution may offer teaching as a plug-gap measure if researchers are unable to secure sufficient funding to cover their salaries. Therefore, although researchers at either type of institution may end up spending equal effort on research and teaching, what they work on would be perceived and thus evaluated differently.

As an early career researcher, it is important to consider the fit between your scholarly identity and an institution's norms around teaching activities. Are you a person who values being in the classroom and having the ability to interact with students directly? Some early career researchers find it acceptable to fully focus their efforts on their research portfolios, while others feel an obligation to teach as a member of the higher education institution. Some prefer to tailor their efforts according to their career stages, i.e., setting up research pipelines as an early career researcher before shouldering greater teaching responsibilities as a mid-career researcher. Many of my colleagues prefer to have mixed research and teaching responsibilities – they highlight that while research is important to them, being in the classroom allows them to nurture the next generation of thought leaders and practitioners, plug the research–practice gap, and generate new research ideas. Depending on the teaching culture, you will also find yourself in the company of different people: institutions with a comparatively stronger emphasis on pedagogy may have more full-time staff members dedicated to overseeing domains such as learning management, learner experiences, or the digitalization of higher education. You may even have peers who are interested in or conducting education research in your own department. Determining your institution's norms on teaching will therefore provide significant clues on the teaching activities that you are expected or encouraged to engage in, how teaching is perceived under what kind of funding conditions, and the kinds of colleagues you would be surrounded with.

Finally, do not forget to assess your institution's expectations and norms on mentorship. Are you expected to mentor undergraduate, master, and/or doctoral students? If so, is there a minimum and/or maximum number for each academic year? Are you expected to mentor them for their thesis projects only, or do you have a role to play in giving career advice? What about students from external universities or departments? Would your mentorship efforts be recognized in that case? Some early career researchers think that it is important to "pay it forward," i.e., mentor others in the same way they benefitted from others' mentorship to be where they are now. Ideally, your institution should have a way to measure, monitor, and/or recognize your mentorship activities (e.g., advising x number of doctoral students is equivalent to y% of salary coverage). If your institution does not explicitly recognize mentorship activities, the general advice is that early career researchers should mentor only to the extent they enjoy it (or have to do it) without overstretching themselves.

Service Activities

Service activities (e.g., serving on an ethics committee, serving as an ad-hoc reviewer for a journal, volunteering time in an academic society) vary widely across institutions and are often discussed less directly than research or teaching/mentoring activities. In part, this is because service requests emerge in an ad-hoc fashion as needs arise, so our institutional leaders and colleagues are unable to fully anticipate the type and amount of service that they require us to engage in. However, by talking with people in leadership positions or who are directly involved in a certain service activity and by observing how decisions come to be made, early career researchers can better assess the institutional norms surrounding service. First, you can understand the structure and composition of committees that drive decision-making within the institution – what are the various committees in existence (e.g., academic affairs, admissions, teaching), how do they contribute to governance, and how are individual members appointed or selected? How does your institution deal with emerging needs that require consensus and input from its members? The service activities of early career researchers, or researchers in general, tend to vary widely, and can be at the department, school, national, and/or international level, as well involve different types of work, such as reviewing papers, convening workshops, or organizing conferences, for example.

Another important question about service is how an institution recognizes contributions both inside and outside its walls. As mentioned above, many of us provide service to communities outside our institutions, including organizing academic conferences; reviewing articles, grants, reports, and applications; and providing advisory consulting to industries. Some of us also take on leadership roles by serving on executive committees in the professional societies within our fields. I presume we enjoy performing these activities as they signal recognition of our expertise and contribution to our field, but it is also important to understand if these efforts are/can be sufficiently visible within the institution. Is there formal recognition of these broader contributions? Many institutions require researchers to submit annual reports of their research, teaching, and service activities when they evaluate individual performance. Even liaising with the popular press and media can be seen as service (see Chap. 15). How is this information being used by your institutional leaders and mentors? Do they provide meaningful feedback? If not, how can you better communicate this information?

Finally, receiving recognition for our service is one thing, but it is also important to understand if your *combined* service activities are being taken into consideration to avoid excessive workloads. Institutions may have safeguards in place to avoid early career researchers from engaging in too many service activities so that they can focus on research and teaching. In addition to the "protected time" mentioned earlier, they may also encourage you to consult your leaders or mentors before you agree to external service requests. If your institution does not have such safeguards, you may need to put them in place yourself or in consultation with mentors or peers who may be able to help. It is also likely that we have more autonomy in saying yes or no to external service requests. Therefore, depending on how your institution accounts for service contributions, you can decide how much bandwidth you have for engaging in service beyond the institution in ways that are aligned with what you want to do (i.e., your scholarly identity).

Professional Development Resources

Assessing our scholarly identities is not a one-time event. It is a continuous process. Often, understanding our work identities prompts us to want to engage in ways to grow further. The Japanese concept of *ikigai* describes identifying the overlap among four elements: what we are good at, what we can be paid for, what we love to do, and what the world needs. These four elements can shift over time as we progress in our careers, thus indicating a need to periodically assess our scholarly identities. As researchers, we value the ability to use our knowledge and skills in our work, but also the opportunity to *develop* our knowledge and skills (see Van der Klink et al., 2016). Early career researchers may therefore anticipate different trajectories given their current scholarly identities – some desire a career ladder oriented toward administrative leadership (e.g., becoming a dean) or being an expert public figure (e.g., writing a *New York Times* best-selling book), while some desire a career that remains fully focused on research.

From this perspective, assessing your institutional environment and norms is not just about whether it supports your scholarly identity currently, but also about where you want to go next. Does your institution offer resources and opportunities related to what you hope to achieve in the future? If you are aiming toward administrative leadership, are there fellowships or programs that you can participate in, such as being paired with an existing leader to learn more about how higher learning institutions operate as a whole? If you are aiming to become an expert public figure, are there people from whom you can learn the art of speaking to and writing for the popular press? While it is challenging to predict how our research careers will pan out eventually, having a sense of how your scholarly identity will grow will be helpful as you assess your fit with your institutional environment to set up for a thriving career.

Conclusions and Practical Recommendations

The fit between what we want to do at work (i.e., our scholarly identity) and where we belong (i.e., our institutional environment, which includes all the people we work with and the broader research and industry landscapes) shapes our research careers. By critically assessing our identities and environments, we can better shape a thriving career for ourselves. Some key recommendations:

- Be strategic – a thriving career is about determining when to deploy what kind and amount of finite resources you have at work.
- Don't let fear of scholarly failure govern your actions. We are unlikely to feel we are thriving if we are driven by fear.
- Create a space to feel novice-like so that you can continue to learn.
- Assess your scholarly identity by asking yourself "what do I wish to do" and "where do I wish to belong."
- Understand how your senior colleagues articulate their scholarly identities by reviewing how they craft their biographies and interact with others.
- Assess your institutional environment by paying attention to existing and emerging norms related to research, funding, teaching, mentoring, and service activities. Some are discussed more than others, but all are important, and you want to avoid doing a lot of "invisible" work!
- Have a clear understanding of your institutional environment so you can make smarter decisions when considering external mentorship or service requests.
- Anticipate how your scholarly identity will grow in order to clarify the professional development activities and resources that you will need.

References

Abma, F. I., Brouwer, S., de Vries, H. J., Arends, I., Robroek, S. J., Cuijpers, M. P., et al. (2016). The capability set for work: Development and validation of a new questionnaire. *Scandinavian Journal of Work, Environment & Health, 42*, 34–42.

Benson, P. L., & Scales, P. C. (2009). The definition and preliminary measurement of thriving in adolescence. *The Journal of Positive Psychology, 4*(1), 85–104.

Boice, R. (2000). *Advice for new faculty members* (Vol. 75, p. 288). Allyn & Bacon.

Gustafsson, H., Sagar, S. S., & Stenling, A. (2017). Fear of failure, psychological stress, and burnout among adolescent athletes competing in high level sport. *Scandinavian Journal of Medicine & Science in Sports, 27*(12), 2091–2102.

Nagpal, R. (2013). The awesomest 7-year postdoc or: How I learned to stop worrying and love the tenure-track faculty life. *The Scientific American*. https://blogs.scientificamerican.com/guest-blog/the-awesomest-7-year-postdoc-or-how-i-learned-to-stop-worrying-and-love-the-tenure-track-faculty-life. Accessed 25 Aug 2021.

Nhat Hanh, T. (1998). *The heart of the Buddha's teaching: Transforming suffering into peace, joy, and liberation*. Harmony Books.

Pratt, M. G., & Ashforth, B. E. (2003). Fostering meaningfulness in working and at work. In *Positive organizational scholarship: Foundations of a new discipline* (Vol. 309, p. 327). Berrett-Koehler.

Ryan, R. M., & Deci, E. L. (2001). On happiness and human potentials: A review of research on hedonic and eudaimonic well-being. *Annual Review of Psychology, 52*(1), 141–166.

Van der Klink, J. J., Bültmann, U., Burdorf, A., Schaufeli, W. B., Zijlstra, F. R., Abma, F. I., et al. (2016). Sustainable employability – Definition, conceptualization, and implications: A perspective based on the capability approach. *Scandinavian Journal of Work, Environment & Health, 42*, 71–79.

Chapter 3
Developing and Maintaining Healthy Work–Life Balance for Early Career Researchers

Lauren A. Fowler

Abstract Careers in research come with many challenges that can hinder or foster your professional and personal goals. One of those challenges involves developing and maintaining a work–life balance that allows you to thrive in your work (and in your nonwork life). Early career researchers are often navigating demanding timelines, unconventional work schedules, and intense pressure to achieve tangible research and career milestones (e.g., publications, funding applications) in a short period of time to stand out in a competitive workforce. This chapter aims to provide an overview of the importance of healthy work–life balance for not only your career success but also your own personal well-being. A brief exercise is presented that allows you to compare how you currently divide your time up between (work, social, personal, family) commitments and how you ideally would distribute your time in valued work/life domains. Actionable strategies and suggestions are discussed to allow you to find what works best for you when developing or maintaining a work–life balance, drawing from social and organizational psychology disciplines as well as personal and anecdotal experiences from other early career researchers.

Keywords Work–life balance · Time management · Job-related stress · Early career researchers · Work–life conflict · Work–life balance inventory

Introduction

The elusive "balance" between my work and my life. How do I find it? Sometimes, I wonder whether it's achievable in this profession, especially as an early career researcher, when it feels like the only way to stand out or get ahead is to keep the scales tipping toward work as much as possible. Writing this chapter certainly

L. A. Fowler (✉)
Center for Healthy Weight and Wellness, Washington University in St. Louis, St. Louis, MO, USA

Department of Psychiatry, Washington University School of Medicine, St. Louis, MO, USA

© The Author(s), under exclusive license to Springer Nature Switzerland AG 2022
D. Kwasnicka, A. Y. Lai (eds.), *Survival Guide for Early Career Researchers*, https://doi.org/10.1007/978-3-031-10754-2_3

awakened that dormant imposter syndrome inside me. Who am I to talk about work–life balance, when I struggle so much to maintain it? What I do know is that I have experienced just how important work–life balance can be for both your work and your life.

In graduate school, there was very little distinction between my work and my life – and this approach to doctoral studies seemed to be the norm. Research-related activities, course work, reading assignments, teaching, and grading happened at all hours of the day, all days of the week. It was a sprint uphill each semester, where life would hit me like a ton of bricks at both intentional and unintentional times. Avoidant coping became my main strategy for handling (or not so much) the consistent self-imposed need to work around the clock. Looking back, my behavior resembled a psychological high-intensity interval workout: work at maximum intensity for as long as you possibly can until you don't just *want* to stop, you physically and mentally *need* to stop. I did not prioritize my mental well-being, nor even acknowledge its slow deterioration. My approach was unsustainable, and it was unlikely I would have completed my program and received my degree if I didn't change my approach to work–life (im)balance.

It was also time to lean on my support network for insight, encouragement, and modeling of healthy work–life balance. I set structured work hours, and gave greater attention to my physical and mental health. I left work at work, and cherished my nonwork time, reintroducing old hobbies in my life that I had left behind when graduate school started, feeling then that they were not useful ways to spend time. I was more efficient and confident in my work during my set work times, and found new fulfillment in my social and family life. To my delight and surprise, I was more prolific and productive in my work when I allowed myself time and space on evenings and weekends for nonwork activities.

Looking back, I can definitively say that finding and working toward healthy work–life balance truly saved my career. I continue to struggle with maintaining that healthy balance, as, my colleague reminded me, the only constant in academia seems to be change. I recognize the necessity of healthy balance for my success in this career path, and I hope to offer you some reasons for and ways to approach a healthy balance in your life.

Varied Perspectives and Insights

Knowing that we all have unique perspectives and experiences, and my experience is but one among many, I contacted some successful early career colleagues, collaborators, and acquaintances about their own experiences with the elusive work–life balance concept. They represent varying stages of early career researchers (e.g., predoctoral, postdoctoral, transitioning to mid-career) and various sectors and fields. Sprinkled throughout the chapter are quotes from these exceptional scientists to offer varied perspectives and experiences. I hope you find their comments as insightful and relatable as I did.

Overall, my nonsystematic qualitative research of other early career researchers provided me with a few important insights. First, work–life balance, in whatever form that looks like for you, seems to be universally important for my colleagues. Second, work–life balance should not be thought of as a dichotomous construct: balance achieved vs. not. I also realized that we all struggle to achieve an ideal work–life balance, even my colleagues who seem to have it all ironed out. Indeed, practicing balance starts with the acknowledgement that (1) balance doesn't come naturally; (2) it will change often; and (3) you will not find the "perfect balance" and stay there. Rather, you will try different strategies, find some strategies that work and others that don't, and your work and life, neither guaranteed to be consistently stable, will require you to adapt your priorities and strategies often.

Any kind of behavior change takes practice, patience, and persistence; finding that sweet spot where the scales aren't significantly weighed down by work (or life) but oscillate in between will also take practice, patience, and persistence. Successful habit formation involves finding what works for you personally and harnessing that (Gardner & Rebar, 2019); hopefully some of the strategies, experiences, and information presented below will resonate with you.

Work–Life Balance: Finding What that Means for You

"All we have to decide is what to do with the time that is given us." I find Gandalf the Grey's words (Tolkien, 1954) particularly appropriate when thinking about work–life balance. After all, balance doesn't just happen; it begins with a decision to inventory what is important to us, decide how we want to spend the time that we have, and practice doing so.

What do you think of when you think of the concept of "work–life balance?" If you're like me, you might picture balance scales, with "work" on one side, and "life" on the other, and the scales are tipping back and forth, with the "work" or "life" side sinking lower or higher, in constant flux. The concept of work–life balance is going to look different for every person and may even look different for different seasons of your life. Broadly, work–life balance is defined as the degree to which an individual can simultaneously balance the emotional, behavioral, and time demands of work and personal life (Hill et al., 2001).

Why do we need work–life balance? For some, the answer to this is obvious. If that's you, you probably find greater value from and satisfaction in your life outside of work; perhaps your family, your social well-being, or your extracurricular activities are priorities in your life and excelling in those areas brings you great joy. In this case, working is a means to an end, the end being when you punch that clock at the end of your day and take home your paycheck. However, I would be willing to bet that most of us had to climb a relatively steep mountain to get where we're at in our respective research journeys, and that many of us find great fulfillment in our work. Regardless of where you fall on this value spectrum, the point is that the ideal "balance" is unique to you and your values. Therefore, what should inform your balancing between work and life demands should be your own values, priorities, and well-being. It might be useful to think about "achieving work–life balance" less in terms of a destination (i.e., achievement) and more in terms of a journey. Ultimately, you will need to determine the right balance for you based on your values. Mapping out your values and ideal time commitments and comparing them to how you currently divide your time up between (work, social, personal, family) commitments can help you identify areas where you want to adjust.

To help you goal-set for a work–life balance that fits your needs, I offer a simple exercise that you can do in the next few minutes below:

Step 1. Start by drafting the table below, and editing the domains (column headers) to encompass all the domains in your life that you value and want to prioritize, including separating various work-related responsibilities if that is useful for you. I provided in the template below the four domains of work, family and relationships, health, and personal projects.

Step 2. Estimate how much time per week, on average, you spend in each domain, expressed as a percentage of all your time (e.g., 15% of my time each week goes toward activities involving my family and loved ones).

Step 3. Estimate how you would ideally spend your time, in terms of the percent of time you would spend in each domain.

Step 4. Determine where your current and ideal percentages do not coincide, to identify areas where you can redistribute your time.

Domain	Work (you may divide this further into different work-related responsibilities e.g., research, clinical, teaching, mentoring, professional development)	Family and relationships	Health (dietary patterns, physical activity)	Personal projects	Etc.
Time spent currently (percentage)	e.g., 60%	e.g., 15%	e.g., 5%	e.g., 20%	
Ideal time spent (percentage)					

Note. You can also quantify it in terms of time, e.g., most of us sleep for 8 h per day so that leaves us with 16 h day (112 h per week) of awake time that you want to roughly divide into the domains above (actual and ideal scenarios)

If you find that the time being spent currently on each domain matches the ideal amount of time you want to spend, that means that you are achieving your definition of work–life balance. Congratulations! However, any difference beyond 10% may indicate a misalignment that you should consider.

Why Is Work–Life Balance Important?

Successful long-term careers in research require a set of skills and competencies. These include technical and scientific training, such as content, methodological, and analytical expertise, as well as experience in all the parts of the research process, from conception to dissemination. Equally, it also includes broader competencies such as scientific writing (see Chap. 12), self-development, networking (see Chap. 8), collaborating capacities, and work–life balance skills (Merritt et al. 2019). Research on workplace productivity across a wide range of jobs consistently demonstrates that we are more efficient and creative at work when we are happy (James, 2014; Rosen, 2018). An essential part of that happiness is of course being happy with your work. This can be fostered through incorporating activities in your work that bring you joy, or pursuing research about topics that you personally are interested in. This also means finding a research environment that is supportive, nurturing, collaborative, person-centered, and promotes healthy work-life balance practices (Maestre, 2019).

However, the competitive nature of research, and especially academia, coupled with the pervasive overwork culture where overtime is the norm and even the expectation (Trust Wellcome, 2020; Woolston, 2017a) can make it challenging to practice healthy work–life balance. The key to changing this culture is dispelling the myth that putting in longer hours will equate to greater productivity (i.e., you'll be more successful if you work more). Of course, there exists a positive relationship between work hours and productivity – but only to a point (Clark et al., 2016). After this threshold, productivity actually decreases, the quality of your work is significantly diminished due to errors and accidents, and fatigue, stress, and illness are likely (see Chap. 4 for more) (Collewet & Sauermann, 2017; Pencavel, 2015). Without adequate rest and breaks, the effects are similar. It is a marathon, not a sprint, to build a career in research, and we should treat it as such. While sprinting may be necessary at times (e.g., when your grant application is due), you'll tire without adequate recovery and rest, which can lead to trips, falls, and burnout (see Chap. 4 about Recovery from Work). Indeed, allowing yourself breaks and developing hobbies can improve your productivity (Oyama et al., 2018; Rosen, 2018). Prioritizing your overall well-being and maintaining balance should be seen as necessities for achieving a successful research career. The increased prevalence of poor mental health reported among academics and early career researchers (Evans et al., 2018; Woolston, 2020) underscores the importance of work-life balance.

Although beyond the scope of this chapter, it is important to mention that there are many structural barriers to achieving balance. Additionally, these structures may be different for different gender identities. For example, a vast literature points toward gender differences in work–life balance, job satisfaction, and burnout in the general workforce, but there is even some research suggesting that this is true for researchers and academics, whereby women may have more challenges navigating work and life demands (e.g., tenure clock may not pause during pregnancy in some areas). Understanding how policies can support or hinder your work–life balance goals can be useful for planning and advocating for your needs (Lola & Meyer,

2007). These systemic problems may take time to address, but I hope providing suggestions for ways that you can address work–life balance in your life on an individual level may additionally empower you to advocate for supportive environments and policies that promote healthy work–life balance at the organizational level.

Navigating Others' Expectations of You

As early career researchers, we are unlikely to have full control over our schedules and how we spend our time. Advancement in our careers typically yields greater autonomy, and the reverse is often true. Particularly in trainee roles, you might find that your ability to balance work and life is dictated by someone else's schedule. Your ideal work–life balance may not match that of your advisor's and there may be an implicit or explicit expectation that you work within their schedule, and it may interfere with your balance goals (e.g., scheduling a meeting for the evening, working on the weekend). Given the power dynamic and your junior role, it can be challenging to advocate for your needs. As before, it will take practice in setting boundaries and keeping them in place when you might recognize an ask from your supervisor to be inappropriate (e.g., to work every day until a grant is due).

These challenging conversations will be easier as you practice having them; expectation-setting is always a useful skill to develop. It is important to remain respectful in situations, and remind your advisor (and yourself!) that you're more productive when you take time away from work to adequately recover. One colleague offers their approach to boundary setting that I found useful: "The biggest challenge I've faced in maintaining work–life balance during my career is working with individuals who are not respectful of my time. In those instances, I found it helpful to set boundaries and say 'no'. What I mean by that is to have a clear amount of time I'm willing to work on a project per week or spend in a meeting and to do my best to not go over those limits. If this leads to needing to excuse myself early from a meeting or discontinue work on something to pick it up the following week, I've tried to hold myself to it and found it best to not automatically supply my reasons why, as this leaves them open for discussion. Of course, this may not work all the time, particularly if one is in a more junior position, but I believe it did help."

Setting boundaries for yourself and your time is important too, and although academia may afford some flexibility in hours, ensuring that you have proper time away from your work to engage in recovery activities is critical. Sometimes when there's not as much structure to your workday (like in graduate school when you can work on your own kind of schedule), the line between work and life can blur to the point where, even if you aren't working all the time, you're thinking about work or about what needs to get done. It can start to feel like work should happen at all times of the day, all days of the week, and life fits in between in the down times. I have personally found that setting and respecting my own work boundaries, leaving work at work (as much as possible) can allow you to maximize your time away from work. My colleague offers their perspective: "I've found it helpful to get some separation from my email – not checking while I'm with my kids in the evenings until they go to sleep or during much of the weekend. I'm finding that having some time to disconnect from email and work is really important in helping me feel more balanced."

Use Technology to Your Advantage

Technology can both foster and hinder your practice of work–life balance. With the constant flow of emails and messaging platforms available on our phones, it is easy to find yourself pulled into work issues outside of your work hours. Consider utilizing tools on your phone to "silence" or halt email notifications outside of your designated work hours, or even remove your work email account from your phone altogether. Even if the expectation hasn't been stated, it can sometimes feel like you're expected to treat email as if you're constantly on call, particularly if the email is from an advisor or supervisor. This can lead to chronic stress, subsequent burnout, and the associated negative physical and mental health effects. Working from home can make it more challenging to disconnect, and boundaries become increasingly important to maintain. Separating workspaces from relaxation spaces can help you further distinguish boundaries between your work and your life and prevent burnout.

Social Support

Do not forget to rely on your social network and relationships, especially if you're struggling with overwhelming demands in your work or your life (Peltonen et al. 2017). Social support refers to social relationships through which an individual receives emotional, cognitive, or material supports to help them in stressful situations (Jacobson, 1986). Developing a strong work-related support system can buffer the impact of work-related stress (Türker, 2017). Recognize that social support can come in many different forms (e.g., words of encouragement, information/resources, feelings of belonging) (Cohen & Wills, 1985), and you might need different kinds of support at different times. A writing accountability group, for example, might provide provisional support and belongingness, while a colleague might offer invaluable insight into the grant application you are writing, including material resources that help you as you prepare your own application.

Effectively Using Your "Work" Time to Maximize Your "Life" Time

Effective time management is also a critical skill to develop if you want to get the most out of your workday, and for researchers, it may be even more important for well-being (Aeon et al., 2021). Time management can be defined as a form of decision-making used to structure, protect, and adapt your time to changing conditions (Aeon & Aguinis, 2017). You have probably heard the phrase "work smarter, not harder" before – this is an excellent application of this phase. While grant deadlines or quick turn-arounds may lead to some work spilling into evenings or weekends, these should be exceptions to the rule.

There's increasing support for the usefulness of reducing work weeks to 4 days or less than 40 h to increase productivity (Woolston, 2017b). However, as early career researchers, the pressure to publish, apply for grants, foster collaborations, network, and navigate our nascent career paths can make it feel like there is always more we can do. To mitigate this pressure while keeping time in your life for non-work growth, you will need to learn how to optimize your efficiency and productivity during your working hours and hone your time management skills. I offer several strategies for building time management skills and point you toward resources for developing these capacities further.

You can't do *everything* at once, but you can do *something* at once.

- *Avoid feeling overwhelmed by your "to-do" list.* When we think of the Yerkes–Dodson law of performance and arousal (e.g., anxiety, stress, perceived workload; see Fig. 3.1), there's a point at which our stress levels interfere with our ability to be productive and efficient in our work (Yerkes & Dodson, 1908). Have you ever found yourself feeling arrested by everything you need to do? Perhaps

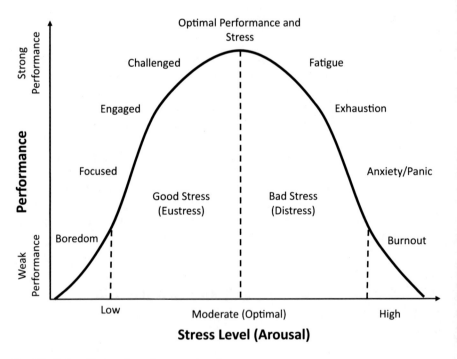

Fig. 3.1 Yerkes–Dodson law of stress and performance

it felt like you had too many tasks to do and not enough time or support to complete it all by the respective deadlines. You might have been in the far-right side of the curve, where perceived stress is so high that your performance is substandard. One way to shift yourself toward the middle of the curve is to break your workload into manageable tasks. You might then start by knocking off a few easier tasks to remind yourself that you're capable and competent (harnessing the power of self-efficacy, i.e., your belief in your ability to successfully execute your work). Importantly, the Yerkes–Dodson law may be less applicable for simpler tasks (Diamond et al., 2007), so use that to your advantage and if you feel debilitated by work-related stress, start with simpler tasks (e.g., send an important email to set up a meeting; create a title page for your manuscript). You might also try reflecting on other times when you've successfully overcome a challenging work deadline, again bolstering your work-related self-efficacy (Bandura, 1977). For example, when I am working on a challenging grant deadline, I remind myself of my experience writing my first NIH grant, how little I understood about the process or components, and how much more experienced I am now to be able to tackle a new grant application.

- *Use the S.M.A.R.T. (Specific, Measurable, Achievable, Relevant, and Time-bound) approach for describing your tasks.* If you find yourself often on the right side of the bell-curve (as I do), practice describing your tasks in more digestible segments. Instead of including "write manuscript" or even "write methods section" on your task list, you might include "write participants section of the methods" or "create draft of participant demographics table." This distills your tasks into manageable activities that are specific and will avoid overwhelming you. You can do *something* at once, not everything, so start with something and go from there.

- *Set deadlines for projects that do not have specific due dates.* Do you find yourself working on projects outside of typical work hours because you can't seem to make progress on them during work time? Or maybe you feel pressure to work more because you're struggling to utilize your work time for projects without specific deadlines (e.g., publishing a manuscript from your dissertation). Again, the Yerkes–Dodson law (Yerkes & Dodson, 1908) can help us understand why setting a deadline can help us follow through on that lingering project that we never seem to have time for. Without adequate arousal and stress (and not all stress is bad!), we don't feel the pressure or urgency to prioritize certain projects. By setting a deadline, particularly when you tell someone else of this self-appointed deadline (e.g., "I will send you the Introduction by this date"), you are increasing its urgency and importance. In a work-world where triaging rules (rescue the tasks that are due first!), sometimes we need to flag nonurgent tasks as "critical" in order to make sure they get attention.

- *Master the art of saying "no."* Ensuring that your work can be completed within reasonable hours includes (respectfully and strategically) turning down commitments when necessary. As early career researchers, we might not find ourselves wanting to turn any opportunity down that comes before us, even if it might not be relevant to our career goals. We also may not have the option to say "no."

However, if taking on something that would not be feasible given your current commitments is necessary (i.e., you cannot say no given your current position), it is important that you feel confident communicating what might need to adjust for you to avoid overwhelming yourself and ending up in the right side of the Yerkes–Dodson curve, paralyzed to move forward. As your career progresses, and with it your independence, you will find that you need to be more strategic in your commitments. After all, you want to be able to contribute meaningfully to everything you are involved in, and this is not possible if you put too many pots on the stove; something is bound to burn or boil over (e.g., a missed deadline, bad quality work). Several of my colleagues agreed on this point, one stating, "I'm also finding that while I pretty much always said "yes" to everything for years and years, I'm needing to learn to say "no." As I get busier and more "senior" in my earlier career, starting to draw limits is really important in terms of helping me work toward balance."

The following flow-chart for researcher decision-making may be useful to refer to when you find yourself trying to decide when and how to respectfully say "no" (Fig. 3.2). The "soft no" is another useful way to avoid overcommitting yourself, where you offer an alternative in lieu of your commitment (see the red circle at the bottom of the flow-chart for an example).

- *Use time management techniques to plan work time.* There are an abundance of techniques and approaches for maximizing your work time so that you can enjoy your nonwork time (Bielczyk et al. 2020). Some ones we have found useful include:
  - *Schedule writing time.* If putting it on your calendar doesn't help, consider relying on your community. Create writing accountability groups during crunch times or to help you finally publish that final dissertation article. Make your scheduled time nonnegotiable. Additionally, be sure to recognize that writing time does not always involve actual "writing," but might take the form of reading, outlining, cleaning or analyzing data, making tables, or anything else that directly contributes to the goal product (e.g., manuscript, grant application).
  - *Time-blocking*, particularly for long stretches of meetings, can help you by creating more blocks of time outside of meetings, so you can avoid having to find ways to effectively use those 15–30 min in between meetings, for example.
  - *The promodoro technique* (Cirillo, 2018), whereby you structure your time with scheduled, short breaks, and often use a timer to do so, might be worth trying. There are various time-setting applications online that might work for you. Don't be afraid to try several different techniques until you find your best fit.
  - *Turn off distractions.* Close your email for periods of time to avoid the distraction and focus exclusively on a task at hand.
  - *Limit perfectionism.* Don't allow perfect to be the enemy of good. As your time spreads increasingly thin across various projects, learning how to dele-

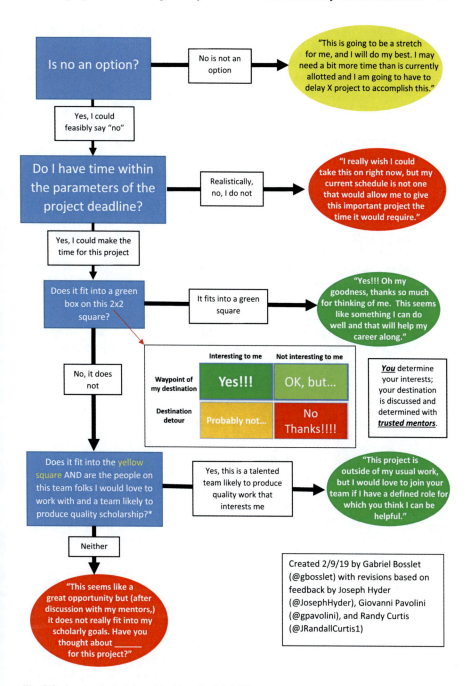

Fig. 3.2 Academic decision algorithm. © Gabriel Bosslet

gate things that are less important but urgent will allow you to focus your time on more important tasks. However, working on recognizing when something is ready to come out of the pan will allow you to maximize your productivity instead of focusing too long on any one task or project. The perfect project or output does not exist, and sometimes it is okay to move on when you have done something relatively well. One colleague shares, "I've learned to be incredibly efficient with my time while working, so I can enjoy other things that are important to me. As a recovering perfectionist, I've learned that any given task will expand to the time allotted to it. I set timers when I write, take frequent breaks, and try to put limits on distractions (e.g., email, texting). I've also learned to not make great the enemy of good!"

- *Use your nonwork time wisely.* See the chapter on recovery from work to optimize your nonwork time to set you up to get the most out of your work hours. Physical activity, hobbies, social activities, and anything else that nourish your soul should not be neglected.
- *One colleague shared a useful approach*: "I take a long approach to work to anticipate times (as best as possible) when I will be busy and times when I can speed up. Similarly, when I will be out or there may need to be more time at home (e.g., spouse has a busy time). I have a weekly calendar with weeks across the top and projects/tasks on the side which helps put things in perspective for what needs to get done this week (big picture items) and how things are moving. I update this throughout the week to keep it in perspective."

Conclusions and Practical Recommendations

Just like with any kind of balancing act, it takes practice to walk that tight rope without falling too often. If you don't get it quite right, don't be hard on yourself. From my own conversations with other early career researchers (and with those in other industries/fields), we all struggle to find the balance that works for us and meets our own personal goals, whether that leans a little more toward work sometimes or more toward prioritizing life. What is important to keep in mind is that finding a good balance between your work priorities and your life priorities (and optimizing your time outside of work through healthy recovery strategies provided in Chap. 4) can be more important for your career success than actually working more hours. Remember, work smarter, snore harder!

I will leave you with some main takeaway messages from this chapter to help you as you pursue your own personal balance goals:

- Start by taking inventory of your current and ideal time commitments to determine what balance goals you want to practice. What areas do you wish you gave more time for?
- The concept of work–life balance is going to look different for every person and may even look different for different seasons of your life. What should inform

your balancing between work and life demands should be your values, priorities, and well-being. Remember that values change over time, so consider taking inventory of how your current practices and time commitments align with your ideal time commitments with the spreadsheet we recommend in this chapter or anything else that helps you reflect on your work–life balance goals.
- Rely on supports to make that balancing easier and more natural. This might include enlisting the support of others who can remind you of your goals for accountability or advocate for you to take adequate time for nonwork-related activities. It may also include using technology to create necessary boundaries between your work time and your time outside of work (see section above). See Bartlett et al. (2021) for suggestions for communities and organizations that can further support early career researchers working toward balance in their professional and personal lives.
- As early career researchers, we may feel the need to sprint, but we're running a marathon, and you can't sprint forever. As we've reviewed, both your physical and mental health will suffer, as well as your work productivity and creativity, if you aren't adequately embracing vacations, boundaries, and a healthy work–life balance.
- Don't hesitate to ask for help, in whatever form that looks like, when you need it. As my colleague, mentor, and friend from whom I've asked for help countless times said, "Know when to ask for help with work (someone review something, etc.) or in life (from a spouse, etc.). We all need it. It's a sign of strength to ask for help." They conclude by reminding me, "At the end of the day, they can replace you at work but not at home."

References

Aeon, B., & Aguinis, H. (2017). It's about time: New perspectives and insights on time management. *Academy of Management Perspectives, 31*(4), 309–330.

Aeon, B., Faber, A., & Panaccio, A. (2021). Does time management work? A meta-analysis. *PLoS One, 16*(1), e0245066. https://doi.org/10.1371/journal.pone.0245066

Bandura, A. (1977). Self-efficacy: Toward a unifying theory of behavioral change. *Psychological Review, 84*(2), 191–215.

Bartlett, M. J., Arslan, F. N., Bankston, A., & Sarabipour, S. (2021). Ten simple rules to improve academic work–life balance. *PLoS Computational Biology, 17*(7), e1009124. https://doi.org/10.1371/journal.pcbi.1009124

Bielczyk, N. Z., Ando, A., Badhwar, A., Caldinelli, C., Gao, M., Haugg, A., Hernandez, L. M., Ito, K. L., Kessler, D., Lurie, D., Makary, M. M., Nikolaidis, A., Veldsman, M., Allen, C., Bankston, A., Bottenhorn, K. L., Braukmann, R., Calhoun, V., Cheplygina, V., et al. (2020). Effective self-management for early career researchers in the natural and life sciences. *Neuron, 106*(2), 212–217. https://doi.org/10.1016/j.neuron.2020.03.015

Cirillo, F. (2018). *The pomodoro technique: The acclaimed time-management system that has transformed how we work*. Currency.

Clark, M. A., Michel, J. S., Zhdanova, L., Pui, S. Y., & Baltes, B. B. (2016). All work and no play? A meta-analytic examination of the correlates and outcomes of workaholism. *Journal of Management, 42*, 1836–1873.

Cohen, S., & Wills, T. A. (1985). Stress, social support, and the buffering hypothesis. *Psychological Bulletin, 98*, 310–357.

Collewet, M., & Sauermann, J. (2017). Working hours and productivity. *Labour Economics, 47*, 96–106.

Diamond, D. A., Campbell, A. M., Park, C. R., Halonen, J., & Zoladz, P. R. (2007). The temporal dynamics model of emotional memory processing: A synthesis on the neurobiological basis of stress-induced amnesia, flashbulb and traumatic memories, and the Yerkes-Dodson law. *Neural Plasticity, 2007*, 33. https://doi.org/10.1155/2007/60803

Evans, T. M., Bira, L., Gastelum, J. B., Weiss, L. T., & Vanderford, N. L. (2018). Evidence for a mental health crisis in graduate education. *Nature Biotechnology, 36*, 282–284. https://doi.org/10.1038/nbt.4089

Gardner, B., & Rebar, A. (2019). *Habit formation and behavior change*. Oxford Research Encyclopedia of Psychology. Retrieved Dec 1, 2021, from https://oxfordre.com/psychology/view/10.1093/acrefore/9780190236557.001.0001/acrefore-9780190236557-e-129.

Hill, E. J., Hawkins, A. J., Ferris, M., & Weitzman, M. (2001). Finding an extra day a week: The positive influence of perceived job flexibility on work and family life balance. *Family Relations, 50*(1), 49–54. https://doi.org/10.1111/j.1741-3729.2001.00049.x

Jacobson, D. E. (1986). Types and timing of social support. *Journal of Health and Social Behavior, 27*(3), 250–264. https://doi.org/10.2307/2136745

James, A. (2014). Work-life 'balance', recession and the gendered limits to learning and innovation (or, why it pays employers to care). *Gender, Work and Organization, 21*, 273–294.

Lola, M., & Meyer, D. M. (2007). Work-life balance – The impact of national policies. A comparative study between Germany and Greece with a special focus on early career researchers. *Science policies meet reality: gender, women and youth in science in central and Eastern Europe*, Prague. https://doi.org/10.5281/zenodo.20724.

Maestre, F. T. (2019). Ten simple rules towards healthier research labs. *PLoS Computational Biology, 15*(4), e1006914. https://doi.org/10.1371/journal.pcbi.1006914

Merritt, C., Jack, H., Mangezi, W., Chibanda, D., & Abas, M. (2019). Positioning for success: Building capacity in academic competencies for early-career researchers in sub-Saharan Africa. *Global Mental Health, 6*, E16. https://doi.org/10.1017/gmh.2019.14

Oyama, Y., Manalo, E., & Nakatani, Y. (2018). The Hemingway effect: How failing to finish a task can have a positive effect on motivation. *Thinking Skills and Creativity, 30*, 7–18.

Peltonen, J., Vekkaila, J., Rautio, P., Haverinen, K., & Pyhältö, K. (2017). Doctoral students' social support profiles and their relationship to burnout, drop-out intentions, and time to candidacy. *International Journal of Doctoral Studies, 12*, 157–173.

Pencavel, J. (2015). The productivity of working hours. *The Econometrics Journal, 125*, 2052–2076.

Rosen, J. (2018). How a hobby can boost researchers' productivity and creativity. *Nature, 558*, 475–477. https://doi.org/10.1038/d41586-018-05449-7

Tolkien, J. R. R. (1954). *The Lord of the rings. The fellowship of the ring*. George Allen & Unwin.

Trust Wellcome. (2020). *What researchers think about the culture they work in*, pp. 1–50. https://wellcome.ac.uk/reports/what-researchers-think-about-research-culture

Türker, T. (2017). Work-life balance and social support as predictors of burnout: An exploratory analysis. *International Journal of Academic Research in Business and Social Sciences, 7*(3), 118–138.

Woolston, C. (2017a). Graduate survey: A love–hurt relationship. *Nature, 550*, 549–552.

Woolston, C. (2017b). Workplace habits: Full-time is full enough. *Nature, 546*, 175–177.

Woolston, C. (2020). Postdoc survey reveals disenchantment with working life. *Nature, 587*, 505–508.

Yerkes, R. M., & Dodson, J. D. (1908). The relation of strength of stimulus to rapidity of habit-formation. *Journal of Comparative Neurology and Psychology., 18*(5), 459–482.

Chapter 4
Work Hard, Snore Hard: Recovery from Work for Early Career Researchers

Eka Gatari, Bram Fleuren, and Alden Yuanhong Lai

Abstract Being an early career researcher often means having to work intensely on projects and articles. Periods with heavy workloads are common, and proper recovery during breaks or after work can sometimes not take place because of limited time. As prolonged periods of intense work with little rest may lead to long-term negative effects, this chapter discusses the importance of recovery and several actionable tips to consider for early career researchers. We begin with a brief personal example that illustrates why sufficient rest is needed. Next, we introduce recovery from work concepts. We explain that optimal recovery from work on a daily basis is necessary to offset negative long-term effects such as fatigue and burnout. Based on research in occupational health psychology, we provide several practical tips on how to recover well and overcome challenges related to recovery from work. The aim is to help early career researchers in preventing exhaustion or eventually burnout, so they can keep doing their work in a sustainable way.

Keywords Recovery from work · Recovery experiences · Sleep · Early career researcher · Mental health

---

E. Gatari (✉)
Faculty of Psychology, Universitas Indonesia, Depok, Indonesia

Faculty of Psychology and Neuroscience, Maastricht University, Maastricht, The Netherlands
e-mail: eka.gatari31@ui.ac.id

B. Fleuren
Faculty of Psychology and Neuroscience, Maastricht University, Maastricht, The Netherlands

A. Y. Lai
School of Global Public Health and Stern School of Business (affiliated), New York University, New York, NY, USA

© The Author(s), under exclusive license to Springer Nature Switzerland AG 2022
D. Kwasnicka, A. Y. Lai (eds.), *Survival Guide for Early Career Researchers*, https://doi.org/10.1007/978-3-031-10754-2_4

Introduction

Being early career researchers ourselves, we are all too familiar with the workload and the temptation of putting in those extra hours to get that submission ready. There is always more you can do, and it is not always clear how much you should be doing. These everyday realities of the academic life can instill a burden on us as early career researchers, particularly because we still have to prove ourselves and move up the academic ladder. At the same time, we're still partly learning the ropes of academic life and do not fully have the life experience to be completely aware of our own boundaries. You can think that being an early career researcher, you may want to sprint to attain your goals, but it is actually a marathon – you may fail if you expend all your energy at the start. In worse cases, you might even lose the will to keep working and burn out altogether. It is time to wake up – if you haven't already – and take the distinction between work and off-work time seriously to avoid accumulating fatigue. Working hard means that you also should play hard, or as we will explain in this chapter, *snore hard* to sustain your own functioning. This chapter aims to make you aware of the importance, pitfalls, and effective elements for good recovery as an early career researcher, so that you can keep solving those social science mysteries.

To illustrate the tension between working as an early career researcher and recovery, Eka would like to share her own experiences:

> When I started my career in academia, I was very idealistic and wanted to give my all to my tasks. I enjoyed working in academia as I learned a lot, and took on many responsibilities to give me new opportunities in my career. As the tasks were enjoyable to me, it felt okay to work long hours and even on the weekends. Who needs rest when your work life is enjoyable anyway? I figured I could just compensate with designated 'revenge sleep' – as I liked to call them – weekends. After some time of living what my colleagues dubbed a 'superwoman' lifestyle, I began to notice that both my physical and mental health were paying the price. I more quickly got nervous or agitated, made more mistakes at work, and found it difficult to focus. These – I now know – classic symptoms of prolonged fatigue/exhaustion caused me to lose several good opportunities, including several offers as both first and co-author and some projects. The 'revenge sleep' weekends were not helping much, and vacations just gave me energy injection for a week or two before I felt again like fighting an uphill battle when working. My curiosity on why I became so easily exhausted physically and mentally made me start to read about recovery and I learned that what happened to me was fatigue accumulation. I then also understood the need to have proper work and rest cycle to get to a healthier state again. I started to be careful with my sleep during workdays, not only on weekends. I slotted break times to detach from work and relax for a while. I regularly engaged in exercise for at least 30 minutes twice a week. Some habits are not easy to change, even until now – I still do some urgent work during the weekends and think about work during off-work times. However, I feel that my health is better when I can recover after work. I can also do work more efficiently when I am in my top condition.

Effort and Recovery

What in hindsight clearly went wrong in Eka's personal story is taking proper care of structural recovery from work. Structured means that you also put attention to have good, sufficient breaks in between work and during your off-work hours as part of your daily routines. Choosing work over your need to recover can, as illustrated, be detrimental to mental and physical health, and this cannot be compensated by your occasional weekend "revenge" sleeping or holiday break (see de Bloom et al., 2013). This reality is based in the theoretical notion of homeostasis, which refers to balance in the internal, physical, and chemical conditions in the bodily system. Working requires effort and thereby draws on bodily resources, bringing the body in disbalance over time. This balance needs to be restored to return to homeostasis, by taking breaks, eating, and sleeping. These ideas align with Meijman and Mulder's (1998) Effort-Recovery model which describes that workers use their resources and effort to meet work demands, which triggers load reactions, such as changes to mood and motivation. These reactions in mind and body need to be reversed by an adequate recovery – which can basically be defined as unwinding and regulating ourselves to restore our energy (Zijlstra et al., 2014). Importantly, the human body has evolved to balance effort and energy expenditure with recovery in daily cycles (i.e., roughly following circadian rhythms). This implies that when you begin working before having reached homeostasis or recovered from a previous day's work, fatigue can accumulate, and you will need progressively more time to recover fully. In an immediate sense, you may experience tiredness and the feeling of needing to spend extra effort to finish work. In the long term, repeated inadequate recovery over time can lead to physical and mental health problems (Meijman & Mulder 1998; Zijlstra et al., 2014).

Recovery Experiences and Activities

To create a better understanding of what the recovery process entails so that you can engage in it, it is important to understand the concept of recovery experiences. Recovery experiences are states of being that people can experience during off-work time, which contribute to their recovery. The main four experiences in the occupational health psychology literature are psychological detachment, relaxation, mastery experiences, and control of leisure time (Sonnentag & Fritz, 2007). By seeking out these experiences during off-work time, you can facilitate your recovery most effectively – and arguably use (your probably) limited recovery time more efficiently. As we will see, you can gain these experiences through engaging in recovery activities (i.e., activities that help you in replenishing resources by obtaining recovery experiences). In this section, we discuss each of the four recovery experiences in more detail, also connecting them to specific types of recovery activities.

Psychological Detachment

Psychological detachment refers to creating mental distance from work and not thinking about work during off-work time (Sonnentag & Fritz, 2007). As you can imagine, continuous thinking about work can negatively affect well-being as it limits people in getting a break from work demands (Sonnentag & Fritz, 2007). Consequently, people who do not detach well from their work, have worse mental and physical health in general (e.g., Steed et al., 2021). It is easy to imagine how an ongoing research project or that last comment from "Reviewer 2" might keep bugging you in the evenings. It is essential, for good recovery, to get away from such thoughts by engaging in activities that occupy your thinking capacity with something else. Social activities (e.g., going for drinks, playing games, good chats), physical activities (e.g., exercising, going for a walk), or activities that require mental effort for things unrelated to work (e.g., reading philosophical books, solving puzzles) can all offer means to avoid work thoughts and thereby detach and contribute to well-being (de Jonge et al., 2018). Another common reason for not detaching in our line of work is having too many different activities going on. If you find yourself running through all the different uncompleted tasks during your free hours, a very easy tool for better detachment is making a list at the end of your working day of things that are still "open" (Sonnentag & Fritz, 2015). Alden, for example, practices the "Bullet Journal" method. This involves having a list of things he manages at the beginning and end of each day, with which elements are marked as complete, moved to a designated time in the future, or eliminated altogether (the lattermost is particularly satisfying). Even though Alden only succeeds in using this method 70% of the time, the list helps him to monitor the things that he has to do as well as what he wants to think about. That way, your mind will be revisiting the tasks-to-be-completed less often, because they are already somewhere in a structured format available. Relatedly, you can include rituals to separate work from nonwork time, such as listening to music on your commute, taking a shower when you get home, or whatever creates a good boundary (Fritz & Demsky, 2019).

Working from home can make detachment particularly challenging because boundaries between work and nonwork are less clear. When you are working from home, having a dedicated space to work can help you. It allows to create a boundary ritual as by leaving that space you establish for yourself that work time is over. You can also leave all your work-related items in that space. Be kind to yourself and switch off that e-mail and text notifications for work during off-work times. You can get even more ritualistic in emulating a work routine to make clear work–nonwork boundaries. For example, some people who work from home like to dress up in complete work attire for work and change back to their casual clothes when work is done. Going out of your house for a bit and then coming back to emulate going home from work may also help your boundary management and detachment (Allen et al., 2021).

Relaxation

Relaxation, as second recovery experience, involves being in a state of positive affect and low activation (Sonnentag & Fritz, 2007). Relaxation is also associated with improved mental and physical health (Steed et al., 2021). The key to experiencing relaxation is to engage in activities that are well-liked, but not effortful (ten Brummelhuis & Bakker, 2012). Some examples include watching a nice TV show in the evening, listening to music of your preferred genre, or – for some people – meditation. Importantly, relaxation can be elicited by such activities, but it is not a necessity. Think of evenings where you are going to watch TV but end up feeling dissatisfied because there is nothing good on Netflix or when you have to engage in an endless effortful selection procedure (Bram has been there often enough). Similarly, reading something complex or watching something engaging but scary or sorrowful is unlikely to make you relax. Importantly, such activities might help in detaching or eliciting the next experience: "mastery."

Mastery

Mastery experiences occur when individuals learn about new things or challenge themselves in aspects unrelated to work (Sonnentag & Fritz, 2007). It is not very relevant what exactly is "mastered," but what matters is that the person doing it experiences it as fulfilling and, for recovery purposes, it should not relate to one's profession. Examples of mastery experiences include experiencing progress in a new language or achieving something new in a hobby (e.g., learning to make your favorite dish from scratch, or running more miles) (Sonnentag & Fritz, 2007). Mastery can additionally boost the feelings of competence, and the skills developed may actually be helpful in future work and nonwork contexts (Hahn et al., 2011). To seek out mastery experiences, obvious activities that can be pursued are sports with clear improvement metrics (e.g., weightlifting, running, archery), any type of creative hobby that produces some form of output you yourself or others may appreciate overtly (e.g., painting, singing, cooking), or engaging in more mentally oriented activities (e.g., learning languages, solving puzzles, video gaming). The key to experiencing mastery is that skill development or progress is noticeable to you in some form. Do note that some mastery-oriented activities may require too much effort to offer relaxation experiences, but they may also help in detaching.

Control Experiences

Last, control experiences encompass experiencing the possibility of choosing how nonwork time is spent (Sonnentag & Fritz, 2007). Obtaining the experience of control can be challenging for people in our career stage for several reasons. For example, since there is always more to be done at work, off-work time can easily be taken up by work tasks that – we think – need to be completed urgently. Relatedly, as we are spending so much time on work, nonwork time can easily get packed with responsibilities in the social, family, and relationship domains that we otherwise don't get attended to. Having weekends and evenings filled with such activities can offer other recovery experiences but may limit the experience of control. Bram, for example, dreads weekends on which both days are prefilled with appointments, especially family obligations such as visiting relatives. Having choice in spending one's free time is crucial for adequate recovery because it allows us to avoid stressful, non-work activities (Hahn et al., 2011), to feel confident (Sonnentag & Fritz, 2007), and to experience vigor (Bennett et al., 2018). Planning and reflecting on the kinds of off-or non-work activities allow us to experience freedom and control (Hahn et al., 2011). The take-home message regarding control experiences is that you should avoid getting your agenda filled with nonwork obligations so that you can choose – in the moment – which activities you want to engage in. Hanging with friends every evening can be great for detachment, but it should not become an obligatory fixed date.

In a general sense, the most effective recovery activities probably combine several recovery experiences. As such, the type of activities you may be looking for may best be characterized as low-effort, social, and physical (Sonnentag, 2001). Research has shown that particularly low-effort social activities offer promising recovery potential, specifically interactions that offer social support without incurring further demands on you (Sonnentag, 2001). Moreover, physical activities may seem somewhat contradictory to the low-effort narrative, but it should be noted that in our case – as early career researchers – we are mostly expending mental rather than physical effort. This is why (remember homeostasis!) physical (rather than additional mental) activities might be particularly good for us (see also Kelley & Kelley, 2017; Puetz, 2006; Sonnentag, 2018). Even though they require physical effort and are exhausting, they also allow us to put our mind on simpler matters. Additionally, if done right, the physical exhaustion involved may also help you sleep better.

Sleeping

We have not yet visited one of the most important aspects of adequate recovery from work, namely sleep (Weigelt et al., 2021). Sleeping enough (quantity) and sufficiently deeply without interruption (quality) is crucial for recovery, and is associated with less anxiety, depression, and fatigue (Litwiller et al., 2017). Since sleep is so obviously important, you may wonder why we only discuss it now and not before the recovery experiences and activities. The reason for this editorial decision is that recovery experiences play an important role in a good sleep.

In our line of work, sleep can be at stake for several reasons, but most of these reasons (i.e., biology-based sleep pathologies aside) are inadequate recovery during off-work and what you do during your nonsleeping time. Insufficient detachment from work and relaxation during postwork hours drives poor sleep (Steed et al., 2021). Perhaps you also recognize that nights following an evening of working until later are much less restful because of a more active mind. Putting sufficient time between working and going to bed is key here. Additionally, presleep relaxation may be compromised by working until late or engaging in too effortful (e.g., physical/social) activities in the evening. Lack of mastery and control experiences can also reduce sleep quantity and quality if a day feels unfulfilling or frustrating because you were unable to engage in things you wanted to do.

On a very physical side, sleep is determined by input and output factors. On the "output" side, we've already discussed that physical activity can be a helpful recovery activity that recurs in both the detachment and mastery echelons of recovery experiences. However, it is important to not get extremely physically active just before going to bed (Kaku et al., 2011). It increases your heart rate and general bodily activity levels such that you will have trouble falling asleep. Ideally, you should leave at least some recovery time between physical activity and sleeping to allow the body to return to homeostasis in a most immediate physical sense. Experts suggest to exercise for some time 5–6 h before going to bed, but to not exercise 3 h or less before going to bed (Morin et al., 1999). In addition to this output factor, the input factors – as we now like to randomly call it – are what you consume. Sleep can be ruined by heavy drinking, smoking (not only cigarettes, obviously), drinking coffee, and eating heavily after work (Bram is an expert on this last one). If you notice troubles sleeping in those scarce free hours, it is very worthwhile to explore breaking any of such consumption habits if you have them. Similarly, consuming too much light before sleeping is also a bad idea (Altena et al., 2020). This relates to the fact that we as humans have evolved to sleep in certain patterns that coincide with the amount of (day)light. This is regulated via the production of melatonin, a hormone that facilitates your sleeping process that is produced less when exposed to light and more when your surroundings get darker. Screen time before bed is therefore a bad idea, which explains both why e-readers that don't have backlight exist and why watching TV all evening or playing on your smartphone might not be the best recovery approach (even if it offers relaxation potential). Don't be like Eka, who loves to play mobile games in the dark just before going to bed and then she is not able to sleep. Other elements of good sleep hygiene are napping (only before 15.00 and not for longer than 1 h, assuming a regular circadian rhythm), taking a body-temperature bath, breathing exercises, and avoiding clock-watching (Altena et al., 2020; Kaku et al., 2011).

Making Your Boss and Colleagues Work

Although recovery by definition happens during off-work hours, it is not only your responsibility. Your employer and colleagues also need to support you (Ejlertsson et al., 2021), because a high need for recovery can result from high demands at work. As such, your employer needs to facilitate possibilities to recover from those demands or to not continuously have high demands at work. Phases of rest or "recovery weeks" can help in reducing backlogs and thereby contribute to recovery opportunities. The culture at work is closely related to recovery as well, particularly regarding how off-work time is spent. If you're in a department where everyone works in the evenings at home, there will be more normative pressure and perhaps even expectations for you to engage in this as well. Some departments may actually find this desirable to keep producing a lot of outputs, but in the long term, it might incur exhaustion and burnout like problems on employees. For a healthy recovery culture, expectations regarding work and nonwork time should be clarified and ideally in such a way that working in evenings and during weekends is discouraged (Fritz & Demsky, 2019). Relatedly, work messages (e.g., e-mails, texts, chat messages) during nonwork times that occur within such a culture should be avoided as much as possible. It is important to set your own boundaries and communicate them clearly, so you don't get bugged in the evening by people expecting you to be available (Fritz & Demsky, 2019).

Break taking at work is an essential, but sometimes poorly handled aspect of recovery. You and your colleagues should remind each other to take breaks (Ejlertsson et al., 2021), even if they are only short (Bennett et al., 2019), and spend them together without talking negatively about work (Tremmel et al., 2019). Your employer can also help you in gaining the aforementioned recovery experiences. Collective physical challenges (Ejlertsson et al., 2021), physical exercise breaks at work (Ricci et al., 2020), reminders to be active (Heath et al., 2012), and off-work personal development can contribute to mastery, relaxation, and detachment experiences. Getting a recovery-culture going is not easy, but these are some things you can do, encourage, or ask for at work.

Conclusions and Practical Recommendations

While working hard is necessary to advance your academic career, it is not as important as preserving your sanity and health in the process. This chapter highlights effort at work and recovery from work as central concepts for early career researchers to be aware of. Inadequate recovery can namely result in more serious fatigue, burnout and functioning impairments that you will want to avoid. By experiencing detachment, relaxation, mastery, and/or control during your off-work time through recovery activities, you can make sure you sleep and recover better. Sleep is a crucial factor that requires clear distancing in the evening and attention to outputs (i.e., physical exercise) and inputs (i.e., drinks, foods, light, and other physical stimuli). Your (work) environment should ideally help you in managing the workload and expectations regarding recovery, and if it doesn't automatically do so, you can ask for it and negotiate. It is important to keep in mind that there is no one "recipe" for good recovery (Hahn et al., 2011), as enjoyment and pleasure in the activities are decisive factors for success (Collins et al., 2019; Oerlemans & Bakker, 2014). We hope that this chapter offers you some inspiration and has illustrated the importance of recovery from work, so that you can transition from being an early career researcher to a senior scholar smoothly!

List of pointers for good recovery:

- Low-effort, social, and physical activities can help with recovery.
- Look for enjoyable and pleasurable activities that help you put distance between you and your work, relax, or let you master new skills.
- Take control of leisure time by not crowding your agenda with appointments during off-work time.
- Plan breaks in during work, even if only for 10 minutes.
- Develop rituals and routines to help your mind to transition between work and rest.
- Sleep is essential for recovery. If you don't sleep well, check your sleep hygiene, avoid excessive unhealthy behaviors during the evening, get enough daylight when you can, and stay away from the gadgets during the night.
- Discuss your recovery with your team or with your supervisor to clarify expectations about off-work hours, have dedicated break time and space, and ask for support or facilities to help you obtain recovery experience.

References

Allen, T. D., Merlo, K., Lawrence, R. C., Slutsky, J., & Gray, C. E. (2021). Boundary management and work-nonwork balance while working from home. *Applied Psychology, 70*(1), 60–84. https://doi.org/10.1111/apps.12300

Altena, E., Baglioni, C., Espie, C. A., Ellis, J., Gavriloff, D., Holzinger, B., Schlarb, A., Frase, L., Jernelöv, S., & Riemann, D. (2020). Dealing with sleep problems during home confinement due to the COVID-19 outbreak: Practical recommendations from a task force of the European CBT-I academy. *Journal of Sleep Research, 29*(4), e13052. https://doi.org/10.1111/jsr.13052

Bennett, A. A., Bakker, A. B., & Field, J. G. (2018). Recovery from work-related effort: A meta-analysis. *Journal of Organizational Behavior, 39*(3), 262–275. https://doi.org/10.1002/job.2217

Bennett, A. A., Gabriel, A. S., & Calderwood, C. (2019). Examining the interplay of micro-break durations and activities for employee recovery: A mixed-methods investigation. *Journal of Occupational Health Psychology, 25*(2), 126–142. https://doi.org/10.1037/ocp0000168

Collins, E., Cox, A., Wilcock, C., & Sethu-Jones, G. (2019). Digital games and mindfulness apps: Comparison of effects on post work recovery. *JMIR Mental Health, 6*(7), e12853. https://doi.org/10.2196/12853

de Bloom, J., Geurts, S. A., & Kompier, M. A. (2013). Vacation (after-) effects on employee health and well-being, and the role of vacation activities, experiences and sleep. *Journal of Happiness Studies, 14*(2), 613–633. https://doi.org/10.1007/s10902-012-9345-3

de Jonge, J., Shimazu, A., & Dollard, M. (2018). Short-term and long-term effects of off-job activities on recovery and sleep: A two-wave panel study among health care employees. *International Journal of Environmental Research and Public Health, 15*(9), 2044. https://doi.org/10.3390/ijerph15092044

Ejlertsson, L., Heijbel, B., Andersson, I. H., Troein, M., & Brorsson, A. (2021). Strengthened workplace relationships facilitate recovery at work – Qualitative experiences of an intervention among employees in primary health care. *BMC Family Practice, 22*, 49. https://doi.org/10.1186/s12875-021-01388-x

Fritz, C., & Demsky, C. A. (2019). Non-work time as individual resource building: A review and research agenda. In R. J. Burke & A. M. Richardsen (Eds.), *Creating psychologically healthy workplaces* (pp. 132–150). Edward Elgar Publishing. https://doi.org/10.4337/9781788113427.00014

Hahn, V. C., Binnewies, C., Sonnentag, S., & Mojza, E. J. (2011). Learning how to recover from job stress: Effects of a recovery training program on recovery, recovery-related self-efficacy, and well-being. *Journal of Occupational Health Psychology, 16*(2), 202–216. https://doi.org/10.1037/a0022169

Heath, G. W., Parra, D. C., Sarmiento, O. L., Andersen, L. B., Owen, N., Goenka, S., Montes, F., Brownson, R. C., & Lancet Physical Activity Series Working Group. (2012). Evidence-based intervention in physical activity: Lessons from around the world. *The Lancet, 380*(9838), 272–281. https://doi.org/10.1016/S0140-6736(12)60816-2

Kaku, A., Nishinoue, N., Takano, T., Eto, R., Kato, N., Ono, Y., & Tanaka, K. (2011). Randomized controlled trial on the effects of a combined sleep hygiene education and behavioral approach program on sleep quality in workers with insomnia. *Industrial Health, 50*(1), 52–59. https://doi.org/10.2486/indhealth.ms1318

Kelley, G. A., & Kelley, K. S. (2017). Exercise and sleep: A systematic review of previous meta-analyses. *Journal of Evidence-Based Medicine, 10*(1), 26–36. https://doi.org/10.1111/jebm.12236

Litwiller, B., Snyder, L. A., Taylor, W. D., & Steele, L. M. (2017). The relationship between sleep and work: A meta-analysis. *Journal of Applied Psychology, 102*(4), 682–699. https://doi.org/10.1037/apl0000169

Meijman, T. F., & Mulder, G. (1998). Psychological aspects of workload. In P. J. D. Drenth & H. Thierry (Eds.), *Handbook of work and organizational psychology: Work psychology* (Vol. 2, pp. 5–33). Psychology Press.

Morin, C. M., Hauri, P. J., Espie, C. A., Spielman, A. J., Buysse, D. J., & Bootzin, R. R. (1999). Nonpharmacologic treatment of chronic insomnia. *Sleep, 22*(8), 1134–1156. https://doi.org/10.1093/sleep/22.8.1134

Oerlemans, W. G. M., & Bakker, A. B. (2014). Burnout and daily recovery: A day reconstruction study. *Journal of Occupational Health Psychology, 19*(3), 303–314. https://doi.org/10.1037/a0036904

Puetz, T. W. (2006). Physical activity and feelings of energy and fatigue. *Sports Medicine, 36*(9), 767–780. https://doi.org/10.2165/00007256-200636090-00004

Ricci, F., Izzicupo, P., Moscucci, F., Sciomer, S., Maffei, S., Di Baldassarre, A., Mattioli, A. V., & Gallina, S. (2020). Recommendations for physical inactivity and sedentary behavior during the coronavirus disease (COVID-19) pandemic. *Frontiers in Public Health, 8*(May), 8–11. https://doi.org/10.3389/fpubh.2020.00199

Sonnentag, S. (2001). Work, recovery activities, and individual well-being: A diary study. *Journal of Occupational Health Psychology, 6*(3), 196–210. https://doi.org/10.1037/1076-8998.6.3.196

Sonnentag, S. (2018). The recovery paradox: Portraying the complex interplay between job stressors, lasck of recovery, and poor well-being. *Research in Organizational Behavior, 38*, 169–185. https://doi.org/10.1016/j.riob.2018.11.002

Sonnentag, S., & Fritz, C. (2007). The recovery experience questionnaire: Development and validation of a measure for assessing recuperation and unwinding from work. *Journal of Occupational Health Psychology, 12*(3), 204–221. https://doi.org/10.1037/1076-8998.12.3.204

Sonnentag, S., & Fritz, C. (2015). Recovery from job stress: The stressor-detachment model as an integrative framework. *Journal of Organizational Behavior, 36*(S1), S72–S103. https://doi.org/10.1002/job.1924

Steed, L. B., Swider, B. W., Keem, S., & Liu, J. T. (2021). Leaving work at work: A meta-analysis on employee recovery from work. *Journal of Management, 47*(4), 867–897. https://doi.org/10.1177/0149206319864153

ten Brummelhuis, L. L., & Bakker, A. B. (2012). Staying engaged during the week: The effect of off-job activities on next day work engagement. *Journal of Occupational Health Psychology, 17*(4), 445–455. https://doi.org/10.1037/a0029213

Tremmel, S., Sonnentag, S., & Casper, A. (2019). How was work today? Interpersonal work experiences, work-related conversations during after-work hours, and daily affect. *Work & Stress, 33*(3), 247–267. https://doi.org/10.1080/02678373.2018.1496158

Weigelt, O., Siestrup, K., & Prem, R. (2021). Continuity in transition: Combining recovery and day-of-week perspectives to understand changes in employee energy across the 7-day week. *Journal of Organizational Behavior, 42*(5), 567–586. https://doi.org/10.1002/job.2514

Zijlstra, F. R. H., Cropley, M., & Rydstedt, L. W. (2014). From recovery to regulation: An attempt to reconceptualize "recovery from work." *Stress and Health, 30*(3), 244–252. https://doi.org/10.1002/smi.2604

Chapter 5
Achieving Balance Between Research, Teaching, and Service at Work

Jorinde E. Spook and Sanne Raghoebar

Abstract Many colleagues and friends in our field of research that we talked to in the early days of writing this chapter have experienced challenges that come along with balancing their work. Why do or should we take on organizing a research seminar when our schedule is already packed? And how do we fit in the supervision of two extra thesis students when we already fulfilled our teaching obligations for the semester? These kinds of 'why' and 'how' questions are at the core of this chapter. We first look into three possible reasons (the 'why') for complying with new tasks and responsibilities that disrupt our balance between our research, teaching, and service respectively, i.e., the three pillars of academia. Second, we discuss four strategies (the 'how') that we have applied to improve our own balance between these three pillars (spoiler: we are no experts in balancing our work either, but we are getting better and better at it. And by talking about balancing our work with our colleagues, we did learn even more and are improving continuously, so keep reading as we share our discoveries with you!).

Keywords Research · Teaching · Service · Management · Academia · Engagement · Support

---

J. E. Spook (✉)
Department of Psychology, Health & Technology, University of Twente, Enschede, The Netherlands

S. Raghoebar
Consumption and Healthy Lifestyles Group, Education and Learning Sciences Group, Wageningen University and Research, Wageningen, The Netherlands

© The Author(s), under exclusive license to Springer Nature Switzerland AG 2022
D. Kwasnicka, A. Y. Lai (eds.), *Survival Guide for Early Career Researchers*, https://doi.org/10.1007/978-3-031-10754-2_5

Introduction

'YES'. Three letters, one word. Do you hear yourself saying this word often at work? Let us share our own stories about pursuing 'balance at work', as it is a phrase we have said so many times in the early stages of our academic careers. We often say yes with great enthusiasm when colleagues request our help to organize seminars, contribute to conferences, review papers, host networking sessions, establish mentor–mentee systems, give guest lectures, or plan social events. While we are convinced that these activities have contributed to the growth of our careers, it is sometimes challenging to balance these tasks together with teaching and research activities. And for example we clearly said 'YES' to the editors on writing this Chapter too. At the end of this chapter, we will explain to you why we agreed to contribute to this book. We hope you enjoy reading about what we learned along the way and that it may be of any help if you need it!

Explanations for an Imbalance Between the Three Pillars of Academia

Let's start with a scenario that is based on experiences of both our colleagues and ourselves. We compiled our experiences in the story of "Dani":

> Monday, November 1st, 08:22 AM. As some of my colleagues are already behind their desks, it feels like I am late when I enter the corridor, even though my first meeting is not until 9 AM. Oh well. I quickly pour myself a cup of coffee in the kitchen, walk back to my desk, open my laptop, and log on. As I have practiced my skill of generating highly secure and complex passwords, it always feels like a win when I enter my password correctly on the first try. Score! A glorious, two-second moment of victory. While sitting there with a smile on my face, a colleague pops their head around the corner. We have a nice chat about the weekend, followed by a request to help organize an upcoming research seminar. 'YES! Of course I can help organize that seminar', I say. 'Can you maybe supervise an extra student on it too?' 'Sure', I say. Even before the first meeting of the week, I have already agreed to perform two significant tasks starting next semester... I wonder 'what just happened?'

Maybe you immediately empathized with elements from the above scenario. Many of our friends in academia have been and are willing to take on tasks like these in one way or another. Some perceive it as part of their jobs, adding fun and meaning to their work. Yet, it can also affect the balance between teaching, research, and service responsibilities when clear boundaries are not set, leading to taking on too many extra tasks across the big three. Why do we do so? Let's dive into some potential (partial) explanations for the onset of imbalance that we have learned and see if you recognize one or some of these situations in your own career (Fig. 5.1).

5 Achieving Balance Between Research, Teaching, and Service at Work

Fig. 5.1 Potential explanations for imbalance between research, teaching, and service at work. Illustrated by Sanne Raghoebar. (© Artistic Scientific Creator 2021)

Explanation #1: "My Colleagues Do It, So It Must Be the Normal Thing To Do?"

The first explanation we recognize is that sometimes we take on extra tasks or responsibilities because we see our colleagues taking on extra tasks too. It seems 'normal'. In novel, ambiguous, or uncertain situations, we tend to follow the behaviour of our colleagues, as they reflect a so-called *descriptive* norm. For example, imagine the following scenario in which Dani joins one of their first team meetings as a new early career researcher. Dani's academic supervisor asks the whole team to take up the supervision of more thesis students as there are still many without a supervisor. Dani already has several students assigned and will also be busy with teaching a course that period. Science suggests that Dani will be more likely to comply with the request if Dani's colleagues agree to supervise more thesis students in that moment. Conversely, science also suggests that Dani will decline the request if Dani's colleagues say no. Following the lead of others is considered 'normal', as our colleagues serve as a social proof for the right thing to do in that situation. Moreover, we tend to follow descriptive norms because we can communicate our (shared) identity via such decisions, and we can save time and cognitive effort by complying with such norms (Jacobson et al., 2011). This may result in (automatically) agreeing to new tasks and responsibilities, as in Dani's scenario.

A slightly different normative explanation for Dani's compliance relates to our need to build and maintain social relationships with others. When we perceive taking on extra tasks as the appropriate thing to do according to our colleagues, this can be seen as an *injunctive* norm in that specific context. Injunctive norms are constructed from our perceptions about what others approve or disapprove of in a certain situation, which in turn tell us how we should behave (Cialdini et al., 1990, 1991). By following injunctive norms, we reduce the chance of being excluded by our colleagues, and we increase our chance of gaining their approval (Jacobson et al., 2011). In Dani's case, even if Dani prefers to reject the request, Dani may still accept based on either believes that colleagues expect this, or to strengthen social relationships and fit in with their new colleagues.

Explanation #2: "If a Perceived Authority Asks It, I Must Do It, Right?"

A second explanation can be found especially at the start of our scientific careers, when we may feel a need to conform to people who are in a real or perceived authority position or whom we consider an expert (i.e., the *authority principle*) (Cialdini, 2007; Guthrie, 2003). In the example of Dani, it is more likely that people comply with a request when a colleague in a higher position of authority is involved, such as a supervisor or the chair of the group. People tend to feel a sense of duty to authority, which governs behaviour (Cialdini, 2007). As such, we may automatically react to the fact that someone is our supervisor, rather than consider other aspects of the situation, such as weighing the pros and cons of taking on an extra task and how it affects our existing work (Cialdini, 2007; Guadagno, 2017). Furthermore, our compliance with authority figures may result out of respect or appreciation for them, and provides us opportunities to learn while we work closely with them. In that case, we may want to engage in the activity because the person has greater power or expertise and provides us an opportunity to develop ourselves too.

Explanation #3: "I Want to Engage in This Activity!"

Sometimes (or maybe even most of the time?) we take on new tasks and responsibilities in academia because we want to. It's fun or meaningful to us. Our intrinsic motivation intensifies when an activity is aligned to our interests as it provides novelty and optimal challenge (Deci & Ryan, 2000). With the example of Dani's colleague asking to help organize a seminar, Dani may feel intrinsically motivated for many reasons. It might be that:

- Organizing a seminar is an interesting activity to begin with;
- The request is in line with Dani's ambitions;
- Dani has the skills needed to organize such a research seminar given previous experiences;
- Dani can also learn new skills from the organizing committee;
- Dani experiences autonomy and ownership over ideas in organizing the seminar;
- It is an opportunity for further collaborations with a colleague with similar lines of research;
- It will allow Dani to build rapport with additional colleagues as seminars can help develop career paths.

The issue though, when we are intrinsically motivated by a new activity that we want to add to our range of responsibilities, is that we will need to find a new balance between our tasks, energy, and time. However, prioritizing between short-term deadlines that require greater attention and non-pressing activities that are intrinsically interesting to us may be hard. And what makes it even more challenging when time is scarce, is that we sometimes try really hard to do them perfectly too. So how can we maintain as much balance among our work activities as possible?

Intermezzo

While we were writing this chapter, we gained a better understanding of why we sometimes get out of balance ourselves. We realized that balancing the three pillars of academia is a continuous process: we strive for balance, something changes in one or more of the pillars, and then we rebalance. Sometimes, we manage to rebalance quickly, and other times it requires more of a slow wave, like changes between teaching periods, semesters, or even academic years. We will now elaborate on four strategies we have applied ourselves to (re)balance our work. Hopefully, applying some (or all) of these strategies will help you better manage as well in case you need it.

Possible Strategies for Balancing Between the Three Pillars of Academia

Strategy #1: Increase Job Control

The first strategy that we apply is to actively control our work whenever possible. This can include our work schedule, when we take breaks, and how we plan our work and breaks. According to research (e.g., based on the Job Control Demand

Model by Karasek, 1979), we see two major ways that can increase our job control. First, we try to exercise autonomy in task-related decisions like the timing of our work. Feeling in control of our own decisions and planning gives us a certain feeling of freedom in how we spend our valuable time and energy. We also try to actively consider which tasks we take on and which ones we don't. Second, we try to maximize the opportunity to apply our professional skills in our work. It allows us to strengthen our skills and to develop ourselves. Yet, what makes it challenging is that typical examples of job demands (e.g., workload and time pressure) can diminish our experience of job control.

Practically speaking, we try to be flexible and look ahead to strategically plan. We want to note that especially in the first year in a new position, it can be difficult to develop a suitable strategy, and we may have to dive into the experience before figuring out what will work. Knowing for example that we will teach more classes in our first semester than in the second can help us plan out our workload over the course of the full academic year. We use calendar notifications to understand and plan for the changing workload dynamics over time. For example, by setting recurring reminders about upcoming deadlines that are time consuming (e.g., reviewing theses) and blocking out sufficient time in our calendars to work on those tasks, we get to limit the number of meetings that may creep into our calendars. Another helpful strategy to us is searching for a common link between our work across the three pillars. Remember that Dani was asked to supervise more thesis students, although it did not directly fit their schedule. Our suggestion would be to create commonalities between the pillars by providing the topic of research as an opportunity for students, allowing them to write their thesis under your supervision while also furthering your own work. Creating systems for students to help each other can provide a beneficial student resource while also taking the workload off you. Maybe it can help to invest a little bit of time in creating a peer-supervision format so that students can help each other throughout the writing process. Note that this strategy as well as the following can work for not only us, but also in some way for our students.

Strategy #2: Create a Support Network

Peer Support What really stands out for us is that peers can become friends. For us, we are co-authors and peers, but we are primarily friends. We, for example, found common ground through scientific interest and activities. When we first met, we started on the same team, at the same time, but in different positions: Sanne had just started her PhD and Jorinde her Postdoc. Over time, we discovered multiple similar interests, like we both played field hockey, shared an interest in healthy foods, and liked spending time with family and friends. But we also connected at a deeper level through conversations about our values in life. As such, we believe that working relationships can truly blossom into long-standing friendships.

Similar experiences are highlighted in literature. For example, McPhail-Bell and Redman-MacLaren (2019) address the importance of peer support for doctoral students, contributing to successful PhD completions and the development of researcher identities. We appreciate how they share their stories about personal and professional growth with other PhD candidates via their co/autoethnography on peer support. We for example recognize this quote: *'Thanks for checking in. I find these weekly check-ins an invaluable part of the thesis write-up process, not only for its practical value but because I enjoy hearing how you are going and being able to share my progress too. I feel very blessed to share this journey with you; thank you'* (p. 1099). Their story on the importance of precious connections in academia supports this second strategy. It is an example of why peer support matters, and how to cope with stressful situations, for example during your PhD.

Supervisor Support Besides peer support, we want to acknowledge the importance of another source of support: supervisors. The relationship between doctoral students and supervisors is in previous research considered the most influential external factor affecting the doctoral students' experience in graduate school (Sverdlik et al., 2018). A supportive relationship with the supervisor is considered part of quality supervision, and a supervisors' commitment and involvement were identified as the most important supervisory selection elements among junior and senior doctoral students (Ray, 2007). Poor supervision was reported by doctoral students as the #2 reason for program attrition (Gardner, 2009). What is clearly shown is that the perceived quality of supervision is important from the start and a key part of facilitating academic accomplishments. In early career research, we believe that it takes two to tango, so it is up to both parties to invest in the relationship. Both should contribute some effort towards understanding the other person. This can be as low-key as starting a meeting with the question, 'How are you today?'

Mentor Support On a final note, we would like to mention that support can also come from senior colleagues, like associate or full professors within or outside your group. These colleagues as mentors may be nice to brainstorm with about managing activities, especially if they are not directly involved in your project(s). This allows them to reflect on the process with you, and they might surprise you with new perspectives and ideas!

Strategy #3: Job Management

We try to manage our work as much as possible, even though we know that teaching obligations can put a great demand on work schedules. What might help is when for example teaching timeslots are pre-defined before the semester starts, it allows to anticipate upon them well ahead of time. We are both very keen on planning our work and filling in our schedule with recurring activities like project meetings, teaching classes, and board meetings. We realize that these meetings also require recurring preparatory time, so it comes in handy to plan the preparatory activities too. When these 'fixed job demands' are clearly visible in our calendar, it increases our opportunity to control our schedules some more, and to gain a better understanding of the upcoming workload dynamics. Like McCrory Calarco (2020) stated, *'One of the things I love most about having a career in academia is that I get to wear a lot of hats. Not literal hats, of course, but hats in the sense of different roles. […] When you have a closet full of hats – student hats, research hats, teacher hats, service hats, and personal ones - it's important to plan which one you'll wear when. If you don't take time to plan, you might end up just wearing your favorite hat all the time or the one that's hardest to take off'* (p. 349–353).

It should be noted that general job management skills are related to project management (also see Chap. 7). Your PhD, Postdoc, or just work-related activities in general can all be approached like it is your own professional (development) project. The important part we want to highlight: *job management is a skill that can be learned.* It is important to realize that job management involves many different subskills such as time management, teamwork, professional communication skills, planning, goal setting, problem solving, and budgeting. They need time and practice. We believe that managing these subskills will contribute to balancing the three pillars of academia too. We also like the diversity in (developing) these subskills, as much as the diversity that comes with our academic jobs.

Strategy #4: Evaluate the Added Value

Fourth, and finally, we think it is key to deliberately weigh the pros and cons of each task that is included and/or added to our list of responsibilities. We have sometimes felt overwhelmed by the pile of work that we added to our job demands by saying 'YES!' because we got inspired. We also note that this pile consisted of great opportunities that contributed to our careers (e.g., committees at work, hosting meetings, joining research projects) which sometimes meant tipping off balance for a bit. However, we do think that too much quantity affects the quality. Meaning that taking on too many tasks may affect the quality of the work you deliver as well as the quality of the experience you have while doing the tasks. So, we think that prioritizing what is important to you is key.

Prioritizing during academic careers has been stated as a key activity by various researchers (Kempenaar & Murray, 2016). McCrory Calarco (2020) stressed that you need to start with deciding what you want to achieve per pillar. For example, if you aspire to become president of an international research community, your current time spent as a member of the board in that community may be more valuable to you than your involvement in the social committee of your department. But if you prioritize to collaborate more closely to direct colleagues in the department, the social committee may be more valuable then a role within an external research committee. As such, you can still take on service commitments at work, but we recommend you align them with your own ambitions as much as possible.

Conclusions and Practical Recommendations

We hope that any or maybe all of these insights help you balance your work in academia. To summarize, it may help to: (1) establish job control, (2) create a supportive network, (3) improve your management skills, and (4) evaluate the added value of the tasks that you do.

We listed below a few bonus tips from colleagues and friends in the field on what helps them to balance research, teaching, and service at work. We hope that sharing some of our experiences in balancing the three pillars of academia has been of help to you. We for sure enjoyed taking on this extra task. Why did we take on the extra task of writing this Chapter? Because we value peer support, and we always said that one day, we would find an opportunity to publish together, despite our different research areas. And here it is. Our first publication as co-authors (and friends).

Bonus Tips from Our Colleagues on Balancing the Three Pillars of Academia

1. Don't be too hard on yourself. Remember: you are doing a great job!
2. If a new task request does not fit your interest or schedule, say 'no' to the task without rejecting your colleague personally.
3. Turn off your email inbox from time to time, e.g., when focusing on a task or at specific timeslots during the day.
4. Simple email requests that take you less than 2 min to respond: do them immediately. Then it's off your list. If it takes more than 2 min of your time: plan it and add it to your to do list.
5. Align your teaching with your research, for example supervise internship students on a topic related to your research.
6. Look for project management courses offered by your University.
7. Find yourself a mentor who you trust.

References

Cialdini, R. B. (2007). *Influence: The psychology of persuasion* (Vol. 55, p. 339). Collins. https://doi.org/10.1146/annurev.psych.55.090902.142015

Cialdini, R. B., Reno, R. R., & Kallgren, C. A. (1990). A focus theory of normative conduct: Recycling the concept of norms to reduce littering in public places. *Journal of Personality and Social Psychology, 58*(6), 1015–1026. https://doi.org/10.1037/0022-3514.58.6.1015

Cialdini, R. B., Kallgren, C. A., & Reno, R. R. (1991). A focus theory of normative conduct: A theoretical refinement and reevaluation of the role of norms in human behavior. *Advances in Experimental Social Psychology, 24*, 201–234. https://doi.org/10.1016/S0065-2601(08)60330-5

Deci, E. L., & Ryan, R. M. (2000). The "what" and "why" of goal pursuits: Human needs and the self-determination of behavior. *Psychological Inquiry, 11*(4), 227–268. https://doi.org/10.1207/S15327965PLI1104_01

Gardner, S. K. (2009). Student and faculty attributions of attrition in high and low-completing doctoral programs in the United States. *Higher Education, 58*, 97–112. https://doi.org/10.1007/s10734-008-9184-7

Guadagno, R. E. (2017). Compliance: A classic and contemporary review. In S. G. Harkins, K. D. Williams, & J. M. Burger (Eds.), *The Oxford handbook of social influence* (pp. 107–127). Oxford University Press.

Guthrie, C. (2003). Principles of influence in negotiation. *Marquette Law Review, 87*, 829.

Jacobson, R. P., Mortensen, C. R., & Cialdini, R. B. (2011). Bodies obliged and unbound: Differentiated response tendencies for injunctive and descriptive social norms. *Journal of Personality and Social Psychology, 100*(3), 433–448. https://doi.org/10.10370/a0021470

Karasek, R. A., Jr. (1979). Job demands, job decision latitude, and mental strain: Implications for job redesign. *Administrative Science Quarterly*, 285–308. https://doi.org/10.2307/239498

Kempenaar, L. E., & Murray, R. (2016). Writing by academics: A transactional and systems approach to academic writing behaviours. *Higher Education Research & Development, 35*(5), 940–950. https://doi.org/10.1080/07294360.2016.1139553

McCrory Calarco, J. (2020). *A field guide to grad school: Uncovering the hidden curriculum*. Princeton University Press.

McPhail-Bell, K., & Redman-MacLaren, M. (2019). A co/authoethnography of peer support and PhDs: Being, doing, and sharing in academia. *The Qualitative Report, 24*(5), 1087–1105. https://doi.org/10.46743/2160-3715/2019.3155

Ray, S. (2007). Selecting a doctoral dissertation supervisor: Analytical hierarchy approach to the multiple criteria problem. *International Journal of Doctoral Studies, 2*, 23–32.

Sverdlik, A., Hall, N. C., McAlpine, L., & Hubbard, K. (2018). The PhD experience: A review of the factors influencing doctoral students' completion, achievement, and well-being. *International Journal of Doctoral Studies, 13*, 361–388. https://doi.org/10.28945/4113

Chapter 6
Climbing the Invisible Ladder: Advancing Your Career as a Woman in Science

Laura Desveaux

Abstract This chapter takes a moment to ground you in the unique challenges women in science face that drive the lack of gender equity across fields of study. More importantly, it harnesses science to support you in articulating the *whys* and *hows* of your career and lays out a series of strategies you can employ in pursuit of reaching the next level. It dives into overcoming imposter syndrome, increasing your visibility, curating a team of mentors and sponsors, and building your bespoke career strategy. It's punctuated with a bit of personality and the blueprint for my career – because you can't lead others somewhere you haven't been yourself.

Keywords Leadership · Professional development · Career strategy · Mentorship · Behaviour change

Introduction

Let's just call out the elephant in the room. I'm a mom to two brilliant little humans who bring me a huge amount of joy 90% of the time (and test my resolve the remaining 10%). But my happiest day as a mother was when I went back to work full time after my first child. Despite colleagues encouraging me to take a full year of maternity leave – a luxury that isn't possible for many women – I came back full time after eight months. And if I'm being totally honest, I started re-engaging with work when my first son was five weeks old. When I had my second son, I came back to work after six months.

Before we dive in, let's be clear on what this story is and what it isn't and what my kids have to do with you advancing your career. This story is part of my experience, and an example that illustrates the unique pressures women face. There are a million others, but the reality is you are likely reading this because the term *career aspirations* resonates deep in your core or you're wondering about (or actively

L. Desveaux (✉)
Institute for Better Health, Trillium Health Partners, Mississauga, ON, Canada
e-mail: laura@lauradesveaux.com

trying to strategize) how to leverage the examples and guidance provided by others and strike that elusive concept of 'balance' between all the things that matter in your life. Because having a career is an essential part of who you are and what you want. And you want to make the most of it. This chapter isn't a recipe for career fulfilment; it's an outline of the essential items you need in your pantry. From there, the power to choose the menu and the magic of bringing it all together lies in your hands.

While this chapter is primarily geared towards women in science, the lessons are applicable irrespective of your gender identity. If you're looking to further elevate your leadership, the insights can help you understand the experiences of women in science and the actions you can take to advance gender equity in your professional sphere. So, if you're looking to level up and design the protocol for your career advancement, read on!

Why Supporting Women in Science Should Be a Universal Priority

Many reading this chapter will know exactly what the problem is, so I'll be brief. The reality is women are underrepresented in sciences, and the common reference to a leaky pipeline is more aptly described as a leaky syringe; it's not simply inertia that is causes the leak – it's the pressure applied through the plunger that is forcing the leak. The plunger in this case represents the structural factors discussed throughout this chapter. While I'm not likening women to a therapeutic, there are parallels to be found in their value to society and investment in their education and career development. And yet, we fail to structure our systems to reflect the unique realities of women in science (e.g., the impact of recovering from childbirth on their program of work and scientific productivity). Why should we care about the representation of women in science or the reality that we lose women, on average, approximately 10 years into their scientific career (Makarem & Wang, 2020)? Because the absence of women limits the achievement of scientific and technological innovations.

Why? Women think differently than men. And I'm not talking about cognitive functioning (not my area of expertise). *What* women think about is different because our social conditioning (West & Zimmerman, 1987) and consequentially, our experiences are different. Let's use health care as an example. We know that health and health care do not work the same for everyone. There are physiological differences between men and women. But the differences don't stop here. Life circumstances and cultural realities influence health and whether and how people experience care. Despite the widespread acknowledgement of these differences, disparities exist. Each year heart disease kills more women than men, but only 38% of patients in heart disease studies are women (Jin et al., 2020). Women experience depression twice as often as men (Bierman et al., 2012) but are three times more likely to experience barriers to accessing care (Bierman et al., 2012). The reality is that care is built around the experiences of men. This is slowly shifting as women bring their experience to the table, making teams and science more inherently diverse. Simply put, we need the science they design and lead.

What Is Driving Poor Representation and Retention of Women in Science?

The issues of equity and diversity in science and leadership have garnered exponential attention in the past year, particularly as it relates to women. The structural and systematic barriers are thankfully well-defined and sadly widespread. The use of biased language is the tip of the iceberg. Inequalities facing women range from unequal pay (Izenberg et al., 2018) to the inequitable allocation of research funding (Witteman et al., 2019) to sexual harassment (Renstrom, 2016). Gendered stereotypes and role expectations are engrained in science (and most other industries) and continue to have an impact on hiring, promotion, career development (Coury et al., 2020) and well-being (Byerly, 2018) as well as women's career choices (Levine et al., 2013) and trajectories. Despite the glaring evidence identifying the problem, progress over the last decade remains marginal (Tecco, 2018).

The journal *The Lancet* recently championed the gender-equity evidence base with a recent themed issue titled 'Advancing Women in Science, Medicine, and Global Health' (2019) that provides robust evidence to inform institutional and system-wide strategies for confronting gender bias, improving diversity, and driving change. At the issue launch in London, UK, the overarching message was clear: *When it comes to moving the dial in science, the burden of work should not be on the underrepresented or the trainees – it's on the organizations and existing system leaders.* While this may be the case, when no one takes clear responsibility, accountability is lost. To advance gender equity, we need people to take ownership of the problem.

Gaps in leadership and opportunity are driven by stereotypes, bias, power imbalance, and privilege. To truly move the needle, we need to be mindful of how our unconscious biases and habits perpetuate micro-inequities. The challenge here lies in the very nature of unconscious bias and habits – we don't engage in conscious thinking during these critical moments. Allow me to provide an example. A group of conference organizers are reflecting on the success of a recent conference and are energized to secure speakers for the upcoming year. In an effort to create a similar experience, they reach out to existing speakers asking for recommendations. Those speakers are statistically likely to be men, who are likely to recommend someone from their network of – get ready for it – mostly men (Spurk et al., 2015). To be clear, I am not saying this is universally true, but there is no debating the evidence (Valian, 2018). So how do we break the cycle of unconscious bias within the professional playing field?

At a system level, we need intentional and explicit leadership that aims to achieve diversity at the executive level to ensure everyone who is interested has an equal opportunity to secure a seat at the table. A range of documents outline strategies for organizations (Women in Global Health, 2018) and leaders (Silver, 2018) with the following key action points:

- Promote equity by closing gender pay gaps;
- Actively encourage women to apply for upcoming positions;
- Include female staff on interview panels;
- Make your commitment to gender equity known;
- Ensure policy solutions are flexible while still aligning with strategic goals;
- Support collective action through partnerships across all levels;
- Mandate that your employees seek diverse speakers for internal events;
- Use a systematic process to measure and evaluate disparities.

How Can Women Take Their Careers into Their Own Hands?

While it is the structural barriers and systematic biases that shape the experiences of women in science, the reality for those reading this is that you want to know what you can do for yourself. Because that's what you have control over. So, let's break down the five things that are most likely getting in your way.

Don't Count Yourself Out – How to Overcome Imposter Syndrome

We've all been there. The insidious, irritating voice in your head that convinces you that you'll fail before you've even tried. A frustrating form of self-sabotage that most struggle to overcome. And we know what triggers it. Major life transitions, success in the face of bias, the pressure of adhering to cultural norms, and who we were raised to believe we are. And no one is immune. Not only have 75% of women executives (KPMG, 2020) experienced it, 85% believe it is commonly experienced by other women. Household names many women admire, including Michelle Obama and Tina Fey, describe vacillating between confidence and the terror that they will be discovered as a fraud.

When accomplished individuals lay their imposter syndrome on the table, it flips a switch. Imposter syndrome thrives on stealth and silence. So, calling it out and modelling authenticity and transparency with one another helps keep it in check. And it teaches us that at its core, imposter syndrome has nothing to do with us. The feeling of self-doubt that leads us to count ourselves out before we've even started stems from our circumstances and how we think others perceive us. Isolation and the absence of feedback from colleagues or peers (Cohen & McConnell, 2019) breed self-doubt. Women are socialized to communicate without being 'aggressive' (Johnson, 2017), which undermines their ability to exercise power at work. It's important to remember that our thoughts do not define who we are – imposter syndrome is a symptom of a systemic disease endemic within our society.

Imposter syndrome divides the individual from the rest of the world. So, what can you do about it?

- Call it out when it happens;
- Create connections around a shared experience;
- Curate your circle with individuals who will remind you of your brilliance.

Don't Hold Yourself Back – How to Increase Your Visibility

While current career structures aren't doing women any favours, we also often hold ourselves back. In a recent survey my team did of approximately 500 women in health care, two thirds of women reported needing support for self-advocacy and confidence building. Two out of three! Recognizing that it takes time to build skills and shift beliefs, there are three key things that women can start doing immediately to get out of their own way. And if it feels awkward, you aren't alone. Remember that 100 small steps will still get you to the same place as 10 giant leaps.

1. *Don't be modest* – take credit for your accomplishments, and make sure this happens publicly. If this feels like a giant leap for you, identify a workplace ally and take turns amplifying one another and graciously accepting the recognition.
2. *Ask for what you need* – it sounds simple, but we don't get what we don't ask for. Whether it's an informational meeting, a stretch assignment, a raise, or a promotion, the sooner you stop waiting for someone else to hand deliver your success, the sooner you'll realize your ability to create it for yourself.
3. *Speak up* – It's easy to sit back and listen when others are filling up the space and tabling their ideas, but this is where the magic happens. Every time you choose to speak up, it's an opportunity to shift thinking and change behaviours – both yours and your colleagues. If a big meeting is too much of a leap, start small with bringing a new idea to a one-on-one meeting with a colleague.

Don't Do It Alone – How to Seek Out Mentorship and Sponsorship

Let's get the distinction straight right out of the gate. Mentors are individuals who share the knowledge they have. They talk WITH you. Sponsors are individuals who have power and influence and are willing to use it on your behalf. They talk ABOUT you.

Mentors provide advice and support, acting as a mirror to help you see yourself more clearly. Great mentors strategize with you in a way that move beyond sharing their experience to help develop your capacity. Mentors in science are more common than any other industry (Olivet Nazarene University, 2018), likely owing to the supervisory nature of scientific training and research environments. Two thirds of mentorship relationships develop organically, with 59% being more casual as opposed to focused on formal goals (Olivet Nazarene University, 2018). This is true of my relationship with my first real mentor – while initially focused on project-specific supervision, the relationship evolved based on trust and continues to be a casual, peer-based mentorship arrangement through which my mentor helps me navigate challenges whenever and however they present themselves.

Sponsors ensure (and sometimes demand) that you be given high-value assignments that serve as a stepping-stone in your career. It isn't something you turn on or off – it's a relationship founded in mutual value that evolves into considerable trust and public commitment. It's also not an all-or-nothing scenario. Sponsorship involves a range of behaviours and therefore includes various types of commitment – connecting you to others, giving you opportunities, and advocating for your promotion and interests in rooms and settings where you are unable to do so yourself.

So, what can you do to assemble your team (that's right – you need more than one team member!):

1. Identify individuals who see your potential (sometimes clearer than you do) and set a strong example;
2. Create connections organically based on shared interests and values – this is the key to enduring relationships;
3. Make the relationship reciprocal – help sponsors see the value or skills you have that help advance their interests.
4. Curate diversity – ensure your team has representation across:

    (a) *All levels* (including those senior to you, your contemporaries, and juniors) – I learn just as much about how to be a leader from those senior to me as I do from those junior to me.
    (b) *Multiple industries* – there's much to be learned by getting out of the weeds and seeing the forest instead of the trees.
    (c) *Your key needs* – identify what you need support in most (e.g., communicating effectively, navigating career politics as a woman, building a network) and make sure you have someone you can turn to for each.

Mentors helps find the right doors, while sponsors stand there and hold them open. Both are essential to get where you want to go. You're hopefully energized by the light bulb that just went off and simultaneously unclear on how or where to find these individuals. Mentors can be 'found' anywhere, so the key is to look for individuals with whom you share some similarity (e.g., similar gender, age, or beliefs) while also having distinct differences (e.g., industry, values, experience). We are often drawn to those who are like us, but we stand to learn the most from those who are different. Sponsors are easier to identify, as they are quite simply part of the conversation or in the room you want to be in – that is, in positions of influence or leadership. Unlike mentorship, sponsorship is often earned through reputation and demonstration of abilities (e.g., stretch assignments).

Don't Fly Blind – How to Create Your Career Strategy

My first mentor did many things which at first blush I described as shaping who I am today. When I think about it, what he really did was help me understand who I was and what that meant for my career. Early on in my training, he sent me an article on academic success by Dr. David Sackett (Sackett, 2001) – one of the founders of Evidence-Based Medicine. While the article touched on some key topics including mentorship and time management, tucked within it was a reflective prioritization exercise that I share liberally and continue to use till this day to assess and refine my career strategy. Sackett describes the list as 'trivially simple' and outlines four categories which I have refined slightly into a set of reflective questions:

1. What do you want off your plate? *Note: This includes things you are doing that you want to quit as well as things you are currently getting asked that you want to say no to.*
2. What do you want to add?
3. What are you doing that you want to continue?
4. How do you plan to shorten the list in response to #1 and add elements from List #2?

Remember that you don't have to do it alone. In working through this exercise, you can draw on your schedule to identify what's on your plate, speak to colleagues to identify what is possible, and connect with your mentors to strategize around how to put this into place. There's an added benefit to leverage here – as you embark on the work of setting your career strategy, the conversations you have with others signal what you are interested in (which builds your narrative) and indirectly communicate what you need to those that are paying attention. Take a second here to cheer yourself – you're weaving your career threads together without even realizing it.

Don't Let the Inspiration Fade – How to Make a Plan

The inspiration people feel after professional development content is often palpable. What's equally palpable is the all-to-common knowledge to action gap (we've all been there) – putting everything this chapter has taught you into practice. Thankfully, there is an entire field of science devoted to change and understanding what drives behaviour. Harness the following three principles from behavioural science to help ensure this moment is the inflection point in your professional journey that you were hoping it would be.

Leverage the Science of Fresh Starts

Fresh starts (Dai et al., 2014) teach us a lot about how to catalyst the transformation we want to achieve. And luckily the concept is already hardwired in your brain. Think about the traditional milestones and time-based events in your life that represent shifts – birthdays, graduations, New Year's Eve, and even the Monday of a new work week. Or maybe you think of your life in chapters – university, your graduate degree, your first job, getting married, starting a family. In whatever way you label these events, recognize the opportunity they present. When we put a plan into motion alongside a *fresh start,* we are more likely to follow through. So, take out the calendar and identify your next opportunity to shift and leverage it to take control over the trajectory of your career.

Open Up a New Mental Account for Professional Change

Now that you've committed to a new chapter, it's time to pick the title. We assign and account for resources in our life (e.g., time, money, mental energy) using categories (Thaler, 1999). The strongest foundation for any chapter is one that is fundamentally connected to what matters to you – so it's time to identify your core values [Brene Brown's list (Brown, 2019) is a great resource]. Pick 2 and 3 and build intentionally around them. Be clear with yourself on how every activity or opportunity you pursue (akin to putting it in your new mental account) aligns with your values and builds towards your career goals. This will help ensure your ladder is on the right wall as you begin your climb.

Understand How to Put Your Plan Into Practice

An intention (or even an innate skill) cannot lead to achievement if it is not put into practice. Given that all activities you undertake involve a specific underlying behaviour, understanding what contributes to a behaviour happening (or not) is central to the success of your plan. There are three core conditions required in order for you to take action (Michie et al., 2011):

1. You need to have the *Motivation*. Between the content of this book and the clarification of your values (see above), you likely have this covered. If you're still searching for clarity, articulate the impact you'd like to have and work backwards from there.
2. You need to have the *Capability*. Reflect on whether there are skills you need to build and set a plan to build them. Where possible, seek out training and skill building opportunities that tailor to the context in which you are looking to apply your skills (e.g., science communication workshops, negotiation skills training).
3. You need to have the *Opportunity*. Once you have the skills you need, find every opportunity you can to apply those skills and build the 'strength' of that muscle.

Be clear about *when*, *where*, and *how* you will apply them to help yourself follow through. Write it down and consider whether you need an accountability buddy to help keep you on track. Increase the odds that you'll follow through by building in a reminder to apply your skills right before the opportunity will present itself (e.g., schedule a reminder to share your new ideas right that pops up right before you walk into a meeting).

Conclusions and Practical Recommendations

Let's bring this final piece of the puzzle together with an example. My core values are growth, leadership, and impact, and they are all inherently motivating to me. From here, I need to not only identify the activities that would be of interest to me, but I need the opportunity to engage in those activities that allow me to put my skills into action (put another way, identifying the activities that align with your values is only half of the equation). For example, writing a book on professional growth that will have impact for a broad audience aligns with all three of my core values. I have debated this for some time and continue to until this day. I could either pursue this independently (bucket list goal) or wait for a more digestible opportunity to present itself (the invitation to contribute to this book). Finally, I need the capability to write a narrative that is compelling to you, the reader. Prior to this chapter, I have given talks and workshops to hundreds of scientists and professionals on career strategy and professional development. I've spoken to more high-performing professionals than I can count. And across each of these opportunities, I have refined my learnings and the key insights that underlie professional success. And I've written a lot (I can thank academia for that one). And if you're reading this, I've succeeded in transitioning these skills to the capability of contributing to a book. Next stop – I'll write the full book myself. Dream big and build a plan to go after what you want – and enjoy the journey.

References

Bierman, A. S., Shack, A. R., & Johns, A. (2012). *The POWER study: Achieving health equity in Ontario: Opportunities for intervention and improvement* (Vol. 2). http://www.powerstudy.ca/the-power-report/the-power-report-volume-2/achieving-health-equity-in-ontario

Brown, B. (2019). List of values. Brené Brown. https://daretolead.brenebrown.com/wp-content/uploads/2019/02/Values.pdf

Byerly, S. I. (2018). Female physician wellness: Are expectations of ourselves extreme? *International Anesthesiology Clinics, 56*(3), 59–73. https://doi.org/10.1097/AIA.0000000000000197

Cohen, E. D., & McConnell, W. R. (2019). Fear of fraudulence: Graduate school program environments and the impostor phenomenon. *The Sociological Quarterly, 60*(3), 457–478. https://doi.org/10.1080/00380253.2019.1580552

Coury, S., Huang, J., Kumar, A., Prince, S., Krivkovich, A., & Yee, L. (2020). Women in the workplace 2020. McKinsey & Company. https://womenintheworkplace.com/

Dai, H., Milkman, K. L., & Riis, J. (2014). The fresh start effect: Temporal landmarks motivate aspirational behavior. *Management Science, 60*(10), 2563–2582. https://doi.org/10.1287/mnsc.2014.1901

Izenberg, D., Oriuwa, C., & Taylor, M. (2018, October 18). Why is there a gender wage gap in Canadian medicine?. *Healthy Debate*. https://healthydebate.ca/2018/10/topic/gender-wage-gap-medicine/

Jin, X., Chandramouli, C., Allocco, B., Gong, E., Lam, C. S. P., & Yan, L. L. (2020). Women's participation in cardiovascular clinical trials from 2010 to 2017. *Circulation, 141*(7), 540–548. https://doi.org/10.1161/CIRCULATIONAHA.119.043594

Johnson, S. K. (2017, August 17). What the science actually says about gender gaps in the workplace. *Harvard Business Review*. https://hbr.org/2017/08/what-the-science-actually-says-about-gender-gaps-in-the-workplace

KPMG. (2020). *Advancing the future of women in business: A KPMG Women's leadership summit report*. KPMG.

Levine, R. B., Mechaber, H. F., Reddy, S. T., Cayea, D., & Harrison, R. A. (2013). "A good career choice for women": Female medical students' mentoring experiences. *Academic Medicine, 88*(4), 527–534. https://doi.org/10.1097/ACM.0b013e31828578bb

Makarem, Y., & Wang, J. (2020). Career experiences of women in science, technology, engineering, and mathematics fields: A systematic literature review. *Human Resource Development Quarterly, 31*(1), 91–111. https://doi.org/10.1002/hrdq.21380

Michie, S., van Stralen, M. M., & West, R. (2011). The behaviour change wheel: A new method for characterising and designing behaviour change interventions. *Implementation Science, 6*(1), 42. https://doi.org/10.1186/1748-5908-6-42

Olivet Nazarene University. (2018). *Study explores professional Mentor-mentee relationships in 2019*. Olivet Nazarene University. https://online.olivet.edu/research-statistics-on-professional-mentors

Renstrom, E. (2016, May 17). 30% of female doctors have been sexually harassed. *TIME Magazine*. https://time.com/4337372/30-of-female-doctors-have-been-sexually-harassed/

Sackett, D. L. (2001). On the determinants of academic success as a clinician-scientist. Clinical and investigative medicine. *Medecine Clinique Et Experimentale, 24*(2), 94–100.

Silver, J. K. (2018). *Be ethical*. https://sheleadshealthcare.com/wp-content/uploads/2018/09/Be-Ethical-Campaign.pdf

Spurk, D., Meinecke, A. L., Kauffeld, S., & Volmer, J. (2015). Gender, professional networks, and subjective career success within early academic science careers: The role of gender composition in inside and outside departmental support networks. *Journal of Personnel Psychology, 14*(3), 121–130. https://doi.org/10.1027/1866-5888/a000131

Tecco, H. (2018, August 1). Gender inequality still plagues the health care industry. Women are fed up. *STAT*. https://www.statnews.com/2018/08/01/gender-inequality-health-care-leadership-women/

Ten Asks: Doing things differently in Gender Equality and Global Health. (2018, September 19). *Women in Global Health*. https://www.womeningh.org/single-post/2018/09/19/Ten-Asks-doing-things-differently-in-Gender-Equality-and-Global-Health

Thaler, R. H. (1999). Mental accounting matters. *Journal of Behavioural Decision Making, 12*(3), 183–206. https://doi.org/10.1002/(SICI)1099-0771(199909)12:3<183::AID-BDM318>3.0.CO;2-F

The Lancet. (2019). Advancing women in science, medicine, and global health. *The Lancet, 393*(10171), 493–610.

Valian, V. (2018, October 9). Two Nobels for women—Why so slow?. *Nature*. https://www.nature.com/articles/d41586-018-06953-6

West, C., & Zimmerman, D. H. (1987). Doing Gender. *Gender & Society, 1*(2), 125–151. https://doi.org/10.1177/0891243287001002002

Witteman, H. O., Hendricks, M., Straus, S., & Tannenbaum, C. (2019). Are gender gaps due to evaluations of the applicant or the science? A natural experiment at a national funding agency. *The Lancet, 393*(10171), 531–540. https://doi.org/10.1016/S0140-6736(18)32611-4

Part II
Research Skills and Competencies

Chapter 7
Managing Research Projects

Anne van Dongen

Abstract Project management is a valuable skill that helps you think about where you want your research project to go, what you need to get there, and how to minimise risks during the process. Unfortunately, most early career researchers do not get much training in research project management and are left to fend for themselves. This chapter starts with useful tips about managing time by giving examples of essential project planning tools like task lists, milestones, charts, and timelines. Next, it discusses managing the research project process including administration, data management, and risk assessment. In addition, it discusses how best to manage people in your project team, from your supervisors to external stakeholders, and shares tips on preparing and chairing meetings and setting up a communication plan. Finally, this chapter emphasises the need to manage your own mental health while making the most of your research project.

Keywords Project management · Time management · Planning · Communication · Mental health · Managing People · Managing Process

Introduction

> My gut is that most conspiracy theorists have never been project managers. Their optimism is adorable. – Merlin Mann (independent writer, speaker, and broadcaster).

Managing your PhD project for most of us will be a daunting introduction to research project management, and most of us were woefully unprepared for it. I started my PhD not even realising I was actually the manager of my PhD project. With three PhD supervisors who did not always agree, and were not always available, I wasted time not taking control of the process more. This partly stemmed from anxiety about telling my supervisors what I needed from them. I didn't realise

A. van Dongen (✉)
University of Twente, Department of Psychology, Health, and Technology, Enschede, The Netherlands

how busy (and let's face it, chaotic) supervisors can be, and just assumed that after sending them my draft I should just wait until they contacted me. In the meantime, I took on other research projects, sat in all sorts of committees, and teaching, which delayed my thesis even more. Even though I loved doing the additional projects, I was mainly doing them to procrastinate. At some point (late in the process, I must admit, as it took me over five years to finish my PhD), I decided enough was enough. I made a plan to finish my thesis, communicated the plan to my supervisors with deadlines for them to review my drafts, and even scheduled two weeks away from the office to finish my thesis introduction and discussion. I learnt that my supervisors actually really appreciated me taking charge and communicating clearly what I needed from them, as that helped them plan my project among all the other projects they had going.

Since then, I have managed or coordinated research projects in the Netherlands, UK, and Australia, and have worked with and for people from different countries. The most important lesson I have learnt when it comes to project management is that no one has a lot of time to contribute, but everyone wants to have their say. In addition, as you are 'only' early in your career, you often will not have the authority that can be used as leverage.

This chapter includes several tips and tricks I learnt along the way, things I have done, things I wish I had done, and things I really need to start doing. In this chapter, I present insights from my own experience, tips I got from colleagues who are managing research projects, and a non-systematic literature search on recent papers or blogs on 'managing research projects'. There are many books, journals, and blog posts dedicated to project management. I have included some in the reference list, and the topics and literature presented in this chapter serve more as suggestions.

Managing from Small- to Large-Scale Research Projects

What Is Project Management and Why Is It Important?

One of the most important goals of project management is that it helps you think about where you want your project to go and what you need to get there. It helps you anticipate how much time a project and its tasks will take and what resources you will need (Howard Hughes Medical Institute and Burroughs Wellcome Fund, 2006). It will also help you minimise risk by being able to take preventative action and detect deviation from the plan early on. In addition, it allows you to update and inform managers, supervisors, and other stakeholders on the project's process and progress.

Unlike classical project management, research programme managers tend to focus on process more than output. This is because the research process is iterative and involves progressive insight. The outcome of one (sub)study may change the direction the project will go in. In addition, research projects are often subjected to factors beyond the control of the project manager. You will have responsibility, but are often unable to assert authority – you will have to get things done through people in your team without having any direct control over them. 'People skills' are therefore as important in research project management as, for example, planning skills.

Furthermore, different types and scopes of projects require different management processes and skills. Projects can range from relatively straightforward in scope, where just you and your manager/supervisor are involved and there is a single research site (e.g., the university), to complex ones, where you have to deal with multiple (internal and external) stakeholders and research sites (e.g., research in several GP practices). 'Stakeholders' are individuals, groups, or organisations who have an interest in can affect or be affected by the outcome of a project. Depending on your field, they can be (external) funders, community leaders, students, policy makers, patients, healthcare professionals, non-profit organisations, industry leaders, etc.

Project management is not an exact science. It should be a tool to get the maximum out of your project and your project members, so use this chapter to gain actionable ideas but implement what works for YOU, and YOUR project and team. As mentioned, as an early career research project manager you will often be dealing with situations that are beyond your control. This chapter describes how to make the most of your project by focusing on the things you *do* have control over.

Managing Time

Whether you are working on a PhD project or managing a postdoctoral research fellowship, you will not have infinite time to complete your research. In this section, I highlight three practical time management templates you can use when planning your projects and listing the tasks involved. A task that should be finished is also called a milestone.

The most basic template is a timeline and task list, which can take the form of a simple Word or Excel table (see Fig. 7.1). A Gantt chart (Fig. 7.2) can be a helpful visual aid for longer term overview. A Gantt chart is a graph (named after Henry L Gantt who introduced the technique in 1903) consisting of horizontal bars that depict the start date, duration, and end date for each activity. Ideally, a task list should also identify task interdependencies. This is when one task cannot start until another task has been completed. For example, data collection cannot start until ethics approval has been obtained, and the submission to the ethics board cannot happen until the whole team has reviewed, edited, and approved the questionnaire or topic guide you will use in your study.

Planning a timeline can be a bit daunting, not least because a research project is often dependent on other people and subject to contingencies. You can have an excellent plan but if your supervisor, the ethics committee, or the engineer programming your app runs over time, your project can be thrown into disarray. Thomas and Hodges (2010, Chapter 8, p. 139) state the following: '*If you want to estimate the*

Task	Who	When	Status
Study 1 - qualitative			
Ethics			
Participant information sheet and consent form	Project Manager	8 Feb	Done
Study protocol	Project Manager	8 Feb	Done
Supervisor final check	Supervisor	14 Feb	Done
Submit to Ethics Committee	Project Manager	15 Feb	Done
Meeting topic guide	Project Manager and Supervisor	2 March	Done
Finalise topic guide	Project Manager	14 March	In progress
Data collection			
Contact participants	Project Manager	15 March	In progress
Interview 1	Research assistant	30 March	Scheduled
Interview 2	Research assistant	2 April	Scheduled
Etc.			
Etc			
Study 2 - quantitative			
Ethics			
Participant information sheet and consent form	Project Manager	23 March	In progress
Study protocol	Project Manager	23 March	In progress
Supervisor final check	Supervisor	29 March	Scheduled
Submit to Ethics Committee	Project Manager	30 March	Scheduled
Questionnaire			
Meeting questionnaire	Whole team	15 March	In progress
Finalise questionnaire	Project Manager	25 March	In progress
Program questionnaire	Project Manager	15 April	Scheduled
Send out questionnaire	Project Manager	1 May	Scheduled
Send reminder	Project Manager	8 May	Scheduled
Etc.			
Etc			

Note: It may be a good idea to underline and highlight the major milestones as we did here

Fig. 7.1 Example of a task list

total number of person hours or days likely to be needed for a project as a whole, a good rule of thumb is to take whatever total you first work out to be a viable estimate and multiply it by two. This is likely to come somewhere close to the actual number of hours or days that will be needed in practice'. This may seem excessive, but I have found this to be a very realistic rule. It will also save you a lot of stress if you are able to adequately allocate the time. In addition, don't forget that after the data collection is finished, articles will need to be written. That takes time. I once worked on an ambitious project where we had lots of cool data at the end, but no one had time to write the articles, because the team members either changed jobs, started different projects, or went on maternity leave.

7 Managing Research Projects

PROJECT TIMETABLE	2022												Notes	
	J	F	M	A	M	J	J	A	S	O	N	D		
Study 1 - qualitative														
Ethics	▓	▓											Deadline 15 Feb	
Topic guide	▓	▓												
Data collection			▓	▓										
Transcription														
Data analysis					▓									
Write paper							▓	▓					Submission deadline 30 Sept	
Study 2 - quantitative														
Ethics					▓								Deadline 30 July	
Hire research student						▓								
Program survey							▓	▓					After results from Study 1 are known	
Data collection									▓					
Data analysis										▓				
Write paper												▓	Submission deadline 24 December	
Group meetings/consultations														
Research team including stakeholders	▓			▓		▓		▓		▓				
Funder					▓				▓					

Fig. 7.2 Example of (part of) a Gantt chart

When planning research projects, be aware that as your project progresses, your goals may change. Therefore, it is good practice to build in periodic reviews of results against objectives and revise the objectives, tasks and timelines where necessary. Organise time backwards from deadlines or planned article submission dates and consider the timing of sequential tasks. For example, you should not plan starting data collection before a reasonable estimated date of ethics approval. In addition, do not forget to take public holidays and your team members' annual leave into account. It is generally no use to send out a questionnaire before the Christmas holidays as people may not be in the mood for surveys. The same goes for summer holidays. Participants, potential respondents, and your team members may not have time or motivation to contribute to your project. And finally, schedule enough time to remind your team members about their tasks. For urgent and/or focused work like writing articles and running complicated statistics, it is good practice to block out time in your calendar, so you will not be interrupted when working on these tasks.

When things get really complex and you have many larger and smaller tasks on your plate, a 3 × 3 planning matrix (Fig. 7.3) can be useful in addition to day-to-day planning. In this schedule, you divide your tasks according to how long it will take you to finish them, and how urgent they are. The columns reflect the former, and the rows reflect the latter. Long tasks (i.e., those that will take you several hours) will need to be scheduled in your agenda. Short tasks (i.e., those that will take less than 2 h) could be done, e.g., between a lecture and a meeting. Emails or calls can be finished quickly and could be done when you have 15 min to spare. Make this work for you – think about how you would like to define long and short tasks by the time period (week, month, quarter) that is most useful for you. In terms of urgency (i.e., the rows), ask yourself, do they need to be finished this week, this month, or is there no deadline? Plan work on the first row and then move your way down to the other rows.

Long – This week	Short - This week	Email or call – This week
Write report on Study 1	Descriptive analyses Study 2	Reminder supervisor
Finish topic guide	Finish consent form Study 3	Call patient 2 to schedule interview
Etc.		
Long – This month or waiting	**Short – This month or waiting**	**Email or call – This month or waiting**
Introduction and methods of paper – waiting for supervisor	Upload documents to Open Science Framework	Wait for reply Patient 4
Finish analyses and script Study 2	Finish poster for conference	
Etc.		
Long – Long-term or no deadline	**Short – Long-term or no deadline**	**Email or call – Long-term or no deadline**
Read book on project management	Write profile for university webpage	
Write new blog post		
Etc.		

Fig. 7.3 Example of a 3 × 3 planning matrix

Managing the Process

Admin and Data Management

When I started my PhD project, I was not very meticulous in making process notes. Instead, I thought I could rely on my memory. I was wrong. It is good practice to take notes on everything, ranging from meetings, changes in the process, and especially the decisions being made. You will need those notes as a few months down the line you will not remember why or how particular decisions were made. Saving your notes and having earlier versions of documents make it possible to retrace editing and decision-making. Sometimes, decisions get casually made in emails, so saving all emails is another way to retrace steps. The best way to keep track of decision-making is to keep an Excel sheet like the example in Fig. 7.4.

It is easy to let project administration slip when you are busy with data collection, article writing, or teaching. And let's face it, it's not the most exciting part of the project. But taking 15 min at the end of each day (when needed) to keep track of the process may save you a lot of time and stress along the way. Another worthwhile exercise is noting down the time it took you to complete specific tasks. A lot of the work you do and the time you spend are 'invisible' to your managers or supervisors, and it can be good to have an overview to show them how long you spend working on each task. In addition, the next time when you plan a project, you will have a much better idea how much time it takes to execute different tasks.

Another good practice to start with early is clear project documentation in a shared folder (Fig. 7.5). This will save you a lot of time looking for specific documents. When saving documents, make sure you add a title and date to the titles of all documents to ensure you are clear on which are previous versions, later versions, and final versions of your documents. And for your data analyses, always save your syntaxes or data cleaning process documents.

7 Managing Research Projects 81

Decision	Date	Made by	Made via	Reason	Documented
Extend deadline for data collection	15022022	Team	Stakeholder meeting	Not enough participants	Meeting minutes 15022022
Drop item 3 and 7 from questionnaire	02032022	Supervisor and PM	Email	Factor analysis	Email from supervisor 02032022
Find MA student for Study 3	07032022	Supervisor and PM	Verbal agreement	Will save time	Not documented

Note: PM stands for Project Manager

Fig. 7.4 Example of an excel sheet on decision-making

Title	Project title at top level folder
Funding application	Applications for funding
Ethics documents	Ethics application, information sheets, consent forms
Communications and meetings	*Subfolders:* - Email messages, - Meeting minutes and critical decision making
Questionnaires / interview scripts	Versions of all the question sets and topic guides ordered by date
Data files	*Subfolders:* - Transcripts - Text documents - Quantitative data
Analyses	*Subfolders:* - Raw data, - Scripts, - Output files
Reports	Research reports for funder with dates
Presentations and manuscripts	All external output like conference presentations and manuscripts
Archive	To store older versions of project documents

Fig. 7.5 Example of a project folder structure

Forecast the Risks

When setting up your project management plan, think through with your team what challenges you may expect for each of the milestones you have outlined in the project plan. Something that all project managers should do is a risk analysis assessment (Fig. 7.6). It is helpful to split risk into two aspects: probability and impact. Probability is the likelihood of something happening, impact is how serious things are, if they do happen.

Common risks to research projects are delays or refusal of approval during ethical review, difficulty in obtaining access to potential research participants, low recruitment or retention rates for research participants (attrition), implementation in the 'real world', data collection methods not working as planned, data processing and analysis being more difficult than anticipated, equipment failure or loss, projects running over budget, and conflict (Streiner, 2011).

There are several strategies that can be used to avoid or reduce some of these risks. Find out what your ethics committee needs in order to approve your project,

Date entered	Last update	Description	Probability	Impact	Possible response actions	Chosen action
15-01-2022		Ethics approval - Delay to approval or significant amendments required	Medium	Medium	Start protocols early to ensure timely submission	Start protocols early to ensure timely submission
15-01-2022	30-01-2022	Failure to recruit participants for trial	Medium	High	Add study site, add research assistant, extend inclusion time period	Add study site
15-01-2022		Patient focus group membership - Maintaining target 12 group members	High	Medium	Continued liaison with local patient groups, decrease number of patients to 8-10	Decrease number of patients to 8-10

Fig. 7.6 Example of a risk assessment overview

and start preparing documents early. Carry out a feasibility or pilot study to test recruitment procedures, questionnaires, or interview topic guides. If you have student research assistants for data collection, set up monitoring systems to check how the data collection is progressing and schedule regular debriefing to discuss progress and problems they are facing.

Finishing Up

As a project is nearing completion, make arrangements to store research data for future use, including re-analysis of the data to confirm the original findings, additional or more detailed analyses, inclusion of data in a meta-analysis, linking the data to other datasets or research resources, or audit of the data to confirm it was collected as stated. If you plan to store your data for future use, it is important to ensure that the types of analyses already performed on the data are adequately documented (e.g., in a codebook or script) and that clear links can be traced from the raw datasets to the reported project results. Preferably, if possible, place everything in an Open Access repository (see Chap. 9).

Now is also the time to reflect on the process to learn from the experience, e.g., did you underspend or overspend, what might you have done differently to better use the resources, and how would you change things for the next project? Take this reflection into your next project, project proposal, or job application.

Managing People

One of the most challenging aspects of project management has nothing to do with the project content and everything with your team members. You may be lucky to be working with only one or two supervisors or colleagues who are clear in their expectations, read your drafts on time, and get along well. If not, this section can help you with the pitfalls of managing your managers and other team members.

Supervising Your Supervisors and Coping with Colleagues

These six tips were kindly written by Lisa Klinkenberg, PhD. She recently finished her thesis and was complemented at her defence on how well she managed her supervision team of four. Such a large supervision team is not common but not unheard of in the Netherlands, and it poses many challenges which Lisa skilfully managed.

Tip 1 Break the Feedback Cycle by Announcing Your Final Version.

When working on a manuscript, a questionnaire or something else, as an early career researcher you are likely to send draft versions to your supervisors or colleagues and receive extensive feedback on these drafts which you will then process into a new draft version, which you will then send back to them again. This cycle can repeat itself many times, with often minimal improvements in the later cycles. And when this cycle continues, you might ask yourself: *when is it finally good enough?* To speed up this process, when you feel confident enough about a version (around the third draft), mention that this is your final version and ask your supervisor(s) or colleagues if it is okay to submit/use it like this, or if they have some minor comments left to share. This urges them to give more clarity on whether it is indeed good enough to be submitted as a final version.

Tip 2 Do Not Expect That All Feedback from Your Supervisor or Colleague Is 'the Truth'.

Your supervisors and colleagues are probably experts in the field. But when it comes to the order in your manuscript, the content of your cover letter or the layout of your research poster, people rely on their personal experiences, opinions, and training. This is also true for your supervisors or colleagues and even though they might mention in their feedback that 'the conclusion of your research should be in the middle of your research poster' or 'the descriptive statistics should be mentioned in your methods rather than your results', these kinds of comments are preferences rather than facts, which have worked in their career but might not work for you. Although it is easiest to just do as your supervisor(s) or colleagues tell you to do, keep listening to your own preferences and feelings. In addition, at some point you do become more familiar with the grant, article, or poster guidelines than they are. If you do, respectfully explain why you are not incorporating their feedback.

Tip 3 Openly Discuss Conflicting Opinions.

Somewhat in line with Tip 2, supervisors or colleagues from your research team might also give conflicting feedback. When supervisor 1 tells you to change the order of some paragraphs, and supervisor 2 tells you to revert the order, it is best to openly discuss this conflicting feedback in a meeting. If you side more with one of your supervisors, you can explain in a respectful manner why you prefer their solution above the solution of your other supervisor.

Tip 4 Give Deadlines and Send Reminders for Feedback.

Your supervisors and colleagues are busy people with other (PhD) students and postdocs to supervise. They probably also need to write grants, teach, and execute management related tasks. So, when you send your draft to them for feedback, they might not reply as quickly as you would hope or maybe not at all. A strategy you can apply is to clearly state in your email (or even in the email title) a deadline for when you want to receive their feedback. In most cases, two weeks in advance should be a sufficient timespan. This deadline should be set a few days earlier than when you actually need the feedback (e.g., for a conference deadline). Also state that when you do not receive feedback, you will assume the version is good as it is and that you will submit it. When one week passes, send a friendly reminder of the draft version you want feedback on and remind them of the deadline. When it is one or two days before the deadline and you have not received all feedback yet, send another reminder with a friendly, but a more urgent tone wherein you again state that you will assume this version is good enough as it is in its current state and that you will submit it.

Tip 5 Celebrate Victories with Your Team.

It is good for team morale to share and celebrate victories, such as an award or a new publication. For example, if you have your manuscript published, bring a cake to your next in-person meeting, or say 'cheers' with coffee and tea in an online meeting. You can also do this with celebratory events that are not work related, such as your or their birthdays. Besides the fun in celebrating victories, it is also good way to bond with your team. And when the relationships between the team members are good, your team is also more likely to help you out and give feedback in time.

Tip 6 Do Not Side Too Much with One of Them. One implication of working as a team is that you may develop closer professional relationships with one of your supervisors/colleagues more than others. Of course, this is a completely normal thing when building relationships: one person's interests, views, and personal traits might align better with yours than that of another person. You should be aware, however, of how this will affect your team dynamics. For instance, you will be more likely to 'side' with the supervisor or colleague you agree with the most while ignoring the feedback of the supervisor or colleague you agree with the least. Also, if you have a more informal relationship with one of your supervisors or colleagues, you should try to be formal when it comes to work related activities. For instance, if the supervisor you like more is often late with his/her feedback or gives very strict feedback, you should professionally handle this situation and not take it personally.

Create a Communication Plan

It is wise to let your team know how you plan to communicate with them, and where they can find the information about the projects. A shared workspace will be the primary source for providing updates to the team and managing project knowledge. It should be a repository for project documentation like meeting agendas and minutes, and planning and task lists.

The easiest shared workspace is a shared folder on the university network drive. This will work well enough if you manage a small team located at the same university. If you work with external team members, there are multiple project software tools available ranging from relatively simple (e.g., Asana, Slack, Teams, Google), to more sophisticated (e.g., Trello, Jira, Monday). Other platforms can also be used to make your research more open (e.g., GitHub, Open Science Framework). Like other software, project management programmes come with bells and whistles you may never need or use. Again, this should be a tool to get the maximum out of your project and your project members, so do what works best for you and your project and team. Before you choose though, it is important to make sure all external stakeholders have access to the software and are able to use it.

If your project involves external stakeholders who are not in the core project team (like a patient advisory group or research assistants), it may be a good idea to produce a newsletter or use (Google drive, Slack, or Teams) groups for updates to keep people engaged with the project. Set expectations for these stakeholders on how often you will distribute updates about the project, and in which format you will provide the communication. Make sure to balance the information provided by including highlights on barriers and facilitators to success and notable achievements.

Meetings

If many people are attending a meeting, it is a good idea to send out a Doodle poll (www.doodle.com) with different day/time options to find out when most people can attend. When choosing a date, consider who actually *needs* to be in attendance, and whose attendance is optional. Send the agenda and documentation you want to discuss at least a week before the meeting, so people have time to read it and prepare for the meeting. If the meeting is long (>1.5 h), schedule a coffee/tea/bathroom break. Especially in online meetings, it is difficult to stay focused for over an hour.

When you are chairing the meeting, clarify the agenda and objectives of the meeting at the start. If the discussion takes too long (for example, when people share excessive background info or start venting), remind them of the meeting agenda and goals in a friendly way. Summarise the conclusions and decisions made at the end, approximately 10 min before the declared meeting end time. Ensure the key decisions and action points are clear to everyone. Give everyone one last option to mention any other business.

After the meeting, share a summary with all attendees and all that could not be present. Full minutes are good but notes of the meeting including the main decisions and action points (including who will take the action) are usually good enough and will save you a lot of time. Check whether these action points have been completed before the next meeting (or sooner in case of deadlines).

Influencing Stakeholders

As an early career researcher, you often do not have authoritative leverage over most of your stakeholders, nor your managers/supervisors. Therefore, it may be good to consider what kind of influencing strategies *are* available to you. If you need someone to do something they may not necessarily want to do, take some time to think about who they are and what they might gain from participating in the project (Daley et al., 2017). Ask yourself questions like:

- What is the bigger picture as far as they are concerned?
- What are their priorities, and how can they be met by this project?
- What are their aspirations, goals, and objectives and how do they fit in with this project?
- What is constraining them?/What is pressuring them?
- What are their strengths and weaknesses?

Influencing factors besides seniority or authority are, for example:

- *Likeability* – people will be more motivated to 'help you out' if they like you;
- *Reciprocity* – if you do something for someone else, they will be more inclined to do something for you;
- *Social* – try to make sure they enjoy working on the project, e.g., by scheduling some time to chat before or after a meeting;
- *Scarcity* – you may have a resource they need (e.g., knowledge, skills, network);
- *Urgency* – if something must be done before a certain date, you can appeal to a sense of urgency;
- *Power allies* – they may not necessarily want to do something for you, but they may want to impress your supervisor;
- *Shared purpose* – The project may serve a similar purpose for both of you;
- *Moral/value-based* – if your research is about making the world a healthier/more social/more equal place, they may feel persuaded by moral reasons;
- *External visibility* – being in the project may increase their visibility in a certain field and may increase their network.

Managing Your Mental Health

Finally, please look after your mental health while managing your projects. Setbacks, impostor syndrome, or negative results can have a real impact on your mood or long-term mental health, and it is important to look after yourself, even (or especially) when no one else does.

Make time for breaks. Go for a walk to clear your head, do some exercises to prevent neck and back pains, take your eyes off the screen for a while, and pet your cat (dog, partner, plant, etc.). Do not think you are alone in this because you are not. If needed, ask for help. Most of the time, someone has done it before, got stuck before, and solved it before. Google is a great resource if you cannot find someone around you who has come across the same issue.

I cannot stress the importance of connecting with other early career researchers and/or project managers. Sharing the burden makes you feel less alone and can occasionally give you great ideas on how to solve problems. At one university where I worked, a group was set up for research project managers who got together (virtually) for an hour once a month. The first half hour was usually spent ranting, and in the second half hour, we tried to help each other with project issues. It was a very wholesome process. If you ever feel the pressure getting to you, talk! To your colleagues, friends, your supervisor if you can, mentor or a professional.

Everyone gets lost sometimes, finding out they have been wasting valuable time, or made a (seemingly huge) mistake. Don't panic! Or panic for a little while (it's only natural) but stop panicking after some time. Then start fresh.

Conclusion and Practical Recommendations

Properly managing your research project from the start takes time and effort, but it will save you even more time, not to mention stress, if you plan adequately. Most universities organise courses or workshops in project management for early career researchers. It can be very useful to enrol in one, as there will always be helpful information or exercises that are not mentioned in this chapter. Research project management can be hard, preparation is key, and you will make mistakes (as we all do!), but at the end, it will be worth it. If not for the scientific result, then for the addition to your CV. Project management is a valuable, key transferable skill that you can utilise within or outside of academia. Finally, I would like to summarise some key practical recommendations to successfully manage projects:

- Project management helps you think about where you want your project to go and what you need to get there.
- Taking some time for planning and management will save you time later on.
- Take notes about the process and all decisions throughout the project.

- Date all project documentation and save it in a clearly defined folder structure.
- Create a clear communication plan for your project group.
- Always look after your own mental health, it is more important than any project.

Acknowledgements I would like to thank Lisa Klinkenberg, Rebecca Woodhouse, Papiya Mazumdar, and Emily Peckham for providing valuable input for this chapter.

References

Daley, R., Guccione, K., & Hutchinson, S. (2017). *53 ways to enhance researcher development*. Frontinus.

Howard Hughes Medical Institute and Burroughs Wellcome Fund. (2006). *Making the right moves: A practical guide to scientific management for postdocs and new faculty*. https://www.hhmi.org/science-education/programs/resources/making-right-moves

Streiner, D. L. (2011). In S. Sidani (Ed.), *When research goes off the rails: Why it happens and what you can do about it*. Guilford Press. https://www.guilford.com/books/When-Research-Goes-Off-the-Rails/Streiner-Sidani/9781606234105

Thomas, D. R., & Hodges, I. D. (2010). *Designing and managing your research project: Core skills for social and health research*. Sage Publications. https://doi.org/10.4135/9781446289044

Chapter 8
Networking and Collaborating in Academia: Increasing Your Scientific Impact and Having Fun in the Process

Elaine Toomey

Abstract Networking is an essential element of an academic career, though it can spark a multitude of reactions ranging from delight to distress. For early career researchers, having a strong network of collaborators can be invaluable in terms of supporting you through the difficult times of academia, as well as helping you to enjoy the good moments. Networking is also particularly important for expanding the reach and impact of your research to a multitude of audiences. In this chapter, I aim to provide an overview of the challenges and benefits of networking. I will explain my core principles underpinning my approach to building networks and collaborations, and provide some practical recommendations and action points based on my experiences or advice given to me that I have found useful. Although there is no one right or wrong approach to networking and building collaborations, this chapter aims to help you reflect on your own core principles and priorities when it comes to networking, and to support you to develop or further enhance your own approach.

Keywords Networking · Collaboration · Impact · Social Support · Social Networks

Introduction

'Research is a team sport'. I heard Professor Jeremy Grimshaw, one of the world's leading health researchers, say this at a workshop in Ireland in 2019. For me, an avid sportsperson, it neatly captured the importance of networking and working collaboratively in academia. Regardless of what academic discipline you work in, none of us can do this on our own. Building effective collaborations is integral to successfully navigating the academic landscape and maximising the overall impact of your work.

E. Toomey (✉)
University of Limerick, School of Allied Health, Limerick, Ireland

© The Author(s), under exclusive license to Springer Nature Switzerland AG 2022
D. Kwasnicka, A. Y. Lai (eds.), *Survival Guide for Early Career Researchers*, https://doi.org/10.1007/978-3-031-10754-2_8

In 2018, while completing my postdoctoral fellowship at the National University of Ireland Galway, I was fortunate enough to spend a few weeks as a visiting researcher at the University of Newcastle in Australia. I had met my hosts at a conference a year previously in Canada and we kept in contact due to mutual personal (exercise, the outdoors, and good food!) and professional (implementation of evidence-based health research into practice and policy) interests, as well as a shared sense of fun. During my visit, a number of people from the department I was visiting attended a Franklin Women's networking event. Franklin Women is an Australian professional community focused on supporting the careers of women working in medical and health research. I could have stayed in my rental apartment working on long overdue papers, but I chose to attend the event and see what happened. What turned out to be the most memorable part of this event was spending time getting to know more about my hosts and their departmental colleagues on a personal level, as we bonded over some of the more cringe-worthy aspects of 'facilitated' networking and enjoyed other aspects of the event. For me, the benefit of attending that event wasn't so much about learning new knowledge about networking, but about investing time in strengthening and maintaining relationships with my existing contacts. This aligns with what I believe are my core principles when it comes to networking and building collaborations – openness, enjoyment, and managing expectations. These essentially involve being open to new opportunities and experiences, striving to enjoy those experiences and to have fun, and not expecting (or wanting) every encounter or experience to yield a career-focused output. I'll expand on these later on in this chapter. I'm privileged to still collaborate regularly with my Australian colleagues – not only because our research collaborations are stimulating and impactful, but also because it's always an enjoyable experience, even when meetings are held at all hours of day or night due to differing time zones!

Why Is Networking Important?

The word 'networking' evokes different reactions in different people. Some people hear the word and light up, others are somewhat ambivalent to it, while others shudder and cringe at the thought. Research tells us that for some, engaging in networking for professional work-related goals is associated with feelings of dirtiness, or a sense of violating our personal moral codes and beliefs (Casciaro et al., 2014). However, the same research also shows that those who experience these feelings engage in networking less frequently, and have lower job performance than those who don't have those feelings. So, like it or hate it, networking is a vital part of an academic career, with many potential benefits.

Academia can be a difficult and arduous career choice. We are constantly faced with rejection, be it in the form of rejected papers, grant applications or job interviews – unfortunately there are plenty of examples! It can also be isolating and overwhelming at times, even during relatively successful moments. For example, securing your first grant funding can initially evoke a sense of delight, followed by feelings of anxiety or worry – will I be able to deliver this? What if I fail? For early career researchers (ECRs), additional issues like precarious contracts and a lack of employment stability are particularly challenging, and research has highlighted that mental health issues like depression and anxiety are common (Cactus Foundation, 2020; Forrester, 2021). For example, a recent systematic review and meta-analysis by Hazell and colleagues found that doctoral students have significantly higher stress levels than the general population (Hazell et al., 2020). The authors also found that social support was one of the most well-established protective factors. As such, establishing a strong, supportive, and collegiate network of colleagues to help you throughout your academic career to work through the difficult times, and to savour the good times with, is critical.

Beyond this, networking and collaborating also help to improve the quality and impact of your research. Expanding your networks can enrich your research with new insights or views. Networking can also maximise the potential impact of your work by disseminating it more widely to different audiences beyond academia, to policy, practice, and public audiences. Having a good network of national and international collaborators can also strengthen your chances of securing grant funding, as you can build a stronger team that is informed by broader experiences and perspectives, with potential for wider reach and impact of research findings. Additionally, many funding streams require you to have existing experience of securing grant funding before you can apply in your own right. For ECRs, this can often be a frustrating stipulation and a difficult hurdle to cross; however, having a good network of collaborators can be helpful in reaching this first milestone.

In the same vein, good networks are important for improving career prospects, through either formal or informal sharing of informal knowledge or opportunities. Evidence suggests that such networks can often be even more influential for career opportunities than individual skills. In 2015, a survey of Australian students found that access to networking opportunities was more influential than skills development on initial job attainment post PhD completion (Jackson & Michelson, 2015). Similarly, a recent survey of ECRs working in science, technology, engineering, math, and medical science (STEMM) fields explored the benefits of career mentoring and found that participants valued being introduced to networks as the second-most valued output of mentoring, which was rated above skills training or writing skills (Christian et al., 2021). Although the ethicality of the importance of 'who you know' over 'what you know' could be debated, it's clear that effective networking plays a big role in career development for ECRs and thus can't be neglected.

How to Network and Build Effective Collaborations – Core Principles

When it comes to networking and building collaborations, after thinking about mine for a while, I defined three core principles that I have found useful for guiding how I approach this. However, it's worth remembering that these principles are naturally quite personal and may not be relevant for everyone. Indeed, taking time to identify your own core principles may be the first step in helping you to network more effectively. Reflecting on or considering your own priorities for networking to help you articulate your own values and principles can be a useful method for approaching networking in a more authentic and personal way and reduce potential feelings of discomfort or awkwardness.

Principle 1: Openness

As a researcher who is particularly passionate about open science, I am somewhat used to trying to conduct my research as openly and transparently as I can. However, I also find applying similar principles of openness helpful for building networks and collaborations. One of the things that can often happen when we attend conferences or events is that we tend to spend time with people we already know. Ingram and Morris (2007) showed in their study of 92 business people, that despite attending a networking event with the intention of making new connections, the majority of people spent time with their existing contacts. While this is important for maintaining and strengthening existing relationships, there is probably a balance to be achieved here in order to optimise your networks. Openness to new experiences and new opportunities, and having the courage to push yourself outside of your comfort zone, is particularly fruitful when it comes to developing collaborations. At a basic level, this could take the form of attending conferences or seminars on your own, and making a point of talking to at least two or three people that you have never met before. Other more structured options could be attending an event specifically set up for networking. This can be often easier said than done, particularly for personality types who are more introverted than extroverted. However, organisational psychology research tells us that we can influence our mindset towards networking, as either a promotion or prevention mindset (Gino et al., 2020). Having a promotion mindset means taking a more open-minded and curiosity-driven approach to networking, by focusing primarily on discovery, learning, and the potential for encountering new opportunities, growth, and ideas that meeting new people can bring (Gino et al., 2020). Focusing on a higher purpose or goal can often help people to motivate themselves to take a more open-minded approach to networking (Casciaro et al., 2016). For example, networking for health researchers could be viewed as an opportunity to disseminate your research to audiences who may be able to bring about change and improve overall patient outcomes. Contrastingly, those with a prevention mindset tend to view networking as a chore they are obligated to participate in for work reasons, a 'necessary evil'. Research shows that people with a preventive mindset are more likely to experience the aforementioned feelings of moral impurity or 'dirtiness' when it comes to networking. They are also less likely to engage in networking and subsequently underperform in aspects of their job such as yearly revenue generated (Gino et al., 2020).

When it comes to building collaborations, I also find it is important to be open, honest, and clear about what you're looking for from people. For example, if your work would benefit from the expertise of another researcher, don't be afraid to reach out to them with an invitation to collaborate on your work, but be clear on what you are asking in terms of work commitment and the timelines involved. On a practical level, this can be done by email or in person, but often works well when some form of personal contact has been first established, for example by meeting that person at a conference and following up later with a polite email invitation. These types of requests can particularly benefit from an introduction by a mutual colleague, but if that isn't possible, don't let it put you off. Many people are very generous with their time and expertise, but it always helps when they know what's expected of them. Likewise, openly reaching out to existing or new networks to address gaps in your CV can also be beneficial. For example, if you are lacking in student supervision or grant co-applicant experience, then an email to more senior colleagues or programme directors and course coordinators identifying what you are looking for, and clearly highlighting what you could contribute, can often result in favourable outcomes. In a similar vein, disseminating your research is a crucial part of maximising its potential reach and impact. Therefore, sending on research updates or summaries to relevant stakeholders with a clear request for what you are looking for, be it to share with their colleagues or to provide feedback, can be particularly useful. While sometimes this variant of 'cold calling' can feel daunting, if done carefully and appropriately, then the worst outcome is usually just a lack of reply (which should not be taken personally). As they say, nothing ventured, nothing gained!

Principle 2: Managing Expectations

One of the challenges I experienced when I started trying to build collaborations in academia was expecting too much from an encounter with someone new, or getting disappointed with myself if something concrete didn't materialise from it. This is something that often comes up in conversation with other ECRs, that we can sometimes put pressure on ourselves to network with an expected end goal or outcome in mind – be it a paper, or a collaborative project, or even just a reply to our email. One colleague recently told me that they find it difficult to turn a new work-related contact into something productive, as opposed to just a new social connection. These concerns resonate with a piece written by ECRs in 2017 about the challenges novice researchers face with networking (Camedda et al., 2017). The article highlighted that despite participating in structured networking events with the intention of building new contacts, ECRs often do not translate these opportunities into academic collaborations or professional activities (Camedda et al., 2017). Although this is a valid concern, over time I've found that managing my expectations as to what I consider 'effective networking' has been really helpful, and even realising that 'effectiveness' can vary depending on the context. For example, when attending conferences or seminars, I avoid being too transactional, and don't view every encounter as a potential collaboration or career opportunity. This ties back into my first principle of openness – being open to meeting a person for who they are, rather than what you think they may or may not be able to help you with from a research and/or career perspective. For me, the initial development of a relationship with someone is the most important outcome, from which academic outputs may or may not follow.

In other contexts, having a clear and focused outcome for a potential collaboration, as well as a structured plan to achieve this, can be equally important. For example, not long after I completed my PhD, I really wanted to write an editorial on the topic with one of the leading researchers in the field to disseminate my findings to a broader practitioner-focused audience. I reached out to her with the help of my mentor and proposed a plan to co-write the editorial which we later published. My mentor gave me crucial advice at the time: to put myself in their 'busy shoes', anticipate *their* expectations of the collaboration, and make it as easy as possible for them to say yes. Additionally, a key part of this for me was working up the courage to reach out in this way, as it can sometimes be daunting for ECRs to reach out to more senior colleagues out of the blue. Previous research has shown that when people view themselves as having less power, they tend to view networking as a negative activity and less justifiable or comfortable from a personal perspective (Casciaro et al., 2014). However, Cohen and Bradford (2003) highlighted that we tend to take a narrower view of what we can contribute, focusing more on aspects like information or expertise, rather than focusing on what we have to offer as an individual with unique perspectives and experiences (Cohen & Bradford, 2003). As Casciaro et al. (2016) state, when we focus on what we can contribute to a senior colleague, such as mentorship opportunities, insights from an ECR perspective, or even just gratitude, we tend to feel less self-promotional and engage more successfully in networking.

Principle 3: Enjoyment

My final, but probably most crucial, principle when it comes to building collaborations is enjoyment and the importance of having fun. Although for some people the idea of networking is diametrically opposed to the idea of fun, focusing on building enjoyable collaborations with people we like and respect, rather than purely on 'networking' for professional gain, can be helpful. Being genuine, passionate, and enthusiastic about your research, and not being afraid to let that passion shine through, can also help to develop new connections as enthusiasm can often be infectious. I've found that a sense of humour and not taking myself too seriously have helped me to build meaningful connections with people, by keeping enjoyment at the core of interactions. Academia can be difficult enough at the best of times, and in my experience, there are more than enough lovely and excellent people to work with out there.

How to Network and Build Effective Collaborations – Some Practical Pointers

There are a number of practical actions that can develop your network of collaborators. Engaging in these actions with your principles in mind may feel like a more authentic, productive, and enjoyable networking experience. I've listed some of these actions below in no particular order:

1. *Get a good mentor*

    No doubt mentoring has been mentioned frequently across other chapters of this book, and for good reason. Mentors play a fundamental role in shaping an academic career, from offering advice on career decisions to connecting mentees with their existing networks and contacts. Often, having multiple mentors with different styles is beneficial for different purposes, and also extends your potential network. However, not all ECRs have a mentor, with as many as 38.1% reporting they did not have a mentor in a recent survey of Australian ECRs (Christian et al., 2021). For example, as outlined previously, my mentor was invaluable for connecting me with a senior colleague to write our joint editorial. Although it can be sometimes difficult to identify a good mentor, there are many resources online that identify the important characteristics to look for in a mentor (e.g., www.vitae.ac.uk), and many institutions run formal mentoring schemes. Talking to your colleagues or other ECRs can be particularly helpful in identifying a suitable person.

2. *Maximise your opportunities*

    For ECRs, we are often restricted in what we would like to do by the availability of our resources, namely time and money. That's why I believe that it's really important to maximise the potential outputs of each opportunity as much as possible, which in turn maximises the scientific impact of your research. For example, many societies and conferences have bursaries available for students and ECRs. If you happen to secure funding to attend a conference, identifying relevant academics working in the locality or nearby universities that you could contact to meet while you are in the area can be really valuable to help build connections. Don't worry if you feel nervous about reaching out (we all do!), or don't have a tangible outcome for the meeting. While a clear focus or goal can be helpful, just being honest and saying that you would like to meet them even for a brief chat to hear about their research and explore potential future collaborations can be equally valuable. Similarly, if you happen to get funding for a research visit, exploring what relevant conferences or seminars that you could attend or present at during your stay is a good idea. Although you might feel daunted by the idea of giving a seminar, most research groups are often delighted to find new content and presenters! Pre-conference or event preparation in terms of finding out who will be there and trying to connect with them during the conference can also be beneficial, but equally important is staying open to meeting others.

3. *Join a society or network that is supportive of ECRs*

Many different societies, networks, and interest groups exist for almost every discipline, as such it can sometimes be difficult to know which ones to invest your time and money in. Membership in a supportive professional society, network, or association can be particularly valuable for ECRs in terms of helping to develop networks and build connections. As an ECR, benefits to look for from a society could include ECR travel bursaries or awards, active ECR networks or mentoring schemes, free or reasonably priced training events and webinars or other continuous professional development opportunities. Investing the time in becoming an active member can also be time well spent. For example, getting involved in organising events, establishing a new special interest group or becoming a committee member can not only help you develop new connections, but also help build your CV and leadership experience.

4. *Invest in maintaining connections as well as building them*

Building contacts initially can be somewhat easy enough; however, maintaining and nurturing those contacts is even more important and requires effort. For example, this can be as simple as following up on initial meetings or conversations with a brief email to share information or just contact details. An important part of strengthening these relationships is also remembering to try and contribute to the collaboration and not just always to take or be on the receiving end. For example, if you come across research or opportunities you think would be valuable or of interest to that person, forwarding these on, connecting others, or inviting them to contribute to work you are leading can be warmly appreciated. As with any academic collaboration, being mindful of others' timelines and following through on what you've promised in time is also key to maintaining positive working relationships – establishing a clear schedule from the outset can be particularly useful for this. As it's probably not possible or necessary to put equal amounts of effort into maintaining all connections, it can be sometimes helpful to conceptualise your contacts as an inner and outer circle, and gradate your level of contact or input accordingly. Try not to worry if some connections fade over time as this is a very natural part of networking.

5. *Utilise social media to your advantage*

In a digital era, having some form of online presence or profile is particularly important for developing and maintaining your professional networks as well as disseminating your research. For example, Niyazov et al. found a 16% increase in citations after one year for papers that had been uploaded to the Academia.edu platform compared to similar articles not available online, rising to 69% more citations after five years (Niyazov et al., 2016). Moreover, having a place to direct people you meet during a conference for more information on your research and interests also takes the pressure off having to explain your life's work in one meeting. In addition, being easily 'findable' for others can be helpful for building international visibility and connections, and can help your work reach non-academic audiences more easily (Jordan, 2019). Several academic social networks exist, such as Academia. edu or ResearchGate. Other platforms non-specific to academia such as Twitter and Facebook can also be useful (see Chap. 16); however, given the multitude of options that exist, and the fact that an out-of-date profile can be unhelpful, it can sometimes be wise to focus on maintaining one or two platforms regularly. Twitter in particular can be a valuable way of disseminating your work more widely, and building your reputation in an area. However, as with all social media, a degree of caution regarding how and what you share is important! Others have provided some key tips for using Twitter as an academic (Mojarad, 2020).

6. *Reflect and work on your communication skills*

Most of what has been discussed in this chapter will be second nature to many, and indeed networking and building effective collaborations often comes down to natural human interaction and our inherent social skills. However, many of us could still benefit from regularly reflecting on our networking and communication skills and being mindful of these when we meet someone new. As most of us are aware, good communication skills involve not just speaking or conveying our own thoughts, but also a process of active listening. In brief, active listening skills involve non-verbal and verbal items, including using appropriate facial expressions and body language, maintaining eye contact, avoiding interruption, and reflecting back the speaker's feelings and content through paraphrasing and summarising key issues (Robertson, 2005). For anyone at any stage of their career, taking the time to reflect on and practice our communication skills if needed, seeking feedback from friends and colleagues we trust, is invaluable. Again, many institutions run networking sessions and communication skills training for researchers, or such training can be found privately also through online searching.

Conclusions and Practical Recommendations

In conclusion, networking and building effective collaborations is a vital part of an academic career whether we like it or not. However, the benefits of developing strong networks cannot be understated, both from a personal support perspective as well as maximising the reach and impact of our work. For ECRs, investing time in developing these networks is time well spent, and to start off, identifying your own core principles such as openness, expectations, and enjoyment that facilitate you to engage in networking more deeply may be a good place to start. Practical action points like seeking out and leaning on your mentor, joining a supportive society or network and building a social media profile may be helpful, as is considering the importance of maintaining networks once they're established, maximising all opportunities available to you to expand and grow your networks, and regularly checking in on your own communication skills. At the end of the day, as Mark Twain said, 'twenty years from now you will be more disappointed by the things that you didn't do than by the ones you did do'. When it comes to networking, this couldn't be truer – the potential benefits of opportunities taken far outweigh the potential embarrassment of rejection. So, take a deep breath, and say 'hello' ☺.

References

Cactus Foundation. (2020). *Joy and stress triggers: A global survey on mental health among researchers*. Retrieved from https://www.cactusglobal.com/mental-health-survey/cactus-mental-health-survey-report-2020.pdf

Camedda, D., Mirman-Flores, A., & Ryan-Mangan, A. (2017). *Young researchers need help with academic networking*. Retrieved from https://www.universityworldnews.com/post.php?story=20170906091434215

Casciaro, T., Gino, F., & Kouchaki, M. (2014). The contaminating effects of building instrumental ties: How networking can make us feel dirty. *Administrative Science Quarterly, 59*(4), 705–735. https://doi.org/10.1177/0001839214554990

Casciaro, T., Gino, F., & Kouchaki, M. (2016). Learn to love networking. *Harvard Business Review.*. Retrieved from https://hbr.org/2016/05/learn-to-love-networking

Christian, K., Johnstone, C., Larkins, J. A., Wright, W., & Doran, M. R. (2021). A survey of early-career researchers in Australia. *eLife, 10*, e60613. https://doi.org/10.7554/eLife.60613

Cohen, A. R., & Bradford, D. L. (2003). Influence without authority: The use of alliances, reciprocity, and exchange to accomplish work. *Organizational Dynamics, 17*(3), 5–17.

Forrester, N. (2021). Mental health of graduate students sorely overlooked. *Nature*. Retrieved from https://www.nature.com/articles/d41586-021-01751-z

Gino, F., Kouchaki, M., & Casciaro, T. (2020). Why connect? Moral consequences of networking with a promotion or prevention focus. *Journal of Personality and Social Psychology, 119*(6), 1221–1238. https://doi.org/10.1037/pspa0000226

Hazell, C. M., Chapman, L., Valeix, S. F., Roberts, P., Niven, J. E., & Berry, C. (2020). Understanding the mental health of doctoral researchers: a mixed methods systematic review with meta-analysis and meta-synthesis. *Systematic Reviews, 9*(1), 197. https://doi.org/10.1186/s13643-020-01443-1

Ingram, P., & Morris, M. W. (2007). Do people mix at mixers? Structure, homophily, and the "life of the party". *Administrative Science Quarterly, 52*(4), 558–585. https://doi.org/10.2189/asqu.52.4.558

Jackson, D., & Michelson, G. (2015). Factors influencing the employment of Australian PhD graduates. *Studies in Higher Education, 40*(9), 1660–1678. https://doi.org/10.1080/03075079.2014.899344

Jordan, K. (2019). From social networks to publishing platforms: A review of the history and scholarship of academic social network sites. *Frontiers in Digital Humanities, 6*(5). https://doi.org/10.3389/fdigh.2019.00005

Mojarad, S. (2020). *A beginner's guide to joining academic twitter*. Retrieved from https://medium.com/@smojarad/a-beginners-guide-to-academic-twitter-f483dae86597

Niyazov, Y., Vogel, C., Price, R., Lund, B., Judd, D., Akil, A., et al. (2016). Open access meets discoverability: Citations to articles posted to academia.Edu. *Plos One, 11*(2), e0148257. https://doi.org/10.1371/journal.pone.0148257

Robertson, K. (2005). Active listening: More than just paying attention. *Australian Family Physician, 34*(12), 1053–1055.

Chapter 9
Accelerating Your Research Career with Open Science

Emma Norris

Abstract We could all benefit from our research and the research of others being more transparent and accessible to all, regardless of our career stage or research field. 'Open Science' provides us with a range of research practices designed to make the processes, data, analysis, and outputs more reproducible, understandable, and accessible. These practices range from making the protocol of your research explicit and publicly available via study pre-registration or Registered Report, to making a final published paper freely available via Open Access publishing or pre-print. This chapter will outline issues and challenges in research that Open Science helps to reduce. It will outline what Open Science is and how it can be integrated into your research workflow and summarise some global initiatives to increase Open Science uptake. The chapter will end by discussing how Open Science can benefit and accelerate your career and give you some tips on how to get started.

Keywords Open Science · Preregistration · Registered Reports · Open Data · Open Materials · Open-Source Software · Pre-prints · Open Access publishing · Open peer review

Introduction

Research is never straight-forward. As you will have experienced, there are challenges underpinning each step of the research process. These challenges include how to define clear research aims and hypotheses, selecting appropriate methodologies, analysing complex data, negotiating collaboration with colleagues perhaps online and internationally: the list goes on! What are examples of problems you've had in your research so far?

E. Norris (✉)
Division of Global Health, Department of Health Sciences, Brunel University London, Kingston Lane, Uxbridge, Middlesex, UK

© The Author(s), under exclusive license to Springer Nature Switzerland AG 2022
D. Kwasnicka, A. Y. Lai (eds.), *Survival Guide for Early Career Researchers*, https://doi.org/10.1007/978-3-031-10754-2_9

I'll start by sharing (some!) of my own challenges. Systematic reviews form an important part of my work. As anyone who's done a review or meta-analysis will know, the process of searching for papers, filtering them for relevance, extracting data on them, synthesising their data is hugely time-intensive (Borah et al., 2017). One major barrier to fully completing a systematic review is not being able to access the raw data you need from past studies to make conclusions on the collective state of play on a topic. Or perhaps you want to get hold of a developed tool, intervention or questionnaire that you've read about but struggle to find who to ask? I've had many instances where I've popped a friendly email to a corresponding author asking for a data file, a few data values, or some details about a study and received no response. There are obvious explanations for this; people move institutions and become difficult to locate, time passes since the study and the study data and materials may become lost or unmanaged. In extreme cases, the reported results may be fraudulent and the data may never have existed! How can we organise science better to ensure data is made routinely publicly available for us to easier learn from each other, as well as facilitate reviews and adoption of our work?

Another challenge I'm sure we've all experienced previously is the long lead-time between finishing a study, getting it peer-reviewed and published. I work in public health and health psychology, where I hope my work has implications for real-world practice and healthcare service delivery. Also, from an early career researcher perspective, we need publications to put us in more favourable positions for job and grant applications. For those of us within academia, we operate in systemic problematic incentive structures where volume of papers and impact factors are primarily valued for recruitment and promotion, rather than research rigour and quality (Higginson & Munafò, 2016). As such, the sometimes multiple year delay in publication of research is not helpful. How can we mitigate delays prominent in the peer-review process?

An additional challenge I've experienced as a researcher is coming into projects partway through, as a Research Assistant or Collaborator. It can be difficult to get to grips with what's been done so far, adding time to the familiarisation process. How can we better organise our work to make its processes more routinely transparent and understandable?

I experienced these challenges primarily during my PhD. Now four years post-PhD, I am fully immersed in Open Science practices within my work which help mitigate these challenges for me. In this chapter, I will attempt to convince you that research practices typically referred to as 'Open Science' practices can help tackle your own research challenges and make your research even more rewarding!

What Is Open Science?

Open Science, also often referred to as Open Research, is a growing global movement aiming to make all aspects of research, education, and scholarship accessible, transparent, and available to all audiences. Open Science involves scientists, funding bodies, and universities working collaboratively to increase reproducibility and transparency in the scientific process, reporting, and teaching (Norris & O'Connor, 2019; Pontika et al., 2015).

The drive towards these more transparent practices is in-part driven by findings that research across disciplines is often not replicable. For example, a survey by the journal *Nature* of 1576 researchers identified that more than 70% of surveyed researchers across disciplines had tried and failed to reproduce the findings of others, and more than 50% had failed to reproduce their own (Baker, 2016). Within psychology, a mass replication attempt of 100 experimental and correlational studies in social and cognitive psychology found that only 36% of replicated studies had statistically significant ($p < 0.05$) results, compared to 97% of the original studies (Open Science Collaboration, 2015).

Academia is rife with problematic incentive structures. Journal publications are often easier for novel and exciting positive findings rather than null or replicative findings (Edwards & Roy, 2017). Promotion and recruitment criteria are commonly based on number of publications and Impact Factor of journals, rather than the actual tacit quality of the work (Nosek et al., 2012). The Journal Impact Factor, as calculated by Thomson Reuters, was originally created as a tool to help librarians identify journals to purchase, not as a measure of the scientific quality of research in an article. These problematic incentives help to drive research error and misconduct. For example, 'questionable research practices' such as selective reporting of outcomes (John et al., 2012) or hypothesising after the results are known (HARKing; Kerr, 1998) are conscious researcher decisions, driven by the need for significant and publishable findings. High-profile cases of uncovered fraudulent researcher behaviour driven by the need for publication success have also driven this need for reform (Ritchie, 2020). For example, Diederik Stapel, former professor of social psychology at Tilburg University in the Netherlands, was found to have manipulated and completely fabricated entire experiments resulting in at least 30 published, peer-reviewed papers (Markowitz & Hancock, 2014).

A range of Open Science reforms to scientific practice have been installed over recent years to increase the reproducibility and transparency of scientific practice. These include specific research practices that can be integrated throughout the research process (Fig. 9.1): before, during, and after data collection. For example, research 'preregistration'is the practice of submitting a research study plan to an online repository (such as Open Science Framework: Sullivan et al. 2019) prior to the research being undertaken (Hardwicke et al., 2021; Lakens, 2019). Preregistration aims to mitigate against questionable research practices and increase transparency (Nosek et al., 2018; O'Connor, 2021) by pre-specifying all hypotheses, methods, and analysis plans and reduced unnoticed flexibility (Nosek et al. 2019). It is hoped that with greater transparency comes greater rigour, and so greater credibility of research (Field et al., 2020; Ihle et al., 2017). Pre-registration of research is also intended to reduce the 'file drawer' problem (O'Connor, 2021), whereby negative and null findings are less likely to be published than positive, statistically significant findings (Rosenthal, 1979).

Open Science practice	Definition and example
Before data collection	
Preregistration	Submitting a research study plan to an online repository prior to the research being undertaken. (Field et al. 2020; Lakens, 2019). Example: Open Science Framework https://osf.io/ and AsPredicted https://aspredicted.org/ provide pre-registration templates and registrations.
Registered Reports	A form of journal article with a 2-stage peer-review and acceptance process. In Stage 1, the proposed methods and analyses are pre-registered and peer-reviewed prior to research being conducted. High quality protocols are then provisionally accepted for publication before data collection commences. In Stage 2, once the study is completed, the author will finish the article including results and discussion sections for this to be peer-reviewed. (Chambers, & Tzavella, 2020; Stewart et al. 2020). Example: Many journals accepting Registered Reports can be found within the Peer Community In (PCI) Registered Reports scheme: https://rr.peercommunityin.org/about/about
During and after data collection	
Open Data	Data that can be freely used, re-used and redistributed by anyone - subject only, at most, to the requirement to attribute and sharealike. Example: FAIR data principles require data to meet the principles of findability, accessibility, interoperability, and reusability. (Wilkinson et al. 2016)
Open Materials	Publishing materials used within research, such as experiments, tasks, questionnaires or intervention content. Example: Journals increasingly offer badges to reward publication of Open Materials alongside papers, as well as for Open Data and Pre-Registration (Kidwell et al., 2016)
Open-Source Software	Computer software released under a licence in which the copyright holder permits users the rights to use, change and distribute the software and its source code (Fortunato & Galassi, 2021). Example: R software for statistical computing https://www.r-project.org/
Publication	
Pre-prints	Version of a scholarly paper that is made publically available online prior to formal peer review and publication in a peer-reviewed journal. Example: OSF Pre-prints offers pre-print services by research subjects https://osf.io/preprints/
Open Access publishing	Making research publications freely available so anyone can read and use them. Example: Sherpa Romeo allows you to check the open access policies in journals globally https://v2.sherpa.ac.uk/romeo/
Open peer review	Scholarly review providing disclosure of author and referee identifies during the peer review process and published alongside the resultant article (Ross-Hellauer, 2017). Example: Wellcome Open Research https://wellcomeopenresearch.org/

Note: See Kathawalla et al. (2021) for a great introductory guide on how to integrate Open Science across the research process as an early career researcher.

Fig. 9.1 Examples of Open Science practices across the research process

Global Initiatives to Increase Open Science

International efforts to facilitate Open Science are ever-increasing. As early career researchers, we are set to benefit from these current and future reforms to the academic ecosystem as we progress in our careers. One development which has provided us all with an infrastructure to work more openly is Open Science Framework (OSF: Foster & Deardorff, 2017): https://osf.io. OSF provides a free platform to create pages for each of our projects: allowing us to pre-register the research, share the data and materials, and publish preprints all in one place. It was developed and is maintained by the Center for Open Science (COS), a non-profit organisation founded in 2013 https:// cos.io/. We can all benefit from OSF by making our own research more accessible but also by being able to search for related work globally and establish new collaborations from this. Global strategies are also working to reduce aforementioned problematic incentive structures within academia. The San Francisco Declaration on Research Assessment (DORA) principles aims to prevent the practice of correlating journal impact factor with scientific merit. It is an opt-in agreement that universities and other institutions can opt-in to which states they will not use impact factor as a substitute 'measure of the quality of individual research articles, or in hiring, promotion, or funding decisions' (Alberts, 2013).

The Transparency and Openness Promotion (TOP) guidelines offer standards as a basis for journals and funders to incentivise or require greater transparency in planning and reporting of research (McNutt, 2016). The TOP guidelines include eight modular standards encompassing Data citation, Data, Materials and Code Transparency, Design and Analysis, Pre-registration, and Replication, each with three levels of increasing stringency: Disclosure, Require, or Verify. Journals select which of the eight transparency standards they wish to implement and select a level of implementation for each (Nosek et al., 2016). This provides clarity for us as authors in the degree of specificity and transparency required ahead of each journal submission, reducing ambiguity. Academic reporting checklists also provide us with structured guidance on how to adequately report all aspects of our research in publications. The EQUATOR Network provides a suite of over 400 developed reporting tools across study designs, disciplines, and populations (Altman & Simera, 2016). For example, the Consolidated Standards of Reporting Trials (CONSORT) statement provides guidance for clear, complete, and accurate reporting of randomised controlled trials (Schulz et al., 2010). By following appropriate checklists for our work, we can be sure to integrate all essential features within our research protocol development and write-up.

How Can Open Science Help Your Career?

Working in a more Open way is clearly beneficial to our understanding and appraisal of science at a global level. However, you'll likely find that upskilling yourself in various aspects of Open Science takes time and adds extra considerations to the research process (Allen & Mehler, 2019; McKiernan et al., 2016). You may see working more openly as admirable but what are the benefits to you as an individual early career researcher? I'll now seek to sell the benefits of Open Science to you from my own experiences. These benefits are informed by the fantastic article by Florian Markowetz 'Five selfish reasons to work reproducibly' (Markowetz, 2015).

Open Science Helps to Avoid Disaster

Have you ever published a paper, been asked some details about the results, and found that you've been unable to replicate your own findings? Have you looked back at your own analysis 6 months, a year, or more down the line and totally forgotten how and why you analysed the data previously? You're not alone! Getting into the routine of logging decisions around your data's structure and analysis whilst you're working on it is beneficial to you in the long-run. Thorough decision-tracking is also beneficial as you work towards managing your own projects. In my own work, keeping a clear decision log of reasons behind paper inclusions and exclusions has been essential for studies involving multidisciplinary teams based in different countries. For quantitative research, keeping clear notes and tracking decisions by logging detailed notes in your syntax or using the R package workflowr (Blischak et al., 2019) are great ideas. However, simple methods are also useful, such as constructing and maintaining a shared Word or Google document of decisions for yourself or your team. For qualitative research, detailed decision logs can help reduce ambiguity in the themes you identify to yourself and other people later on.

Open Science Helps Reviewers See It Your Way

Peer reviewers are becoming increasingly prepared to see data, a pre-registration or a detailed Open Science Framework page to accompany papers they review. This allows them to better appraise the quality and transparency of your work. Providing additional detail like this allows you to tell a clearer story of your research: filling in the gaps that a 3000-word journal article just doesn't have space for. Additionally, the increase in Open Peer Review means that reviewers can appraise your experience in-line with the research you have submitted (Wolfram et al., 2020).

Open Science Helps to Build Your Reputation

For me, using and speaking about Open Science practices within public health and health behaviour change has opened a range of opportunities: such as writing this book chapter! Firstly, being open about your use of Open Science can grow your reputation in your existing institution. Although use of Open Science is on the increase, uptake in many disciplines is still relatively low and varies highly between institutions. I work in a Public Health department where understanding and uptake of Open Science is currently low. Showing an interest and being an advocate for Open Science has enabled me to start conversations across my own university on how to develop tailored initiatives: all beneficial for future promotion attempts! Secondly, being engaged and active in Open Science can lead to fantastic collaborations. For example, I am a co-Chair of the European Health Psychology Society's Open Science Special Interest Group (Norris & Toomey, 2020), which involves developing initiatives to increase Open Science with colleagues from across Europe. Members of the Group have quite diverse research interests and so working together to promote Open Science provides a legitimate and important reason for collaboration which is not tied down to a specific research project.

Open Science Helps You Build Your Research Competence

Perhaps most importantly, putting extra thought into Open Science considerations has made me personally feel increasingly competent as a researcher. I completed my PhD in January 2017 and was totally unaware of Open Science at this time beyond Open Access publishing and Open Data. Emerging from a PhD where I was supervised by four multidisciplinary experts, I felt nervous about being able to maintain quality of research under my own steam. However, immersing myself in Open Science has enabled me to increase my confidence as an independent and thorough researcher. For example, the practice of preregistering a study plan before data collection has enabled me to be far more detailed and explicit in study design and analysis plans than I was before, reducing ambiguity when dealing with the data subsequently. Additionally, grant funders and journals are increasingly requiring Data Management Plans and evidence of Open Science prior to submission. It is reassuring to think that Open Science is now integrated into my workflow, and I can now concentrate on the content and scientific contribution of the research itself.

Conclusions and Practical Recommendations

As we've seen, a range of Open Science practices have been established across academic disciplines in recent years to improve the transparency and reproducibility of research. Using principles of Open Science is the present and future of best research practice. As early career researchers, we have much to benefit from these initiatives in terms of contributing to and spearheading higher quality scientific research and increasing our own research competence. Looking at the range of Open Science practices that exist (Fig. 9.1 provides a snapshot of these) can be somewhat daunting. My one top tip is to not try and integrate all of these Open Science practices in any given project! Try and integrate one new Open Science aspect into each new project. For example, add a pre-registration or try publishing a preprint. Take time to evaluate how you found your experience and consider if you'll seek to improve this or try another practice in your next project.

I'll end with one of my favourite Open Science quotes from the outstanding Open Science advocate and co-founder of ReproducibiliTea Open Science Journal Clubs Dr. Amy Orben from University of Cambridge, UK: 'Open science is a process, not a one-time achievement or a claim to virtue' (Orben, 2019). Open Science is not a virtue signalling exercise. It serves both as for the collective benefit for science, as well as for improved personal confidence and competent in science. Open Science is here to stay: Get involved!

References

Alberts, B. (2013). Impact factor distortions. *Science, 340*(6134), 787–787.
Allen, C., & Mehler, D. M. (2019). Open science challenges, benefits and tips in early career and beyond. *PLoS Biology, 17*(5), e3000246.
Altman, D. G., & Simera, I. (2016). A history of the evolution of guidelines for reporting medical research: The long road to the EQUATOR network. *Journal of the Royal Society of Medicine, 109*(2), 67–77.
Baker, M. (2016). 1,500 scientists lift the lid on reproducibility. *Nature, 533*(26), 353–366. https://doi.org/10.1038/533452a
Blischak, J. D., Carbonetto, P., & Stephens, M. (2019). Creating and sharing reproducible research code the workflowr way. *F1000Research, 8*, 1749.
Borah, R., Brown, A. W., Capers, P. L., & Kaiser, K. A. (2017). Analysis of the time and workers needed to conduct systematic reviews of medical interventions using data from the PROSPERO registry. *BMJ Open, 7*(2), e012545.
Chambers, C., & Tzavella, L. (2020). Registered reports: Past, present and future. https://doi.org/10.31222/osf.io/43298
Edwards, M. A., & Roy, S. (2017). Academic research in the 21st century: Maintaining scientific integrity in a climate of perverse incentives and hypercompetition. *Environmental Engineering Science, 34*(1), 51–61. https://doi.org/10.1089/ees.2016.0223
Field, S. M., Wagenmakers, E. J., Kiers, H. A., Hoekstra, R., Ernst, A. F., & van Ravenzwaaij, D. (2020). The effect of preregistration on trust in empirical research findings: Results of a registered report. *Royal Society Open Science, 7*(4), 181351. https://doi.org/10.1098/rsos.181351
Fortunato, L., & Galassi, M. (2021). The case for free and open source software in research and scholarship. *Philosophical Transactions of the Royal Society A Mathematical, Physical and Engineering Sciences, 379*(2197), 20200079. https://doi.org/10.1098/rsta.2020.0079
Foster, E. D., & Deardorff, A. (2017). Open science framework (OSF). *Journal of the Medical Library Association, 105*(2), 203.
Hardwicke, T. E., Thibault, R. T., Kosie, J., Wallach, J. D., Kidwell, M. C., & Ioannidis, J. (2021). Estimating the prevalence of transparency and reproducibility-related research practices in psychology (2014–2017). *Perspectives on Psychological Science.* https://doi.org/10.1177/2F1745691620979806
Higginson, A. D., & Munafò, M. R. (2016). Current incentives for scientists lead to underpowered studies with erroneous conclusions. *PLoS Biology, 14*(11), e2000995. https://doi.org/10.1371/journal.pbio.2000995
Ihle, M., Winney, I. S., Krystalli, A., & Croucher, M. (2017). Striving for transparent and credible research: practical guidelines for behavioral ecologists. *Behavioral Ecology, 28*(2), 348–354.

John, L. K., Loewenstein, G., & Prelec, D. (2012). Measuring the prevalence of questionable research practices with incentives for truth telling. *Psychological Science, 23*(5), 524–532. https://doi.org/10.1177/0956797611430953

Kathawalla, U. K., Silverstein, P., & Syed, M. (2021). Easing into open science: A guide for graduate students and their advisors. *Collabra: Psychology, 7*(1), 1–12.

Kerr, N. L. (1998). HARKing: Hypothesizing after the results are known. *Personality and Social Psychology Review, 2*(3), 196–217.

Kidwell, M. C., Lazarević, L. B., Baranski, E., Hardwicke, T. E., Piechowski, S., Falkenberg, L. S., … Nosek, B. A. (2016). Badges to acknowledge open practices: A simple, low-cost, effective method for increasing transparency. *PLoS Biology, 14*(5), e1002456. https://doi.org/10.1371/journal.pbio.1002456

Lakens, D. (2019). The value of preregistration for psychological science: A conceptual analysis. *Japanese Psychological Review. 62*(3), 221–230.

Markowetz, F. (2015). Five selfish reasons to work reproducibly. *Genome Biology, 16*(1), 1–4.

Markowitz, D. M., & Hancock, J. T. (2014). Linguistic traces of a scientific fraud: The case of Diederik Stapel. *PLoS One, 9*(8), e105937.

McKiernan, E. C., Bourne, P. E., Brown, C. T., Buck, S., Kenall, A., Lin, J., McDougall, D., Nosek, B. A., Ram, K., Soderberg, C. K., Spies, J. R., Thaney, K., Updegrove, A., Woo, K. H., & Yarkoni, T. (2016). How open science helps researchers succeed. *eLife, 5*, e16800. https://doi.org/10.7554/eLife.16800

McNutt, M. (2016). Taking up TOP. *Science, 352*, 1147.

Munafò, M. R., Nosek, B. A., Bishop, D. V., Button, K. S., Chambers, C. D., du Sert, N. P., … Ioannidis, J. P. (2017). A manifesto for reproducible science. *Nature Human Behaviour, 1*(1), 0021. https://doi.org/10.1038/s41562-016-0021

Norris, E., & O'Connor, D. B. (2019). Science as behaviour: Using a behaviour change approach to increase uptake of open science. *Psychology & Health, 34*(12), 1397–1406.

Nosek, B. A., Ebersole, C. R., DeHaven, A. C., & Mellor, D. T. (2018). The preregistration revolution. *Proceedings of the National Academy of Sciences, 115*(11), 2600–2606.

Nosek, B. A., Beck, E. D., Campbell, L., Flake, J. K., Hardwicke, T. E., Mellor, D. T., ... & Vazire, S. (2019). Preregistration is hard, and worthwhile. *Trends in cognitive sciences, 23*(10), 815–818.

Norris, E., & Toomey, E. (2020). Open Science in Health Psychology: Launching the EHPS Open Science SIG. *The European Health Psychologist., 21*(5), 679–682.

Nosek, B. A., Spies, J. R., & Motyl, M. (2012). Scientific utopia: II. Restructuring incentives and practices to promote truth over publishability. *Perspectives in Psychological Science, 7*, 615–631.

Nosek, B. A., Alter, G., Banks, G. C., Borsboom, D., Bowman, S., Breckler, S., & DeHaven, A. (2016). *Transparency and openness promotion (TOP) guidelines.* https://osf.io/vj54c

O'Connor, D. B. (2021). Leonardo da Vinci, preregistration and the architecture of science: Towards a more open and transparent research culture. *Health Psychology Bulletin, 5*(1), 39–45.

Open Science Collaboration. (2015). Estimating the reproducibility of psychological science. *Science, 349*(6251).

Orben, A. (2019). A journal club to fix science. *Nature, 573*, 465.

Pontika, N., Knoth, P., Cancellieri, M., et al. (2015). Fostering open science to research using a taxonomy and an eLearning portal. In *Proceedings of the 15th international conference on knowledge technologies and data-driven business.* Association for Computing Machinery.

Ritchie, S. (2020). *Science fictions: Exposing fraud, bias, negligence and hype in science.* Penguin.

Ross-Hellauer, T. (2017). What is open peer review? A systematic review. *F1000Research, 6*, 588

Rosenthal, R. (1979). The file drawer problem and tolerance for null results. *Psychological bulletin, 86*(3), 638.

Schulz, K. F., Altman, D. G., & Moher, D. (2010). CONSORT 2010 statement: Updated guidelines for reporting parallel group randomized trials. *Annals of Internal Medicine, 152*(11), 726–732.

Stewart, S., Rinke, E. M., McGarrigle, R., Lynott, D., Lunny, C., Lautarescu, A., & Crook, Z. (2020). *Pre-registration and Registered Reports: A primer from UKRN*. https://osf.io/8v2n7/download?format=pdf

Sullivan, I., DeHaven, A., & Mellor, D. (2019). Open and reproducible research on open science framework. *Current Protocols Essential Laboratory Techniques, 18*(1), e32.

Tenopir, C., Rice, N. M., Allard, S., Baird, L., Borycz, J., Christian, L., & Sandusky, R. J. (2020). Data sharing, management, use, and reuse: Practices and perceptions of scientists worldwide. *PLoS One, 15*(3), e0229003. https://doi.org/10.1371/journal.pone.0229003

Wilkinson, M. D., Dumontier, M., Aalbersberg, I. J., Appleton, G., Axton, M., Baak, A., ... Mons, B. (2016). The FAIR guiding principles for scientific data management and stewardship. *Scientific Data, 3*(1), 1–9.

Wolfram, D., Wang, P., Hembree, A., & Park, H. (2020). Open peer review: Promoting transparency in open science. *Scientometrics, 125*, 1033–1051.

Chapter 10
Being Agile: Honing New Skills and Fostering Curiosity for Increased Scientific Impact

Olga Perski

Abstract As early career researchers (ECRs), our work and scientific practices are situated in a fast-changing and ever-evolving research landscape. We also live in times of great geopolitical and economic uncertainty. At the time of writing, we are in the midst of a global viral pandemic, with a need for rapid scientific insight into how the SARS-CoV-2 virus spreads and what behavioural and pharmacological interventions are effective. In this chapter, I'd like to share a personal story about working as an ECR in a rapidly changing and uncertain research landscape – i.e., the COVID-19 pandemic – and what this has taught me about being 'agile' thus far. Specifically, I'd like to invite you to reflect on (i) what it means for us ECRs to adopt an 'agile' mindset, (ii) why it's increasingly important to be agile as an ECR, and (iii) what key barriers are to being agile. I'd also like to share my top tips for how to overcome (or at least not to be overwhelmed by!) these barriers.

Keywords Adaptation · Being agile · COVID-19 · Constructive feedback · Curiosity · Diffusion of Innovation · Intellectual humility · Living review · Open science · Skills acquisition

Introduction

We find ourselves in a rapidly changing research landscape: new hard- and software developments – including personal devices with high processing power, the proliferation of social media platforms, and inexpensive cloud storage – have forever changed the ways in which we collect, store, analyse, and disseminate data and research findings. Scientists can now run complex statistical analyses within a matter of minutes. In addition, the recent, positive shift towards practices relating to the

O. Perski (✉)
University College London, Department of Behavioural Science and Health, London, UK

Open Science movement (see Chap. 9) – including the sharing of research data and analytic code and the posting of pre-prints to open platforms prior to journal submission – enables more rapid dissemination and synthesis of research findings. Although these changes are largely positive, we are also seeing a growing number of publications each year – it has been estimated that the global scientific output doubles every nine years (Van Noorden, 2014). This means that it's becoming increasingly difficult for researchers to stay on top of what's going on in one's field and ensure that one's work stands out from the crowd and reaches its intended audiences.

In addition to these rapid changes to data gathering methods, analytic techniques, and dissemination practices, we also live in times of great geopolitical and economic uncertainty. At the time of writing, we are in the midst of a global viral pandemic, with a need for rapid scientific insight into how the COVID-19 virus spreads, why some people develop severe disease and die from COVID-19, and what behavioural and pharmacological interventions are effective at different time points. In this chapter, I'd like to share a personal story about working as an early career researcher (ECR) in a rapidly changing and uncertain research landscape – i.e., the COVID-19 pandemic – and what this has taught me about being 'agile' thus far. Specifically, I'd like to invite you to reflect on (i) what it means for us ECRs to adopt an 'agile' mindset, (ii) why it's increasingly important to be agile as an ECR, and (iii) what key barriers are to being agile. I'd also like to share my top tips for how to overcome (or at least not to be overwhelmed by!) these barriers. Let's kick things off with my personal story!

Being Agile During the COVID-19 Pandemic

When my colleagues and I first learnt about the COVID-19 outbreak, we were keen to apply our diverse skill sets to contribute to the limited knowledge base. As smoking cessation and infectious disease researchers, we understood from existing evidence that current and former smokers are at increased risk of catching and being hospitalised with respiratory viruses, such as influenza (Lawrence et al., 2019). Our starting point was therefore that smokers may be at an increased risk of catching COVID-19 and – as smoking involves repeated hand-to-mouth movements – that smoking may play an important role in community transmission (Simons et al., 2020a). However, when we started looking into the (at the time) little evidence generated during the first few months of the evolving pandemic, a different, unexpected pattern had started to emerge. Within the early observational studies conducted in China, fewer than expected patients requiring hospitalisation were current smokers, suggesting to some that tobacco smoking may protect people from becoming infected with and/or critically ill from COVID-19 (Farsalinos et al., 2020). However, my colleagues and I didn't want to jump to any conclusions before looking closely at the available evidence and – following the lead of an impressive ECR that we knew from Twitter (Wynants et al., 2020) – decided to set up a 'living review' on the topic. Living reviews are a relatively new scholarly output which supports the ongoing synthesis of research findings through regular updates of literature searches and analyses (Elliott et al., 2014). Particularly during times of uncertainty when new evidence is continuously produced and released, ongoing evidence syntheses can enable rapid learning and help inform social/health policy formation and clinical decision-making. Living reviews stand in contrast to traditional approaches to evidence synthesis, which typically take several years from conception to publication.

Since we started working on this project (March 2020), we have updated our living review on the association of smoking status with COVID-19 outcomes 12 times on a pre-print server (https://www.qeios.com/read/latest-UJR2AW), with v7 published in the peer-reviewed journal *Addiction* (Simons et al., 2020b). As our living review grew – and following extensive debates with colleagues in the tobacco research community and helpful reviewer comments (both solicited reviews by the journal and unsolicited reviews via the pre-print server Qeios, Twitter and e-mail) – we adapted our methods. For example, as we were regularly adding new data to our meta-analyses, we opted for a Bayesian statistical approach, which means that prior knowledge was incorporated into subsequent analyses via the specification of a 'prior distribution' (Dienes, 2011), and thus avoiding issues of family-wise error inflation through multiple testing. In line with Open Science principles (see Chap. 9), we also wanted to ensure that the data extracted from the studies included in the review and the accompanying R code were made openly available to reviewers and other researchers. We also decided to dedicate a substantial section of the living document to discussing methodological issues that complicate interpretation of the findings. In the last version of the review, with literature searches conducted up to July 2021, the results pointed towards current (compared with never) smokers being at reduced risk of SARS-CoV-2 infection but increased risk of greater disease severity once infected. However, it is important to note that our meta-analyses were unadjusted, with potential for confounding variables (e.g., age, socioeconomic status) to have clouded the results.

Engaging in this challenging work during a period of substantial uncertainty has highlighted to me the importance of being agile as an ECR. Many different definitions of 'agility' are being used across different domains, typically referring to the ability to adapt or change one's approach or practices in an evolving environment. To me, adopting an agile mindset means being open to continuously developing new research skills (e.g., living reviews, Bayesian meta-analysis). As such, being agile is closely related to innovative thinking – i.e., thinking outside the box and challenging the status quo, and not necessarily listening to nay-sayers who claim that something is too difficult or that it doesn't neatly fit within traditional scientific practices. In addition, being agile means being open to receiving feedback from others, reflecting on – and adapting to – constructive feedback and learning from things that did not initially work out as planned, pivoting instead to new approaches which may be better suited to addressing the problem at hand. As such, adopting an agile mindset can help ECRs make progress and learn to thrive in a rapidly changing and uncertain research landscape, which necessarily requires innovation and out-of-the-box thinking. Being agile is by no means an easy feat and requires ongoing efforts – my ECR colleague and I estimate that we jointly spent over 1500 h over the 18 months during which we worked on the living review, conducting searches, screening studies, extracting data, writing R code, learning new statistical techniques, engaging in critical debate (written and verbal) with colleagues, and writing several versions of the living review. In the following sections, I will discuss what I see as noteworthy barriers to being agile and share my top tips for overcoming these.

Balancing Skills Acquisition with the Need to Produce New Evidence

PhD students, post-docs, and junior lecturers are often encouraged to spend time acquiring new skills, either informally via supervisors/mentors or formally via research institutions (EURAXESS, 2016; Vitae, 2021). Learning new skills is crucial to being an agile ECR. However, despite skills acquisition generally being seen as a core part of an ECR's day job, we're often left with a nagging feeling that one ought to prioritise producing new research outputs, hence deprioritising skills development. It has also been acknowledged that ECRs are sometimes treated as 'paper-writing machines', with little support from senior academics to block out time for learning new skills and self-development (Bogle, 2018). In addition, ECRs are often employed on temporary contracts, live miles away from family and friends, find it difficult to maintain a good work–life balance, experience financial stress, or are looking to start/have recently started a family – all of which may negatively influence one's opportunity to adopt an agile mindset. For example, a survey of >7500 post-docs across 93 nations conducted by the journal *Nature* found that 49% of respondents regularly work on weekends and days off (Woolston, 2020), suggesting that many ECRs struggle to stay on top of their workload, likely having to deprioritise ongoing skills development.

Although it can be challenging for ECRs to carve out time for learning new skills – particularly given the barriers mentioned above or if finding oneself in an unsupportive environment (and the best solution may then be to try to move to a different research context) – I'd encourage you not to be afraid to try to learn new methods/approaches with an initially steep learning curve. As learning requires regular practice, it can be helpful to draw on evidence-informed techniques commonly used by behavioural scientists, such as goal setting or action planning (i.e., detailed planning of the behaviour, including the context, frequency, duration and intensity of the behaviour) (Michie et al., 2013). For example, it may be useful to block out time in your diary to learn how to produce a colourful graph with the *ggplot2* package in R (Wickham, 2009) or set a broader goal (with smaller sub-goals!) to conduct the entire statistical analysis for a given project in R, despite this initially being much quicker with a familiar statistical programme, such as SPSS. Drawing on behaviour change techniques can help ensure that skills development is regularly prioritised over other tasks that may feel more urgent in the moment (such as paper writing).

Another common barrier to being agile is that specialist training materials/courses are often costly, requiring competitive bursaries to be secured or goodwill from employers – both of which are difficult for ECRs to control or plan for. A recent positive change, facilitated at least partly by new hard- and software developments, is that many resources are now available for free online, including resources for learning to code in R (Wickham & Grolemund, 2016; https://r4ds.had.co.nz/) or Bayesian statistical inference (McElreath, 2018; https://github.com/rmcelreath/rethinking). There is also a rapidly growing number of short courses available for free or at low cost (covering topics from data science to artificial intelligence) via online platforms such as *Coursera* (https://www.coursera.org/) or *edX* (https://www.edx.org/), and it may be useful to create a Twitter account and start following handles such as @rstatstweet or @rstudiotips. I'd encourage you to start by looking online for high-quality, free resources – chances are that you won't have to pay in order to learn about a new topic!

Swimming Against the Current

It can be (or at least feel!) very challenging to try to persuade senior academics or funders that it's worth the effort to try new methods or to think outside the box. It has been argued that barriers to challenging the status quo (e.g., in relation to open peer reviews, continuous evidence syntheses, or other practices related to the Open Science movement) are primarily social (rather than financial or technical), with researchers themselves having the power to change research culture (Nosek & Bar-Anan, 2012). For example, as most journals now exist in a digital format, allowing for continuous evidence syntheses and open peer reviews is not technically difficult to facilitate. What is needed, though, is the willingness from all involved – particularly senior academics and those in editorial roles or funding committees – to try new approaches/practices.

According to the 'Diffusion of Innovation' theory, the adoption of new technologies or practices is a socially driven phenomenon, with 'early adopters' (i.e., trendsetters who are quick to abandon old practices for new, improved ones without necessarily relying on social approval) acting as important accelerators of change (Rogers, 1995). By making the early adopters' activities salient to others (e.g., junior and senior colleagues), the adoption of new practices will likely become more widespread (Berwick, 2003). If trying to persuade 'unimpressed' senior colleagues or funders that it's worth trying or investing in a new approach, it may therefore be helpful to identify examples of other cutting-edge projects that have used a similar approach and highlight what impact this has had on the field in terms of citations, media coverage, Twitter impressions, or patient/participant testimonials. For example, our living review has to date been viewed >75,000 times on Qeios.

Following the Science and Fostering Curiosity

Being agile also means being open to following the science (i.e., showing willingness to change one's prior beliefs according to the current state of the evidence), as opposed to sticking to one's 'pet theories' (i.e., theories or hypotheses in which one has an intellectual or financial stake). Returning to my previous example of studying the association of smoking status with COVID-19 outcomes during times of uncertainty, researchers must be careful when planning and executing studies and interpreting findings so as not to fall prey to 'pet theories', irrespective of whether one strongly believes that tobacco smoking or nicotine exacerbates the risk of or protects against COVID-19 infection at the outset.

Research shows that people are not always very good at judging the accuracy of their beliefs (Kruger & Dunning, 1999), with meta-cognitive skills such as 'intellectual humility' (i.e., the recognition that one's beliefs are fallible) required for accurate self-assessment of one's beliefs and knowledge (Leary et al., 2017). Intellectual humility is closely related to curiosity, with people who score highly on intellectual humility taking pleasure in seeking new information that contradicts their beliefs (Leary et al., 2017). Those high in intellectual humility also appear to be more agile, as they have been found to be more receptive to critical feedback and more willing to invest effort to learn about a new topic (Porter et al., 2020). In fact, meta-cognitive skills such as 'the recognition of the boundaries of one's knowledge, skills and expertise' form part of the UK Researcher Development Framework and are encouraged within academia. Although it may feel a bit tricky to try to foster an abstract meta-cognitive skill such as intellectual humility, I'd encourage you to try to stay curious in your scientific work. For example, I find that reading scientific articles/books or listening to podcasts from outside my immediate scientific discipline (e.g., biology, epidemiology, computer science, philosophy) keeps me on my toes and feeds my scientific curiosity!

Learning from Constructive Feedback

Closely linked to staying curious and following the science, being agile also means being open to learning from things that did not initially work out as planned. This means that it's important not to be afraid of failure (as it provides a learning opportunity), trying instead to pivot to new approaches that may be better suited to addressing the research problem at hand if one's initial approach didn't work out. I believe some of these critical aspects of an agile mindset are encapsulated within the Loss-of-Confidence Project (Rohrer et al., 2021). Here, researchers (many of them ECRs) were invited to disclose loss of confidence in (their own) previous research findings and reflect on the reasons why they no longer feel confident in the results. In-depth interviews with the participating researchers highlighted that it takes a lot of courage to revisit and learn from prior mistakes, also acknowledging that researchers at all career stages need to balance continuous learning (driven by curiosity) with the need to produce new knowledge and publish findings, which is not a walk in the park. Rather than feeling afraid or embarrassed to disclose mistakes or acknowledge when one's knowledge base and skill set has outgrown prior work (hence devaluing it), an agile researcher would instead try to view the detection or realisation of errors or methodological/logical flaws as learning opportunities that can help one grow as a scientist.

As discussed above in relation to the living review on the association of smoking status with COVID-19 outcomes, how one reacts to and engages with the peer review process (whether formal or informal) also constitutes an important part of the agile mindset. It can be daunting to invite/receive critical feedback on one's work – particularly when learning to apply new methods or 'swimming against the current' (e.g., having convinced senior colleagues to place their bets on an approach with as yet unknown benefits). However, learning to adapt to feedback from colleagues will only help to improve your work and ensure that inferences are valid. A useful way of looking at peer review comments is that it's a real opportunity (rather than a punishment!) to be provided with comments from an expert in the field who has critically engaged with your research question and scientific practices. It's also important to try actively not to take peer review comments personally – reviewers are commenting on the quality of the science rather than us as individuals. In the event of tricky reviewer comments, it can be useful to consult with more experienced team members who are likely able to bring an extra pair of eyes to critical reviews of our work and help think through how to adapt and respond to these.

Conclusions and Practical Recommendations

The research landscape we currently find ourselves in is rapidly changing and uncertain, and this requires ECRs to adopt an agile mindset in order to thrive. Being agile means not being afraid to try new things and to teach yourself new skills, thinking outside the box and challenging the status quo, and – most importantly! – staying curious and learning from things that didn't initially work out as planned. To pivot to an agile mindset, it may be helpful to use behaviour change techniques such as action planning to ensure you regularly block out time to learn new skills and to highlight to currently 'unimpressed' colleagues the impact of projects that have used cutting-edge methods, with a view to persuading them that investment in new methods has multiple benefits. They won't stay unimpressed for very long!

- Consider making use of evidence-informed techniques commonly used by behavioural scientists, such as goal setting or action planning, to help ensure that you regularly prioritise skills development.
- To support your learning, search for free, online materials via educational platforms such as *Coursera* or *edX*, or social media platforms such as Twitter.

- If trying to persuade 'unimpressed' senior colleagues or funders that it's worth trying or investing in a new approach, it may be helpful to identify examples of other cutting-edge projects that have used a similar approach and highlight what impact this has had on the field in terms of citations, media coverage, Twitter impressions, or patient/participant testimonials.
- Foster curiosity in your scientific work by regularly reading scientific articles/books or listening to podcasts from outside your immediate scientific discipline.
- Learn to adapt to critical feedback – try actively not to take peer review comments personally, view it as an opportunity (rather than a punishment!) to be provided with comments from an expert in the field and consult with more experienced team members on how to respond if needed.

References

Berwick, D. M. (2003). Disseminating innovations in health care. *JAMA, 289*(15), 1969–1975.

Bogle, D. (2018). What the research system needs to be doing to improve the world that postdocs face. *Naturejobs Blog.* http://blogs.nature.com/naturejobs/2018/06/27/how-could-universities-and-funders-improve-the-situation-for-postdoctoral-scientists/#/

Dienes, Z. (2011). Bayesian versus orthodox statistics: Which side are you on? *Perspectives on Psychological Science, 6*(3), 274–290. https://doi.org/10.1177/1745691611406920

Elliott, J. H., Turner, T., Clavisi, O., Thomas, J., Higgins, J. P. T., Mavergames, C., & Gruen, R. L. (2014). Living systematic reviews: An emerging opportunity to narrow the evidence-practice gap. *PLoS Medicine, 11*(2), e1001603. https://doi.org/10.1371/journal.pmed.1001603

EURAXESS. (2016, March 23). *Research profiles descriptors.* https://euraxess.ec.europa.eu/europe/career-development/training-researchers/research-profiles-descriptors

Farsalinos, K., Niaura, R., Le Houezec, J., Barbouni, A., Tsatsakis, A., Kouretas, D., Vantarakis, A., & Poulas, K. (2020). Editorial: Nicotine and SARS-CoV-2: COVID-19 may be a disease of the nicotinic cholinergic system. *Toxicology Reports, 7,* 658–663. https://doi.org/10.1016/j.toxrep.2020.04.012

Kruger, J., & Dunning, D. (1999). Unskilled and unaware of it: How difficulties in recognizing one's own incompetence lead to inflated self-assessments. *Journal of Personality and Social Psychology, 77*(6), 1121–1134. https://doi.org/10.1037/0022-3514.77.6.1121

Lawrence, H., Hunter, A., Murray, R., Lim, W. S., & McKeever, T. (2019). Cigarette smoking and the occurrence of influenza – Systematic review. *Journal of Infection, 79,* 401–406. https://doi.org/10.1016/j.jinf.2019.08.014

Leary, M. R., Diebels, K. J., Davisson, E. K., Jongman-Sereno, K. P., Isherwood, J. C., Raimi, K. T., Deffler, S. A., & Hoyle, R. H. (2017). Cognitive and interpersonal features of intellectual humility. *Personality and Social Psychology Bulletin, 43*(6), 793–813. https://doi.org/10.1177/0146167217697695

McElreath, R. (2018). *Statistical rethinking: A Bayesian course with examples in R and Stan.* Chapman and Hall/CRC. https://doi.org/10.1201/9781315372495

Michie, S., Richardson, M., Johnston, M., Abraham, C., Francis, J., Hardeman, W., Eccles, M. P., Cane, J., & Wood, C. E. (2013). The behavior change technique taxonomy (v1) of 93 hierarchically clustered techniques: Building an international consensus for the reporting of behavior change interventions. *Annals of Behavioral Medicine, 46*(1), 81–95. https://doi.org/10.1007/s12160-013-9486-6

Nosek, B. A., & Bar-Anan, Y. (2012). Scientific utopia: I. Opening scientific communication. *Psychological Inquiry, 23*(3), 217–243. https://doi.org/10.1080/1047840X.2012.692215

Porter, T., Schumann, K., Selmeczy, D., & Trzesniewski, K. (2020). Intellectual humility predicts mastery behaviors when learning. *Learning and Individual Differences, 80*, 101888. https://doi.org/10.1016/j.lindif.2020.101888

Rogers, E. M. (1995). *Diffusion of innovations* (3rd ed.). The Free Press.

Rohrer, J. M., Tierney, W., Uhlmann, E. L., DeBruine, L. M., Heyman, T., Jones, B., Schmukle, S. C., Silberzahn, R., Willén, R. M., Carlsson, R., Lucas, R. E., Strand, J., Vazire, S., Witt, J. K., Zentall, T. R., Chabris, C. F., & Yarkoni, T. (2021). Putting the self in self-correction: Findings from the loss-of-confidence project. *Perspectives on Psychological Science, 1745691620964106*. https://doi.org/10.1177/1745691620964106

Simons, D., Perski, O., & Brown, J. (2020a). Covid-19: The role of smoking cessation during respiratory virus epidemics. In: *The BMJ Opinion*. http://web.archive.org/web/20200415110656/https://blogs.bmj.com/bmj/2020/03/20/covid-19-the-role-of-smoking-cessation-during-respiratory-virus-epidemics/

Simons, D., Shahab, L., Brown, J., & Perski, O. (2020b). The association of smoking status with SARS-CoV-2 infection, hospitalization and mortality from COVID-19: A living rapid evidence review with Bayesian meta-analyses (version 7). *Addiction*. https://doi.org/10.1111/add.15276

Van Noorden, R. (2014). Global scientific output doubles every nine years. http://blogs.nature.com/news/2014/05/global-scientific-output-doubles-every-nine-years.html.

Vitae. (2021). *The Vitae researcher development framework* [page]. https://www.vitae.ac.uk/researchers-professional-development/about-the-vitae-researcher-development-framework/developing-the-vitae-researcher-development-framework

Wickham, H. (2009). *ggplot2: Elegant graphics for data analysis*. Springer. https://doi.org/10.1007/978-0-387-98141-3

Wickham, H., & Grolemund, G. (2016). *R for data science: Import, tidy, transform, visualize, and model data*. O'Reilly Media, Inc..

Woolston, C. (2020). Postdoc survey reveals disenchantment with working life. *Nature, 587*(7834), 505–508. https://doi.org/10.1038/d41586-020-03191-7

Wynants, L., Calster, B. V., Collins, G. S., Riley, R. D., Heinze, G., Schuit, E., Bonten, M. M. J., Dahly, D. L., Damen, J. A., Debray, T. P. A., de Jong, V. M. T., Vos, M. D., Dhiman, P., Haller, M. C., Harhay, M. O., Henckaerts, L., Heus, P., Kammer, M., Kreuzberger, N., & van Smeden, M. (2020). Prediction models for diagnosis and prognosis of covid-19: Systematic review and critical appraisal. *BMJ, 369*, m1328. https://doi.org/10.1136/bmj.m1328

Chapter 11
To Come, to See, to Conquer: Practical Pointers in Applying for Funding and Securing Your Initial Grants

Daan Westra and Bram Fleuren

Abstract Obtaining your doctorate degree not only implies that you are able to design and conduct rigorous scientific research independently but also that you are expected to be able to get your projects funded. Your ability to acquire research funds can have large implications for the type of research questions you can pursue, the articles you can publish, the societal impact you can have with your work, and whether or not you will get a permanent position. Therefore, applying for funding can be one of the most daunting aspects of being an early career researcher. In this chapter, we reflect on our attempts at acquiring funding as early career researchers for the past five years of our careers. We share some lessons we have learned during this bumpy road, which was filled with (many) rejected and (some) successful grant applications. We hope that these will help early career scholars to feel more prepared for their own funding endeavors.

Keywords Funding · Grants · Effective writing · Peer-review · Funding bodies

Introduction

Twenty-twenty was a crazy year, crazier than anyone could foresee when it started. In February, COVID-19 hit the Netherlands and our province of residence in particular. The wild sounds of the prespring festivities were still echoing in our ears as the 'COVID-call' was dropped on the Dutch scientific sector on May 1st. Wanting to help in handling the challenges that COVID-19 and its 'intelligent lockdown' posed, as well as – let's be honest – to secure a slice of that sweet grant pie, we had a phone call. Daan: 'The call was just released, do you want to submit that research

---

D. Westra (✉)
Maastricht University, Faculty of Health, Medicine and Life Sciences, Care and Public Health Research Institute (CAPHRI), Maastricht, The Netherlands

B. Fleuren
Maastricht University, Faculty of Psychology and Neuroscience, Maastricht, The Netherlands

© The Author(s), under exclusive license to Springer Nature Switzerland AG 2022
D. Kwasnicka, A. Y. Lai (eds.), *Survival Guide for Early Career Researchers*, https://doi.org/10.1007/978-3-031-10754-2_11

idea we talked about regarding hospitals and their workers? I'll do the organization part, you'll do the employee part?' Bram: 'Yes!' The deadline to submit initial ideas was short, so this exchange meant that for the following two weeks, our evenings were instantly booked.

A few weeks later, we received the news that *'the committee has regretfully decided against inviting your initial research idea to be submitted as a full research proposal'*. Twenty percent of the submitted research ideas were selected, and their teams invited to submit a full research proposal. Ours was not one of them, and it felt like a slap in the face – all the evenings of hard work we had put into it had gone to waste. Even worse, we now had to take the bad news to our team. To our surprise, one of our mentors indicated that formally, the bad news was 'merely' an advice of the committee not to pursue the proposal any further and not a definitive rejection. He still believed in our idea and encouraged us to submit a full proposal for the next round regardless of the committee's advice not to do so. We felt like that was probably a pointless endeavor...

But was it? Five weeks later, after another week of evenings filled with hard work and (multiple) existential crises, which was followed by several weeks of hoping for the best, Daan opened an incoming e-mail from the funding agency while on vacation, to the dismay of his fiancé (trying to prevent your work from invading your time off? see Chap. 4 on recovery). *'The committee considers your research proposal to be both highly relevant and of excellent quality and has decided to award the requested funding'*. Daan took a screenshot of the e-mail immediately and threw it on the WhatsApp group, leaving the whole team in disbelief. We had carefully studied the committee's initial negative advice, indicated to the funding agency why we believed it was unwarranted, received permission to submit a full proposal, and, against all odds, now were awarded with EUR 500,000 to study hospitals' adaptations to the COVID-19 pandemic and their effects on employees' sustainable employability. In an instant, 2020 – and the next two years – went from crazy to utter madness.

The above is one of our experiences applying for research grants in our fields. Certainly not all of our experiences have such happy conclusions. For us too, the rejected funding applications outnumber the successful ones. In this chapter, we share some lessons learned from these experiences, both the good and the bad. We will not focus on specific funding agencies or schemes, as we cannot possibly be comprehensive, and many resources on these topics exist already (e.g., Yang, 2012 for NIH grants). Instead, we focus on the common denominators across our applications and aim to provide general strategies that early career researchers can use, regardless of their operational context. We will illustrate these approaches with examples from our own experiences and hope that they are helpful to our peers.

Target Your Efforts

You. Need. Money. That is, if you want to work in academia, you need money to fund your projects, to secure a permanent contract, and – basically – to build a successful research career (Bloch et al., 2014). Of course, it feels like your peers are – seemingly – more successful in their applications. So are you even a legit scholar if you do not have many successful grant applications? As early career researchers, these thoughts can push us on a – often frustrating – path to grant writing. Particularly if you (like us) are not affiliated to a university that provides their newly appointed assistant professors with formal startup grants (Koziel, 2016). Do not let the pressure of all the reasons for 'having' to secure funding become the main driver of your grant writing efforts though. If it does, you will find yourself chasing any kind of funding in a desperate attempt to get your hands on some money. Unfocused grant chasing will lack a clear direction, impose many (tight) deadlines on yourself, increase your work pressure, and limit your ability to align with what funders look for. Our first lesson learned is thus to target your efforts; deliberately select the funding opportunities to go for and those to ignore!

An awareness of the different funding options in your environment is essential for targeted grant-writing. We distinguish between three main routes of funding: *industry funding* (i.e., from private organizations, sometimes in your research field, and other times organizations that have a scientific need that you can fulfill), *project grants* (i.e., from scientific funding agencies), and *personal grants* (i.e., for individual scholars). These routes come with different requirements and expectations as well as different levels of prestige, which become apparent at different levels. For example, an individual grant from the European Union such as an ERC Starting Grant features different requirements and, depending on your context, might be considered more or less prestigious than a project grant from your own research institute. Getting acquainted with the funding options relevant to your field and department is thus a must, especially if you have recently transitioned into a different department, university, or discipline. Mentors, peers in your discipline, your university's research office (if applicable), and direct colleagues can typically provide you with insights into the optimal funding routes to target and the prestige associated with each route.

Once you have a sense of the lay of the funding landscape, you should attempt to 'preempt the call' as much as possible. You will not be the first person with a great research idea who spotted the call for proposals too late and is left with too little time to build a strong proposal and/or consortium before the deadline (trust us on that one!). A big part of why we managed to successfully apply to our country's COVID-19 funding scheme is because we discussed a potential project before the call for proposals came out. We had a rough idea of the focus and research questions of the project before the call formally appeared. The tight deadline of the COVID-19 call made such a small head start particularly useful. It is essential to keep yourself informed about upcoming calls.

Leveraging our network and tracking funding agencies have proven to be valuable ways for us to do so. Supervisors and mentors with close(r) connections to funding agencies are an obvious source of information. However, it is important to also talk to your faculty/university's funding advisor or equivalent offices. If your funding advisors do not communicate upcoming opportunities regularly (e.g., through a newsletter), simply reach out and ask them for advice based on your research interests and expertise. Similarly, funding agencies' formal calendars specify which calls come out when and thus form an excellent way of preempting recurring funding schemes as well. Unfortunately, your competitors also have these options, and now they are definitely aware of them.

To ensure that you stay ahead, you can keep up with wider discourse relevant to your fields. Specific topics on the policy agenda might very well require new or additional research and could thus result in formal funding opportunities. Sensing which topics are pertinent, to whom, and at what time is also crucial in securing industry funding, which typically follows less formalized application procedures. The specifics of this funding route can differ greatly by research field but in general, industry partners will decide to fund your research project if they see a (direct) benefit for their own agenda. Here, alignment with ongoing policy discussions is also an important factor. Relatedly, being aware of the goals that potential industry funders pursue and being able to articulate how your research aligns with them can provide you with an important source of research funding. Daan, for example, has generated a considerable research budget from health insurers by articulating how important it is for the insurers' goal of keeping healthcare affordable, to understand the behavior of healthcare providers. As an extra plus, the research you will end up doing with this money likely generates direct societal impact.

Skipping funding opportunities that are not a good match is as important as seizing the right ones. There is no point in chasing a prestigious personal grant with a CV that simply does not meet the requirements for it. Ask yourself whether your CV provides funders with sufficient grounds to feel comfortable entrusting you with a substantial amount of their resources. Can you make a compelling case that you are able to lead that large research consortium as principal investigator (PI) for example? This does not mean that you should limit your own ambitions when it comes to acquiring research funding. In fact, we have witnessed how several colleagues have obtained (personal) grants for which they were told by others that 'their CV was not good enough'. Instead, we encourage you to contemplate whether applying for such a grant is worth your time and effort. If you are an 'aim for the stars' type of person, go for it! But at the very least, let it be a deliberate choice. If you would rather not want to aim for the stars, you might be able to get involved in a proposal in a smaller role in order to build up your CV for larger roles in future applications. Think about roles as co-PI or as PI of a specific work package within a grant project. If you do, though, make sure that you get a fair share of the funding and the corresponding recognition. Most importantly, allow yourself the time to grow into roles so that you can confidently apply for later opportunities.

Skipping opportunities is not only a matter of considering your seniority and CV, but of your research interest and establishing a clear research profile as well. If you are passionate about your research topic (like us), saying no will be a difficult but important challenge in targeting your fund-generating efforts. After all, how can you pass that opportunity that could perhaps, maybe someday, if you actually get the money, and the project works out as it is supposed to, become one of your best articles? But think about whether that money (if you get it) will in fact allow you to do something that is relevant for your research profile and topic. Does it help you in meeting your formal requirements (e.g., for obtaining a permanent contract, to cover your fixed-term contract, or both)? How long will it take you to craft this proposal and is this time not better spent on doing actual research and writing articles? Is getting this money realistic enough (i.e., are you adhering to the tips in this chapter?)? And when you do get the funding, do you have the time to execute the project properly and deliver on the promises in the proposal (be honest now)? We realize that saying no becomes easier after you have already secured some funding in the past. However, even if that is not the case, we learnt that spreading yourself too thin – both quality and quantity wise – will not help you to acquire funding at any stage of your career.

Recognize and Mobilize the Resources at Your Disposal

The first time we were asked to participate on a grant proposal (as one of many coapplicants on a project of our mentors, as per our advice to apply in a manner adequate for the career stage), we did not have the slightest idea how applying for funding actually worked or what was expected of us in the process. We just went with what everybody else on the team did and felt like we were barely keeping our heads afloat. This realization underscores the importance of resources in obtaining more resources, such as funding. Resources can come in many shapes and forms, but essentially boil down to anything that facilitates you in obtaining your goal of writing the proposal and securing that money. Knowing which resources are available and how to effectively mobilize them has proven instrumental in our successful applications and therefore constitutes the second part of this chapter. We discuss some of the ones that have been most important to us, to offer you a basis for identifying the resources available to you in your own environment and enable you to mobilize them.

A first crucial resource is 'the others'. Oliver Wendell Holmes Sr once wrote that *'Many ideas grow better when transplanted into another mind than in the one where they sprang up'*. While you may have a great research idea yourself, it is extremely useful to get others' perspectives on it before you use it in a proposal. Our successful funding applications are typically team efforts or based on getting other peoples' perspective on our ideas before applying rather than purely solitary endeavors. Solitary grant applications are not only relatively uninspiring and dreadful, but also simply do not turn out as competitive as they could be (Guyer et al., 2021). Your peers and mentors are thus arguably the most important resource in grant writing. Get feedback from people whose opinion you appreciate, even if it is unfavorable. Brainstorm ideas with them and ask for their perspective on issues (e.g., based on their expert knowledge, skills, background, or insights into practice). In our experience, peers and mentors are surprisingly willing to help you craft a competitive proposal, even if you cannot offer a formal project role in return (e.g., in individual grant applications). Once you start putting this advice in practice though, do make sure that you also return the favor when peers ask your input on their proposals!

A second important resource are the 'ABC-experts', the Anything-But-Content-Experts. They are more commonly known as research officers, grant support officers, or funding advisors. Our university employs several of these officers and their main tasks are to provide detailed feedback on grant proposals and their associated budgets and to communicate funding opportunities to the appropriate departments. Initially, we were a bit reluctant to work with our grant support officers since it felt a bit like we were being 'checked' unnecessarily ('what do they know about this topic anyway?!'). However, working with our funding advisors has proven to be very worthwhile and enjoyable, not only because they are simply very nice people. ABC-experts are not there to scrutinize your work for the sake of it but rather to contribute their unique financial expertise and tacit knowledge to your mutual(!) goal of acquiring research funding. They are familiar with various funding schemes and know all about things like eligibility criteria, formatting guidelines, budget requirements. You can probably estimate how much money your project requires for example, but grant proposals typically require a budget that includes nitty gritty details you may not know that exist. The financial experts of our grant support office think about these all the time. They have pointed out missing obligatory items on the budget or identified insufficiencies in cost estimates for the activities we proposed in the applications on multiple occasions. Without their advice, your proposal can get shot down early for not ticking all the required boxes (see Sect. 11.4 of this chapter), or you can end up having to deliver on unrealistic promises being made in your proposal. Additionally, funding advisors have had countless successful and unsuccessful proposals pass through their hands. They thus have a pretty good idea of what funders are looking for. Where your peers and mentors can help with the scientific content and merit of your proposal, funding advisors will help you to frame it appropriately, use the right language, and emphasize the elements funders are looking for. Finally, their knowledge of the funding landscape also enables them to point you to funding and networking possibilities you may never have thought about yourself.

Third, connections to nonacademic partners constitute another valuable resource. That is, organizations or individuals that are relevant to the proposal you are working on. Examples include those that can help you to get access to secondary data or in which you can collect primary data (in the case of our COVID-19 project, these are hospitals for example), those that are willing to cofund your application (either in cash or kind), those that can help you disseminate your results, those who can become a member of a user committee for your project, or even those that helped to define the research questions of the project. Such partnerships with 'the real world' give you a major edge in the grant competition, because they give funding committees confidence that you can actually carry out the ambitious project you are proposing beyond the confines of the academic ivory tower. The best way to mobilize this resource depends on the content of your specific proposal, but you can try several approaches. The most convenient is through relationships you or any of your peers or collaborators have established through prior research projects. A second (and overlooked) approach is through your teaching activities. A surprising number of alumni from your institution may hold positions that are of added value to your project. Whichever approach you take, reach out and pitch your idea (with a story that resonates, see the following section on how to ensure that) to potential partners.

Third, your university might have relations with industry partners through a formal office. Our university has a so-called knowledge transfer office for example, which actively seeks to bridge the gap between academia and industry partners. Other names for it are Industry Liaison Office (Jones-Evans et al., 1999) or Technology Transfer Office (Macho-Stadler et al., 2007). In case your university offers a similar office, it is a great place to reach out to. Last, but definitely not least, if you feel that your grant proposal would benefit from a specific partner with whom there are no prior ties, consider cold-calling them. You might need to get over the initial hesitation, but it worked for us in several of the hospitals that now participate in our COVID-19 project.

Fourth, when a topic makes it into either the 'For Dummies' or 'The Complete Idiot's Guide to' book series, you can be quite sure that a lot has been written about it before. In the case of grant writing, there is a book in both of these series (Browning, 2016; Thompson, 2011). If that is not proof that there are many written resource available on the topic, beyond the chapter you are currently reading, we don't know what is. Exploring some of these written resources such as books, chapters, manuals, and papers can definitely be helpful. When you do start to navigate these resources though, remember that some are generic while others are very field-specific. This chapter is an example of the former and there are many examples of the latter. Be particularly cautious with applying the tips and tricks of the latter because customs and expectations can be quite different across fields. In the further reading section at the end of this chapter, we have listed a few of these resources that might be useful for you.

Finally, as a minor suggestion, it might be useful to consider outsourcing administrative burden to specialized agencies. Although we have not used these services personally, our colleagues have had positive experiences, as these agencies can help to avoid risks of 'tripping up' over nonscientific content (e.g., administrative requirements for an application). This particularly applies to larger (e.g., EU-level) applications. Some of these agencies use a no-cure-no-pay model in which you only have to pay them when you actually acquire the grant. In some cases, your university might even cover the costs of such agencies, minimizing the impact on your research budget.

Make It Resonate

Our successful applications simply have a more convincing story than the unsuccessful ones. In some proposals, a clear theoretical or methodological knowledge gap needs to be filled for the advancement of a research field. In others, like our COVID-19 proposal, the project directly contributes to solving pertinent societal issues. Yet in others (not necessarily our own), a bold and groundbreaking idea has the potential to fundamentally change the way we view specific parts of our lives. Whatever the story of your proposal is, it helps tremendously if you are able to communicate it in a clear and concise manner. When we had trouble convincing colleagues – or even ourselves – of our proposal's narrative, we never succeeded in convincing the assessment committee of it either. Luckily, the art of conveying a convincing grant-story can be learned (Jones et al., 2017). Daan attended a pitching workshop for academics hosted by an actor/director and fine artist. In an early stage of writing the proposal, they filmed him pitching the main project idea, pointed out where it was difficult to follow for a nonscientific audience, and helped to structure the main message using appropriate and accessible vocabulary, which significantly improved the flow of the proposal. Once he made it to the final interview round, they helped him deliver a convincing presentation to the committee. Here, we share some of the other ways in which we have made our stories resonate.

You have probably ventured into the social sciences hoping to understand and improve the world we live in. Logically, societal improvement is thus a major part of the story behind successful proposals. Our COVID-19 proposal for example, made it very clear that the main aim of the project was to help keep hospital staff employable amidst the crisis, which was a major challenge for hospitals. The entire proposal was written toward this specific end goal; the theoretical perspective, empirical setting, study design, and deliverables directly connected to sustaining staff employability. Additionally, we extensively pitched the project idea to the organizations involved in the project (as per our advice regarding partners from outside academia) and included them as partners on the application, both to ensure the immediate societal value and to signal it unambiguously to the funder. When you get powerful stakeholders in the field on board, a funding agency will have a hard time disagreeing with the value and feasibility of the proposal. The key is to make this signal of societal impact and feasibility as explicit and tangible as possible: Having stakeholders from the field as coapplicants for the proposal, flashing signed agreements or letters of intent in the early stages, and getting stakeholders to pledge cofinancing the project are all good ways to do so.

Another tip for resonance is to make your proposal 'programmatic' (Bradley, 2017). To us, this means that any grant application you submit fits in your logical research narrative. Even if you are currently unaware of it, there is probably a 'deeper story' that ties together all of your research projects (regardless of how they are funded). Explicating that story and positioning the proposed project as the logical next step in that program helps funders understand why you are targeting a specific grant and why you will be able to successfully execute the project. That story can be theoretical, it can be methodological, it can be through societal relevance (which is usually at least part of the story), it can be a combination of these, or it can be something else. Fitting your proposed project into a (successful) bigger picture can help to convince funders that you can be trusted with the money: This applicant knows what they are doing and this grant aligns perfectly with their expertise. When your proposal fits into your overall research narrative, chances are also high that you will be able to recycle some of the work for other grant opportunities or short papers (which might even be considered resources for future endeavors) in case the proposal does not receive funding.

A research narrative is NOT something that is exclusively reserved for senior scholars. As an early career scholar, you also have a story to tell that ties together all your research in some way and it is up to you to formulate it convincingly. This does not mean that you should embellish your biography or leave out less successful projects; you may actually use these to signal that (and why) you are moving from one line of inquiry to another (more focused) research line. Importantly, when working with a grant team, you should try and build a team narrative that makes sense given individual narratives. In our joint application, Daan's healthcare management focus matched perfectly with Bram's work on sustainable employability for example.

Please, Tick the Boxes!

Last but definitely not least, there is the obvious, rather boring, yet crucial aspect of grant writing: Make sure that you tick all of the boxes! Most funders have specific judging criteria they use to assess incoming proposals, in terms of the (quality of the) academic content as well as criteria such as formatting and budgeting. Luckily, they usually communicate these clearly in their call for proposals. Follow them meticulously and repeatedly check whether you adhered to all of them before hitting the submit button. To avoid being caught off guard by some additional form you need to attach on the final page of the submission system a few minutes before the deadline, it is wise to check the exact requirements by going through the submission process (as if you are about to submit) in an early stage of crafting your proposal. For example, some grants might require your dean or head of school to sign in order for the application to be eligible and that is not something you want to become aware of only minutes before the deadline. In other words, check the requirements for all of the details that funders could easily reject you for. Decision makers will have hundreds of proposals to go through and are happy to rule one out easily because it does not fulfill all requirements. Your job is to make sure that your proposal is not among the ones that they reject for not meeting all of the requirements. Do note that not all boxes that need to be ticked are always explicit and that 'reading between the lines' is thus essential in responding to a call well. A call might be based on a set of values or expectations that are not formally communicated as requirements, but that you can make yourself aware of. If, like us, you have a difficult time reading between the lines the first few times you apply to a funding scheme, your research office can probably be of added value. They have seen plenty of successful as well as unsuccessful proposals and thus have a good sense of what is expected from a particular scheme. Use that awareness to avoid being rejected for not being congruent with the informal expectations of a particular call for proposals!

Where Does All This Leave Us?

Applying for research funding can be one of the most daunting aspects of early career in academia. Whereas your PhD project was most likely relatively confined and predictable, once you have obtained your PhD, you are expected to bring in external funding, and usually without any formal training in doing so. We are both still early career researchers and we do not consider ourselves experts in acquiring research funding. For the most part, our experience is based on trial and error. We hope that sharing some of these experiences and suggestions can help you as an early career researcher to feel more prepared to acquire research funding and make the ordeal a bit less daunting. At the very least, writing this chapter has helped us in identifying some of the hidden reasons behind our own failures and successes, so we will be looking to apply these in our future applications.

Conclusions and Practical Recommendations

We want to conclude by emphasizing that even in the best-case scenario, applying for research funding is a very bumpy road. Similar to publishing research articles, getting rejected is part of the game in applying for funding. In our environment for example, not (a whole lot) more than 10% of the applications for a typical call for project or personal grant proposals will receive funding. For the COVID-19 call that we applied to, 12% of the projects received funding. In this case, our proposal ended up on the good side of the line. However, most proposals do not. Remember that *'consistently failing to obtain research support is a realistic prospect for many excellent researchers'* (von Hippel & von Hippel, 2015, p. 5). We hope that you will not let yourself get discouraged by one or multiple failed attempts at acquiring funding. Rejected research proposals still feel disappointing to us, but once the disappointment fades, the grounds on which a proposal was rejected always contain valuable lessons for future applications. If there is one thing we have learned from our experiences, it is that informed persistence pays off!

The tips in brief:

- Target your efforts.
  - Acquaint yourself with the (prestige and expectations) of the various funding routes through peers, colleagues, and mentors.
  - Pre-empt the call by keeping up with funding calendars and ongoing policy discourse, leveraging your personal network, and connecting to your funding advisors.
  - Learn to say no to applications for which you do not fancy the odds and situations in which you are unable to meet expectations.
- Recognize and mobilize the resources available to you.
  - Teamwork makes the dream work; involving peers and partners in your application will make it more competitive.
  - Funding advisors are here to help you, so make sure to utilize their knowledge and experience.

- Get out of the ivory tower and into the field. Connecting to 'real world' partners will make your proposal more relevant to funders and boost the societal impact of your work.
- Make your application resonate.
  - Identify the 'story' of your grant proposal and (learn to) communicate it in convincing fashion. Unable to convince your peers (or yourself)? You are unlikely to convince funders.
  - Making the world a better place is an integral part of social sciences, so it should be a (big) part of your application's story.
  - Make your research programmatic. Identify the story that ties your (previous) research activities together and position your proposal in this larger story.
- Tick the boxes.
  - Do not give funders an easy reason to put your proposal on the 'no' pile. Make sure that you ticked all the (administrative) boxes. Go through the submission system early to avoid surprises.
  - Read between the lines of the call text to identify the implicit expectations of a call and make sure you adhere to them.

References

Bloch, C., Graversen, E. K., & Pedersen, H. S. (2014). Competitive research grants and their impact on career performance. *Minerva, 52*(1), 77–96.

Bradley, M. M. (2017). The science pendulum: From programmatic to incremental—And back? *Psychophysiology, 54*(1), 6–11.

Browning, B. A. (2016). *Grant writing for dummies* (6th ed.). John Wiley & Sons.

Guyer, R. A., Schwarze, M. L., Gosain, A., Maggard-Gibbons, M., Keswani, S. G., & Goldstein, A. M. (2021). Top ten strategies to enhance grant-writing success. *Surgery, 170*(6), 1727–1731.

Jones, H. P., McGee, R., Weber-Main, A. M., Buchwald, D. S., Manson, S. M., Vishwanatha, J. K., & Okuyemi, K. S. (2017). *Enhancing research careers: An example of a US national diversity-focused, grant-writing training and coaching experiment.* Paper presented at the BMC proceedings.

Jones-Evans, D., Klofsten, M., Andersson, E., & Pandya, D. (1999). Creating a bridge between university and industry in small European countries: The role of the industrial liaison office. *R&D Management, 29*(1), 47–56.

Koziel, J. A. (2016). Successful grant-writing strategies for junior scientists: An American public university perspective. *Puls Uczelni, 10*(4), 21.

Macho-Stadler, I., Pérez-Castrillo, D., & Veugelers, R. (2007). Licensing of university inventions: The role of a technology transfer office. *International Journal of Industrial Organization, 25*(3), 483–510.

Thompson, W. (2011). *The complete Idiot's guide to grant writing.* Penguin.

von Hippel, T., & von Hippel, C. (2015). To apply or not to apply: A survey analysis of grant writing costs and benefits. *PLoS One, 10*(3), e0118494.

Yang, O. O. (2012). *Guide to effective grant writing: How to write a successful NIH grant application.* Springer.

Part III
Research Dissemination

Chapter 12
Being an Effective Writer

Sarah Krull Abe

Abstract In this chapter, I will share my story of becoming an effective writer. Common types of outputs you may be working on include manuscripts, reviews, grant proposals, white papers, and blogs. Versatility should be expected as an early career researcher. Academic writing is not just about writing but also paying attention to your audience and platform. Two habits I developed as a PhD student that continue to support my writing are open trusting communication with my supervisor and a well-organized timeline to effectively manage my time. Personal habits like organizing, mapping out timelines, devoting space, and advisor meetings are good habits that yield better writing. Here, I also share specific writing techniques. Going back to the basics, using flashcards or post-its, is useful for organizing your thoughts. The "paragraph hamburger" or "sandwich" format also supports the organization and logical thought processes. Finally, keep these three action points in mind: first, identify authors who demonstrate excellent writing style and apply these as templates for your own writing. Second, participate in writing workshops and peer review journal manuscripts. Third, make the time for your writing. In conclusion, effective writing is a process and an important communication tool.

Keywords Effective writing · Writing skills · Journal articles · Systematic reviews · Grant proposals · White papers · Reports · Blogs · Writing habits

My Story of Becoming an Effective Writer

My primary research interest is international public health with a focus on cancer, nutrition, and social epidemiology in Japan. I hope that some of the topics touched on in this chapter transcend my field to offer a broader group of early career

S. K. Abe (✉)
National Cancer Center, Division of Prevention, Tokyo, Japan

© The Author(s), under exclusive license to Springer Nature Switzerland AG 2022
D. Kwasnicka, A. Y. Lai (eds.), *Survival Guide for Early Career Researchers*, https://doi.org/10.1007/978-3-031-10754-2_12

researchers tips on effective writing. I draw inspiration from different sources. Keeping an open mind pays off. Recently, I connected with my cousin and PhD candidate who is researching an unpublished papyrus letter from 500 Common Era (CE). How cool is that? Hearing about her project got me excited and motivated. I realized an effective writer can find motivation beyond our own immediate field. In fact, something new may trigger ideas and fresh approaches, perspectives, processes that can be applied to our own work. The topic has nothing to do with my background or professional field, but all types of academic writing exist, an important point to keep in mind. Particularly in the social sciences and health, a silo approach leads to narrow views while an interdisciplinary approach can tackle long-term issues.

A year and a half ago my supervisor asked if I could take over an article that a former student was drafting. Before her, two other researchers had worked on the topic body mass index (BMI), height and weight change, and risk of lung cancer in Japan. I willingly obliged. I was familiar with the data, the analyses had all been performed, and the manuscript drafted. I set it on the back burner for a year and finally attacked the coauthors' comments written in Japanese, adding to the challenge. The comments seemed mundane; however, they required reanalysis. I consulted with my supervisor on how to categorize the BMI categories replacing the standard World Health Organization (WHO) cut-offs with Japanese-focused ones as very few participants fell into the obesity category (BMI ≥ 30). This was an easy task. However, working on multiple other projects and raising two young kids meant that it was difficult to find time to update the tables and revise this manuscript. Finally, I decided to go to the office on a weekend and finished all hard tasks within two concentrated days. This experience was so satisfying, proving I could do it, if I set aside time to focus only on this project and taking compensation days in exchange. I have since recommended this approach to others, especially working mothers. Finally, a decade on, the journal *Cancer Epidemiology Biomarkers and Prevention* published our article (Abe et al., 2021). Lessons learned: concentration, persistence, and finding the right home (journal) will pay off and lead to a successful contribution.

Researchers juggle between easy tasks and hard tasks. An easy strategy is to pick the low hanging fruit first. This warrants a note of caution, following this approach means quick easy tasks such as responding to emails will be completed in a timely manner. However, bigger projects will remain on the "to do" list. Therefore, it is important to set aside chunks of time dedicated to comprehensive writing projects such as manuscripts.

Writing Experiences, Skills, and Habits

Academic writing is not JUST about writing, but also paying heed to the audience and platform. As PhD students, many of us learn how to write research articles and grant applications. Growing into early career researchers, our writing requires more variety. I have contributed to different types of academic writing, including peer-reviewed articles, systematic reviews, reports, blogs, etc. I would like to share some lessons I have learned from these experiences and introduce common writing styles that early career researchers will likely use.

Types of Academic Writing

Journal Articles In my field of epidemiology, manuscript writing follows a systematic, cookie cutter-like approach. Elements to include and order have been described extensively (Rothman et al., 2008). Most of my manuscripts focus on survival analysis such as cancer and lifestyle risk factors, e.g., diet and infection. When I write these types of manuscripts for academic medical journals, I use formal scientific jargon. Analytic and literature search skills are useful for this type of writing. During the peer review process, I have received useful project-specific tips and general advice. For example, comments from a *British Medical Journal* review – avoid all but the most common abbreviations. Tables and figures should stand alone. This means they must contain all relevant information including defining of the included abbreviations, identifying the population and time.

Systematic Reviews I contributed to reviews on anemia, green tea, and health outcomes, most recently polymorphisms and calcium status (da Silva Lopes & Abe, 2021) for the World Health Organization. Systematic reviews are unsurprisingly systematic in nature, generally following a rigid preregistered protocol. Review studies synthesize data applying a narrative or quantitative approach. The process of writing a review can be challenging comparing individual studies in a meaningful way. Themes within studies can be grouped to structure a review in a form that is understandable to the reader. The purpose of a review is to present unbiased evidence for clinicians and policy makers in the context of health reviews.

Grant Proposals I also write grant proposals for my research. I am a coinvestigator on numerous grants and successfully received a grant. This did not come easily; I was finally successful on my fifth attempt. Rejection is part of the process, and try to reflect on what went well and what was missing. Carefully check the funder's expectations and goals and align your application accordingly. In initial attempts, I focused on the content, however after consulting with several successful awardees of similar grants, I understood the format was equally important. The funder has published a whole book specifying the format to follow. Unfortunately, currently this is only available in Japanese, while applications in English are also accepted. Effective writing needs to be coupled with other strategies such as flowcharts. A useful strategy is reading other researcher's successful grant applications to see how they structured them etc.

White Papers White papers are official reports (Purdue University, 2021). Researchers working for or in collaboration with companies, nonprofit organizations, international organizations, ministries and other entities may contribute to white papers. The World Health Organization (WHO) for example has a lengthy and rigorous guideline development process which includes both intense verbal discussions and oral documentation. Guidelines are developed for clinical, public health, health systems, health promotion and implementation. This opportunity opened my eyes to complexities in the field and at country level, community specifics which must all be considered. With a team, we are developing key guidance documentation for our consortium members. Skills required include striking a balance between a compact, easily digestible overview to outlining details from project proposal to submission. This is an example of a concise, succinct user-friendly solution.

Blog Posts Aside from my "official work," I cofounded Women in Science Japan (WISJ). We keep a blog, another form of writing output. In comparison to manuscripts, where you usually start with a pyramid model – going slow and then save the big findings for later, in blog posts you usually put all the content in the first two paragraphs. Blog posts are useful ways to communicate your science to the broader audience, e.g., to policy makers, practitioners, and to the general public. They are usually easy to read and understand and free from academic jargon. A good way of assessing a readability of your post is giving it to your nonacademic colleagues or friends. You can ask them to give you feedback, and to say if the message is clear and if they understood the post.

Writing in a Multicultural Environment

Working internationally has opened my eyes to different backgrounds, cultures, and work styles which represent core pillars in writing. For example, I was invited to contribute to a curriculum for an elementary school based in Germany, where communication with international stakeholders was primarily in English and French. For this project, I used a casual tone and applied creative problem-solving skills with short snapshot texts. This work required communicating via formal emails, preparing invitation letters, codrafting the president's opening speech, proofreading the 200-page program booklet several times. Beyond manuscripts contributing to scientific literature and grant writing, verbal and written daily communication is extremely important for all career level researchers. After all we are human and fostering these relationships may provide an underlying basis for formal writing.

The versatility outlined in the types of writing section and multicultural environment should be expected as an early career researcher. The earlier you get involved with different forms of writing the easier it will become. Many academics feel overwhelmed, and this may partially come from unpreparedness. Our PhDs train us to do isolated, self-reliant work while this is the opposite in the real world. In an academic setting, some researchers may worry about their ideas being stolen or others getting ahead and fail to realize how enriching collaboration is, and this attitude may also depend on the cultural setting. What goes around comes around. This is to say that the time you invest in supporting and mentoring others will also benefit you.

Writing Habits

Think of your PhD as a process, not merely a final product. The skills you learn will support you in becoming a successful early career researcher. Writing was never my forte, hopefully I can share some insights to help others overcome challenges by sharing my experiences and useful skills for effective writing as a researcher. Over the course of the past decade, I've become an effective writer thanks to habits I developed during my PhD.

Two key points I learnt in the process of working on my PhD are open trusting communication and a well-organized timeline to effectively manage my time. Frequent formal and informal meetings with my supervisor lead to a trusting relationship and successful completion of my PhD with a first author publication in just over a year of initially proposing the topic and receiving the data. An open trusting relationship as a PhD student and researcher may also mean sharing some personal information so that you can make adjustments or get advice beyond your immediate research project as needed. As for time management, everyone has individual preferences. Again, it is important to communicate or arrive at a mutual understanding with your supervisor. For my PhD timeline, I had a hard deadline, i.e., submission in order to graduate on time. I worked backward from final submission, adding milestones along the way to understand the pace I needed to achieve to complete each task. For other types of writing there may or may not be hard deadlines. I've found it helpful to self-impose deadlines and create project-specific timelines. Personal habits like organizing, timeliness, devoting space, and advisor meetings are good habits that yield better writing.

How to Start and Finish a Writing Project

Especially for longer pieces such as books, chapters, manuscripts, and grants, most of us will need several days or weeks to complete a first draft, not to mention a final draft ready to publish. I recommend using post-its, cards, PowerPoint, or other media in the brainstorm phase to initially organize your thoughts. When I was in school, just starting to use computers, we used flashcards. Each flashcard contains one idea and can be reshuffled so that they become organized as coherent thoughts. For example, in a manuscript on coffee and mortality, one card might include quantity of consumption in different countries, another card may include a suggested mechanism, another a different possible pathway, another mortality trends, and a final one coffee consumption, also separately for men and women. These can then be organized and reshuffled to create a coherent story. There's something to be said for taking a break from the computer screen and jotting down notes throughout the day, putting pen to paper, then arranging and organizing can be rewarding and satisfying. Engaging your hands and body rather than keeping all the ideas in your mind.

PowerPoint or other presentation software may also be more intuitive as it is designed to present to an audience, tell a story, and be more interactive than black and white words on paper. Visual aids make the descriptions more vivid. Even in scientific writing conjuring images can be helpful to the reader. I haven't tried audio or video recording that transcribes to text, but there are tools out there (e.g., otter.ai). This tool is used for interviews and qualitative research as an established form of writing and may also be applicable to other writing styles.

Another simple technique I recall learning in school that is still applicable as an early career researcher in terms of effective writing is the "Paragraph hamburger" or "sandwich." In English-speaking countries, this concept is taught in lower elementary school and well ingrained throughout school years so that students are well equipped to present their ideas and thoughts logically. The basic concept is to start with an introduction/title sentence (top bun), add three supporting details (patty, lettuce and cheese), and the conclusion sentence (bottom bun). This paradigm can be applied to an entire piece of writing. Using this strategy to the process of outlining an article will help ensure the reader receives a complete package of logically organized ideas and can follow the entire process. The advantage of this method is that it provides a simple, flexible structure, starting with an idea, providing supporting evidence, and finally concluding. The sandwich writing approach may be cultural, yet applicable to different languages. Individual linguistic preferences such as longer sentences in German, poetic forms in French, and nuanced writing in Japanese are enriching and should be kept in mind when writing and reading.

While multitasking received praise in the past (Male, 2013; Zhan, 2020), it seems to be less popular now and research has shown that focusing on one task at a time may be preferable and improve the quality of the final product (May & Elder, 2018; Sanbonmatsu et al., 2013). This does not mean the whole document needs to be written in one session or without working on other projects. Rather, I've found it helpful to dedicate time to a given project. Mindset and mood also must be in the right place to tap into your creativity and prepare a manuscript or other document. During the pandemic, I started working from home two days a week. At our center, researchers must apply to work from home the following month with a rough outline of what they will achieve. At the end of each "telework" day, we submit a brief report of our activities. While this seems overly bureaucratic, having this structure, even drafting the report as goals in the morning has helped me focus on completing tasks in a shorter period of time.

Many of us are perfectionists, and there is always more we can add and revise when it comes to academic pieces. However, the art of writing is completion, sharing with others and then making final adjustments if necessary. Chronic perfectionism among young academics underpins the effectiveness of writing (Sherry et al., 2010; Shih, 2012). Academic manuscripts, particularly, often drag on forever, after momentum is lost with no clear deadline submission or publication in sight, endless coauthor, and reviewers comments. At some point, it is time to release your document!

Effective Writing

Now, I'd like to focus on effective writing, not just any writing. *Nature Education* offers some valuable tips: "Effective writing is readable — that is, clear, accurate, and concise. When you are writing a paper, try to get your ideas across in such a way that the audience will understand them effortlessly, unambiguously, and rapidly" (Nature Education, 2004). That pretty much sums up this whole chapter in a nutshell! Go back to the basics: keep it straightforward, short and sweet and *one idea per sentence* is a good rule of thumb. Keep your writing compact so that the key messages are easily understood by the reader. Keep sentences and paragraphs short. Follow a logical sequence at each level: sentence, paragraph, sections and entire piece. The best advice I got during my Masters was to read more to improve my writing. Not only scientific literature, novels, newspaper articles, magazines, and other forms of writing can help improve your writing. For my PhD, "A done dissertation is a done dissertation" was my ultimate guiding principle ensuring I graduated in the designated three years and later helping students organize their theses.

As for style, writing is a form of communication. End on a hopeful, positive note with one to three key messages. Initially, it may be easier not to bog yourself down with nitty gritty formalities and the audience. First, get your ideas down on paper, audio, or other media as mentioned above. Then organize and group concepts. In the process of fleshing out the details, consider the audience, grammar, word choice. Focus on who your target audience (manuscripts, reports, grants), not all work is appropriate for *Nature, The Lancet,* or *The New England Journal of Medicine.* Choose a journal or other medium that is suitable for your field.

Share your work with others in the field and outside to get fresh perspectives and ensure your writing is meaningful and understandable. Sharing your work during the process, getting feedback from peers and senior staff, at conferences verbal feedback often helps me with the logical flow, argumentation. Finally, take a break and get a good night's sleep, recheck your work in the morning. Time permitting of course, in some cases you may need to finalize a document within a day or a matter of hours or minutes. For more casual writing such as emails some of these steps may be skipped. However, before pushing send, it is always good to check the basics such as correct addressee, date (if applicable), formality level and grammar/spelling. In the meantime, several options exist in addition to Microsoft Word spell check, e.g., Grammarly. I still refer to Strunk and White gifted to me in elementary school for basic grammar questions and rules (Strunk & White, 2009).

Resources

Identify resources available at your institution such as books and the library. Several universities such as Duke provide open scientific writing materials. *Nature* offers a masterclass in scientific writing and publishing. Springer has an author tutorial on Writing in English. Coursera and Edx offer several courses on scientific writing. Be sure to cite references appropriately and check for plagiarism with iThenticate or other software. During the initial brainstorming phase, be sure to jot down where you obtained the information, e.g., article (author, year, title), website link, etc., in order to keep track of resources.

Action Points for Effective Writers

In conclusion, effective writing is communication and is part of a process. For most of us it does not happen overnight, Rome wasn't built in a day. Different approaches and styles may work better for different people, so try different methods to find your groove. Welcome change, throughout our lives and careers we are constantly developing along with the world around us, so keep your eyes and ears open to new trends, while falling back on the tried and true.

Conclusions and Practical Recommendations

I'd like to end this chapter with a few action points for effective writing:

1. Identify authors who demonstrate excellent writing style. Ideally find examples in your field or industry or writing project, e.g., grant application, manuscript, report, and follow their example as a template.
2. Participate in writing workshops and peer review journal manuscripts. Reflecting objectively on the writing of others is often easier than criticizing and revising one's own writing.
3. Find concentrated uninterrupted time to focus on your writing. Simultaneously, keep it flexible and be persistent. As a grad student during the final months of my PhD, I was often at the lab until 10 pm and dedicated most of my weekends to my research. Now, as a working mother, in principle I don't work on weekends. However, occasionally I dedicate a weekend to work, if, for example, there is an upcoming deadline "real" or "self-imposed" to finish one of those never-ending research projects. Writing requires hours of concentrated time which often aren't available on weekdays with meetings, etc.
4. Try your best to be in a good frame of mind to attack your work. Being in the right mindset greatly expedites the writing process and improves the quality.

This can give you space to create and improve the whole experience. Especially, time outdoors can help generate fresh ideas and perspectives.

References

Abe, S. K., Narita, S., Saito, E., Sawada, N., Shimazu, T., Goto, A., & Tsugane, S. (2021). Body mass index, height, weight change, and subsequent lung cancer risk: The Japan public health center-based prospective study. *Cancer Epidemiology, Biomarkers & Prevention.* https://doi.org/10.1158/1055-9965.EPI-21-0195

da Silva Lopes, K., & Abe, S. K. (2021). Polymorphisms contributing to calcium status: A systematic review. *Nutrients, 13*(8), 2488.

Male, A. (2013) Communication arts and the polymath principle: Intellectual Multi-tasking and the creation of knowledge bearing imagery. Critique 2013: Creative practice reflecting in art, architecture and design. *One.* ISSN 978–0–9923943-1-8.

May, K. E., & Elder, A. D. (2018). Efficient, helpful, or distracting? A literature review of media multitasking in relation to academic performance. *International Journal of Educational Technology in Higher Education, 15*, 13. https://doi.org/10.1186/s41239-018-0096-z

Nature Education. (2004). Unit 2 of english communication for scientists. Retrieved July 31, 2021, from https://www.nature.com/scitable/topicpage/effective-writing-13815989/

Purdue University. (2021). *White Paper: Purpose and Audience.* Retrieved November 24, 2021, from https://owl.purdue.edu/owl/subject_specific_writing/professional_technical_writing/white_papers/index.html

Rothman, K., Greenland, S., & Lash, T. L. (2008). *Modern epidemiology* (3rd ed.). Lippincott Williams & Wilkins.

Sanbonmatsu, D. M., Strayer, D. L., Medeiros-Ward, N., & Watson, J. M. (2013). Who multi-tasks and why? Multi-tasking ability, perceived multi-tasking ability, impulsivity, and sensation seeking. https://doi.org/10.1371/journal.pone.0054402

Sherry, S. B., Hewitt, P. L., Sherry, D. L., Flett, G. L., & Graham, A. R. (2010). Perfectionism dimensions and research productivity in psychology professors: Implications for understanding the (mal)adaptiveness of perfectionism. *Canadian Journal of Behavioural Science / Revue canadienne des sciences du comportement, 42*(4), 273–283. https://doi.org/10.1037/a0020466

Shih, S. S. (2012). An examination of academic burnout versus work engagement among Taiwanese adolescents. *The Journal of Educational Research, 105*(4), 286–298. https://doi.org/10.1080/00220671.2011.629695

Strunk, W., & White, E. B. (2009). *The elements of style.* Penguin Press HC.

Zhan, M. (2020). Generation Z in Hong Kong: Simple While Multi-tasking. In E. Gentina & E. Parry (Eds.), *The new generation Z in Asia: Dynamics, differences, digitalisation (the changing context of managing people)* (pp. 39–53). Emerald Publishing Limited. https://doi.org/10.1108/978-1-80043-220-820201006

Chapter 13
Dealing with Rejection: Critical Thinking, Constructive Feedback, and Criticism in the Peer-Review Process

Kim M. Caudwell

Abstract The following chapter is about the experience of the peer-review process for early career researchers. It introduces readers to what it is like to have a manuscript rejected, as well as what it is like to receive a 'revise and resubmit', and most importantly, what to do from this point onwards in the academic process. The chapter is based on viewing dealing with rejection and critical thinking as an essential element in developing oneself as a scientific writer and emergent contributor to the peer-review process. More broadly, the chapter discusses the ways in which feedback can be effective and ineffective in contributing to the process of academic writing and, finally, how criticism may be an unavoidable yet manageable part of this process. These themes are then integrated into a discussion on how key personal and institutional elements can support academic writing and being an effective peer reviewer, which are fundamental to the scholarly success of early career researchers.

Keywords Peer review · Publication · Rejection · Critical thinking · Feedback · Criticism · Academic writing

Introduction

I remember how it felt to have my first manuscript rejected. I remember being pretty devastated, and upon reading beyond the preamble to the forensic analysis, I started catastrophising. *Was I up to the challenge of PhD? Should I have taken that graduate job after all? Had I made a huge mistake?*

Luckily, my downward spiral was interrupted by my supervisor, who gave me a valuable piece of timely advice that I have carried with me throughout my time in

K. M. Caudwell (✉)
Researchers in Behavioural Addictions, Alcohol, and Drugs, College of Health and Human Sciences, Charles Darwin University, Casuarina, NT, Australia

© The Author(s), under exclusive license to Springer Nature Switzerland AG 2022
D. Kwasnicka, A. Y. Lai (eds.), *Survival Guide for Early Career Researchers*, https://doi.org/10.1007/978-3-031-10754-2_13

academia: '*There are academics who* have *been rejected, and there are academics who* will *be rejected*'.

That was a reassuring comment, sure, but I wondered what was next for me. Although the decision was 'rejection', the reviewers and editor had provided some valuable feedback. There were a few barbs, here and there, but some ideas. I left it for a day or so, then read back through the comments again. This time, I managed to shrug off the barbs, and I found a few comments landed differently. It was clear that there were some good points that, if addressed, would strengthen the manuscript once submitted elsewhere.

I set up another meeting with my supervisor, and we came up with a plan. There was quite a bit of work to do – some reading, some rephrasing, and some judicious editing. There were also more mundane tasks, like restructuring the manuscript to suit the next journal's submission guidelines. Still, I got to work.

Then, a desk rejection. Though another setback, a succinct and painless one, and quite probable. Over the period 2007–2017, an average of 10,624 manuscripts were submitted to *Nature* for review, with 7.8% of those eventually accepted for publication (Nature, 2021). The acceptance rate for *Psychological Science* is slightly higher – at 9% from 2015 to 2019 (Association for Psychological Science, 2021). In retrospect, my journal choice was likely a bad 'fit' – the manuscript got bogged down in theory, limiting its ability to 'cut through' to the readership, who were more interested in intervention within applied settings. To me, the theory was too important to limit the description of it.

So, my supervisor and I thought a bit more about a better journal pairing, then submitted somewhere more theory-oriented. This time, a 'revise and resubmit' – with few but pointed suggestions for revision. By this point, I felt a bit more practised at responding to reviewers, and having had some time to think, I saw some of the reviewers' comments coming, which better prepared me to respond. And, sure enough, at the end, the manuscript was accepted! I can clearly remember throwing up a 'success' fist like Bender from *The Breakfast Club* when I read through the email.

Dealing with Rejection

Since then, I've had mostly rejections, some 'revise and resubmits', but never an outright acceptance. Perhaps I have habituated to rejections, or simply grown a much thicker hide. As Jefferson et al. (2002) put it, '*the doubts contributed by peer review are an intrinsic and essential part of science, layered over the critical reviews that take place during the process of doing the work*' (p. 2785). So, it would seem that peer review – and the rejections that come with it – is simply part of the job. For those fairly new to the peer-review process, or interested to learn more about it, I would recommend Kelly et al. (2014) as a starting point.

Most of us have no major issue interpreting and acting upon probability when it comes to statistical analyses; however, those analyses rarely have an impact on our self-esteem. So why does rejection bring about feelings of inadequacy and fear? There are likely many reasons, though some may be par for the course in academia and simply unlikely to change anytime soon. As academics, and perhaps especially so as early career researchers (ECRs), we should *expect* rejection and learn to take it in our stride. Rejection is rarely a reflection of our personal failings, but it *is* one of the only ways we can hope to develop as academics, and ultimately, it reflects the high bar that peer review sets for the academic community.

On the other side of the fence, though they are our peers, perhaps we don't use that term in the way it is intended – often we see reviewers as cruel, punishing pedants. Though some can be quite cruel, I think it's fair to say that most are just like us – trying to be helpful and do a good job. So, it becomes an important task to resist the cognitive dissonance trap that comes with rejection (e.g., *'it's not me, it's Reviewer #2'*), and start thinking about anything other than acceptance as a probable, but not overly problematic outcome.

Similarly, it is incumbent upon ECRs to become good reviewers, if not just to avoid being lumped in with the 'bad', but also to help manuscript authors succeed – that is, to apply critical thinking in a way that might avoid outright criticism, and to provide feedback that is constructive rather than punitive. And so, my aim here is to explore three facets that often revolve around rejection and the peer-review process: critical thinking, constructive feedback, and criticism. I also want to discuss how these things map more broadly into the ECR experience. Hopefully, this makes future rejections easier to endure, helps you recognise strengths and weaknesses when they're pointed out to you, and inspires you to publish better work. If you are already a publication wizard, then I congratulate you – and hope you read on, if only to avoid becoming Reviewer #2 – or perhaps Reviewer #3 (see Peterson, 2020, for an amusing analysis that reveals the reviewer we should *really* be concerned about).

Critical Thinking

Several scholars have worked to define 'critical thinking', and my favourite is that of Ennis (1991), who defines it as *'reasonable reflective thinking focused on deciding what to believe or do'* (p. 6). To me, this a brief but encapsulating definition of critical thinking, as it imposes some thoroughness (i.e., reasonableness), introspection (i.e., reflection), and leads to an action (i.e., believing or doing something).

Ennis' definition makes me think back to receiving that first thorough rejection – I think it's fair to say that I jumped to the *'what to do'* (e.g., quit academia and start a band) before I had engaged in the *'reasonable reflective thinking'*. Once I had given myself a bit of space to process the emotional component of rejection, I found taking a more objective view of the comments of the reviewers and editor allowed me to prepare my next move.

As ECRs – new experts – we have amassed a range of skills and competencies that lead us to make decisions about what to believe or do. We decide what to do when confronted with the outcome of intricate statistical analyses, what to believe when faced with evidence for and against the contributions of theories, perspectives, and paradigms. It is fair to say that a lot of what we believe, or what we do, can have far-reaching implications in relation to innovation and advancement. There is a lot of faith placed in academics in relation to the correct assessing of statements, and increasingly, there has been much debate around the world about whether or not that faith has been misplaced. In 2016, then Lord Vice Chancellor Michael Gove said that people in the United Kingdom were fed up with *'experts… saying that they know what is best and getting it consistently wrong'* (Sky News, 2016). To be fair, academics *do* get things wrong – in developing and testing theories and models, and in research design, analysis, interpretation, and dissemination. However, science is cumulative – and as such, we should work towards improving it. All in all, it seems critical thinking is something that ECRs can start to work on as soon as possible, to try and avoid 'wrongness' in the first place, and to think about how we can get closer to 'rightness'.

So, Ennis' preamble that critical thinking must be reasonable reflective thinking implies some deductive aspects, and a bit of healthy introspection. An important metaphor that I find helps research methods students is this: when we come to a fork in the road, we make a decision, yet we inevitably find another fork down *that* road. After a while of fork-related decision making, looking back means justifying *why* we chose those paths – the decisions we made in relation to what to think or do, need to be justifiable, and this makes them defensible.

Ennis (2018) has since outlined a range of components related to critical thinking, including *dispositions* (i.e., things critical thinkers are prone to do), and *abilities* (i.e., the skills of critical thinkers). A fair few of Ennis' critical thinking components seem important to consider or develop during the early career period, especially as they relate to preparing a manuscript for peer review, and refining rejected manuscripts, or those for which resubmission has been invited, to increase the chances of success. Similarly, given you will be invited to review the manuscripts of your peers, it is important to consider aspects of critical thinking that will help authors improve their manuscripts – whether or not they are accepted by the journal.

Dispositions of Critical Thinkers

As an Author Critical thinkers should be well-informed, using credible sources, keep an open mind, and consider other points of view. The 'funnelling' approach often talked about at undergraduate levels of writing instruction is by no means vestigial at the graduate and early career levels. Rather, it is an approach that continues to be useful throughout an academic career. I think a lot about the importance of *synthesis* in writing – the ability to not only present a range of contextual information that leads the reader to your study, but to weave a strong impression through presenting this information that demonstrates you are an authority – that you know your stuff.

According to Emerson (2012), senior academics consider writing to be intrinsically scientific, and ultimately about the construction of knowledge. That is to say, that the development or crafting of a story requires an innate understanding of the connection between writing, science, and meaning, developed over years of immersive experience. It is difficult to develop this understanding without being well-informed, and without the use of credible sources. So, how do we achieve synthesis? Unfortunately, I think it can only come from reading, reading, and more reading, and a bit of writing too. In fact, I tell students in university preparation courses that they should aim to spend about three times as much time reading, as they do writing. Becoming an ECR may mean that you have to read beyond the scope of your PhD, but I would reassure you that this is going to build on your existing knowledge (which at this point is already quite developed).

As a Reviewer Ennis believes that critical thinkers should display a range of behaviours that I would say fall under what is *reflexivity*. Reflexivity is the process of constantly examining your own beliefs and worldview and checking whether or not it is influencing your behaviours – especially applicable to the reviewing process. To me, reflexivity is a key skill of a peer reviewer, but is difficult to develop until you have lasted a few rounds on both sides of the submission portal. All academics have certain pet theories, and theorists, as well as loathed theories and theorists. The task as a reviewer is not to critique the theories so much as their application to the current study (unless, of course, you are reviewing a theory that is being proposed or modified in some way).

Abilities of Critical Thinkers

As an Author Ennis also suggests critical thinkers use 'advanced clarification' – endeavouring to define key terms and judge definitions. Definitions are an important thing to get right, especially in the social sciences, where perspectives and theories overlap, and the ideas that extend from them 'come and go' (see Hagger, 2014). Authors (and reviewers) need to ensure that definitions are as accurate as they are consistent. Defining a variable incorrectly, or at least failing to provide some justification for pursuing a certain definition or perspective regarding that variable, will likely irritate a purist reviewer. As for dealing with equivocation, being as specific and precise in your language as possible, so that your intentions are clear, and 'owning up' to the shortcomings of your manuscript, is important.

As a Reviewer Here, Ennis includes judgements – of credibility, and of background knowledge, as important things when guiding a decision. While you may review articles outside or extending from your area of emerging expertise, it's important to chase up leads – when authors are citing the same source multiple times, or multiple sources from the same author/s, and you are less familiar with these sources or authors, it's time to study. In some cases, consistent citing of the same author may be indicative of self-citations (e.g., in blind review). While this isn't always an issue (see Gálvez, 2017), it may warrant some further investigation. Be especially alert to sources that are 'under review' or 'submitted' – you likely won't be able to access these sources to make judgements about the credibility of statements.

I think one of the most time-consuming tasks of the reviewer is to follow along with the authors' rationale for conducting the research that is detailed in the manuscript. Again, the 'funnel approach' that starts with a broad introduction section, narrows to the scope of the manuscript's inquiry, and lands on the research question or hypotheses the remainder of the manuscript sets out to answer or test. It is important to ascertain how reasonable these reasons, assumptions, and conclusions are. Similarly, there are sections of the methods section where being the critical thinker is essential – is this a reasonable population with which to test these hypotheses? Do the measures seem appropriate? Are the analyses likely to yield meaningful and trustworthy outcomes? Again, in a discussion section, conclusions need to stem logically from the evidence presented.

Constructive Feedback

It should be the aim of every reviewer to provide constructive feedback – and it should be their hope to receive it in the peer-review process! So, getting constructive feedback right is essential for the ECR. Denton (2018) defines constructive feedback as that which (1) identifies a specific problem, (2) explains the problem, and (3) provides a concrete solution for how the authors might solve the problem (p. 22). In my experience as an author, it is rare that a reviewer's comment covers these three elements. Perhaps the *least* helpful comment is the one that stops after the mere identification of a problem – often, it's one I'm already aware of (sometimes I have even addressed it in the manuscript), or, if I'm made aware of it, I may well have no idea how I might solve it (or at least not immediately). Comments that therefore provide *and* explain a problem are more helpful, and usually require a mix of thinking and work to address. In my view, this process is highly valuable to the development of an ECR as an academic and science communicator. The ultimate comment, though rarely seen, is one that provides a *concrete* solution that *might* solve the problem – and the emphasis here is important. I do not think we should rely on reviewers to pick up the scientific slack of poor science work, but I do think that offering potential solutions is much better than not offering anything but outright criticism (see Shashok, 2008). Of course, sometimes the solutions are not tenable, but for those, their respective problems are usually forgivable, if alluded to honestly and openly.

Generally speaking, social support is thought to heavily influence post-PhD engagement and disengagement, and so it is important to seek constructive criticism from your colleagues. According to Vekkaila et al. (2018), *co-constructional support* (i.e., having collaborators to help generate ideas, or 'bounce' ideas off) is thought to facilitate the more concrete aspects of conducting research, but also engender an 'optimal emotional research experience' (p. 1449) that can facilitate the development of researchers. Perhaps we can consider peer-reviewers as collaborators in a similar fashion. Sure, some reviewers volunteer their expertise and commentary, and are sometimes acknowledged in published manuscripts; however, some reviewers will also be your contemporaries – even competitors. Whether or not this competition impacts the peer-review process, and the nature of the feedback, depends on various factors, such as whether or not the review is blinded (Ali & Watson, 2016). I have had reviewers provide immensely helpful constructive feedback (some even offering compliments), and I have also had reviewers provide feedback that is next to useless.

Castelló et al. (2017) sought to ascertain how academics' perceptions of writing relate to their engagement, perceptions of the researcher community, productivity, and burnout. They found that academics with more adaptive perceptions of writing reported higher engagement and lower burnout. And, if you needed a good reason to adopt a more positive outlook, adaptive perceptions were positively correlated with the number of peer-reviewed publications as a first author. Easier said than done? Well, it turns out that more adaptive perceptions of writing were linked to perceived support from the researcher community.

Criticism

Criticism is often synonymous with peer review, and I think it can be said that some criticism is fair, and some is unwarranted. It is my belief the latter may be a symptom of the peer-review system – a space where, strangely, work that requires expertise and research training is not directly financially compensated (but otherwise tolerated by employers, or expected by the profession). It is also likely a reflection of the burden on reviewers who consistently volunteer their time and effort, with others passing on requests. Modelling of papers from the biomedical research field by Kovanis et al. (2016) concluded that 1 in 5 researchers conducted 69% to 94% of the field's reviews – dubbed 'peer-review heroes'. Though most reviewers dedicate 1% or less of their work time to peer review, 1 in 20 spends as much as 13% of their work time on it. It should be no surprise then, that honest mistakes or oversights could draw the vicious ire of a reviewer who is normally quite the mellow academic.

Criticism – in any form – can come at a bad time for ECRs. Though they have already earned their degrees, and are no longer students, they may lack recognition or a sense of legitimacy compared to that of their superiors (Hudson et al., 2018), finding it difficult to prove themselves 'as legitimate scientists in their own and others' eyes' (p. 622). As such, criticism sensitivity during the ECR period is likely quite detrimental to academic development and wellbeing.

Chan et al. (2021) conducted a range of interviews with academics of varying levels of experience in the health sciences field, asking about their experiences in relation to research rejection. The emergent themes were linked a popular cognitive psychology framework, showing that while the stimulus (i.e., rejection or criticism), and emotions that accompanied that stimulus (e.g., disappointment, confusion), remained the same, thoughts and beliefs that stemmed from the rejection or criticism stimulus could differ, and have concomitant effects on behaviour. For example, upon having an article rejected, an academic may engage in negative self-evaluation (e.g., *'what a waste of time!'*) and this may lead to concordant behaviours (e.g., avoiding submitting an article in the future). Alternatively, a belief accompanying rejection or criticism stimulus may be *'what next?'*, leading the researcher to adopt a new approach from that point. So, knowing that there is a strong chance of any author having their article rejected, the ECR who asks *'what next?'* will likely publish sooner.

Hyland and Jiang (2020) reviewed criticisms academics had shared online, analysing them for *evidentiality* (commitment to the reliability of statements, including hedges and boosters), *affect* (attitudinal expressions), and *presence* (e.g., first person pronouns). Almost a third of reviewer comments were classified as boosters (e.g., 'clearly'). The least frequent were hedges, in which reviewer comments were more tentatively-phrased (e.g., 'perhaps') comprising 14.4% of responses. Essentially, these peer reviewers may think they are right, but risk being perceived as mean. Though the sample obviously includes the worst of peer-review comments, there is something to be said for keeping criticism about the work (i.e., constructive criticism), and not about the author. It is worth remembering that the nature of feedback can depend on the review process itself – when open, a reviewer may be less likely to be honest and critical; when closed, anonymity may encourage outright criticism (see Ali & Watson, 2016).

An interesting study by Mur-Dueñas (2012) looked at research article introductions and both coded and counted *critical acts* – that is, critiques of other research (positive or negative). Though not its main purpose, it contained two key observations: (1) published articles exhibited positive and negative critical acts (but mostly positive ones); and (2) positive critical acts tended to be self-referential, whereas negative critical acts tended to refer to previous research in a broader sense. It would seem that reviewers – the gatekeepers of research – need to see that critical acts tilt positive, and that any critical act is aligned with the overall contribution of the manuscript. Criticism is not always bad, either. Rigby et al. (2018) found that engagement with reviewers (i.e., through the back-and-forth of the review process) leads to more citations. They view reviewing as knowledge production, rather than error correction.

Finally, it is important to consider the most insidious type of criticism – that of one's self! An insightful study by Castelló et al. (2017) looked at identity development in ECRs, collecting their beliefs regarding *writing* (i.e., knowledge creation, productivity, procrastination, perfectionism, 'innateness', and experience of writer's block); *burnout* (i.e., cynicism, exhaustion); and *engagement* (i.e., with supervisors, and the research community). Correlation analyses revealed interesting relationships between perceptions of writing. Viewing writing as productive was negatively correlated with procrastination, perfectionism, and writing blocks. It seems those who write regularly and produce writing may be less likely to put writing off, endlessly revise it, and become 'stuck'. Unsurprisingly, perfectionism was strongly correlated with experiencing writing blocks and viewing writing as an innate ability. So, try not to be your own worst critic; know that both manuscripts and people can be improved, but will never be perfect. Ultimately, a growth mindset will go a long way in developing your writing.

The Role of Organisations and Individuals in Dealing with Rejections

A lot of my research uses Self-Determination Theory (SDT; Deci & Ryan, 1985) as a framework to understand how individuals arrive at decisions and actions related to their health behaviour. A central component of SDT is that we all have innate psychological needs – autonomy, competence, and relatedness (Deci & Ryan, 2000). Put simply, if we feel agency in doing things, reasonably proficient at doing things, and supported by others in doing things, we tend to thrive. The ECR experience makes for a challenging environment for these needs to be met. We may experience less autonomy than we enjoyed in our PhD; competence may be tethered to our PhD experience, making onboarding and skill transfer difficult; and, the competitive nature of the academic industry may mean there is little support to go around. Constructive feedback may be difficult to find when you aren't well-supported by peers, and criticism may sting a bit more if you feel you are lacking in competence.

Perhaps unsurprisingly, Crome et al. (2019) found that competence, relatedness, and organisational support were significant predictors of work engagement among ECRs, suggesting that institutions focus on providing training and other resources (to ECRs and supervisors alike), ensuring timely feedback and quality performance reviews, and fostering social support. Pyhältö et al. (2017) found that academics receiving 'adequate support' (based on cluster analyses of various organisational psychology constructs) were more likely to be involved in research groups, and were less likely to report intentions to leave academia; they also exhibited less cynicism, and reported greater engagement.

However, in a sample of postdoctoral researchers at two Dutch universities (van der Weijden et al., 2016), 44% did not complete any form of training or course during their postdoctoral period. Of those who did, around one in eight completed a written communication course. Unless you are provided with training and development opportunities that hone your writing and reviewing skills, the peer-review process may be the only avenue for developing them – which may instil some bad habits! If you feel you would benefit from training or mentorship, you should approach your line manager or collaborators. Hollywood et al. (2020) have suggested mentoring and career planning would greatly support ECRs, allowing them to conduct the 'best possible science' (Signoret et al., 2019).

And the perception of success is important, too. Hollywood et al. (2020) looked at intrapersonal and experiential factors that would relate to ECR perceptions of career development and wellbeing. Perceived research success was correlated with the likelihood of being in academia in the next five years, as well as the likelihood of gaining promotion in those years. Factors that were related to increased job satisfaction included finding one's feet, 'stepping up' to challenges, variety, and surviving stress.

Conclusions and Practical Recommendations

So, although the ECR experience is not devoid of setbacks, remember that it is a journey. There is a near certainty of rejection, but applying critical thinking skills, taking on constructive feedback, and taking criticism in your stride with a *'what's next?'* attitude will see you embark on a smooth and rewarding one. On the other side of the reviewer portal, it is important to remember to apply critical thinking skills, which will in all likelihood help you to provide constructive feedback, and ensure your criticism is warranted, and will be unlikely to contribute to a negative ECR experience.

Practical recommendations for ECRs when dealing with (or in) rejection:

- Take a moment to process rejection (and feedback) when it comes your way, before asking *'what's next?'*;
- Seek avenues to foster critical thinking dispositions and abilities throughout your ECR experience, both as an author and a reviewer;
- Look for and provide constructive feedback, and seek co-constructional support from those around you (e.g., line managers, mentors, research teams);
- Bear in mind that criticism may not be a reflection on you as an ECR, but as a reflection on the peer-review system (e.g., overworked 'heroes'), and, be mindful of the impact of criticism on others (e.g., in relation to feelings of legitimacy);
- Pay attention to hedges and boosters when processing feedback, and use more hedges than boosters when providing it;
- Be mindful of your own beliefs and the impact that can have on your scholarly work – and consider the bigger picture of contributing to the cumulative endeavour that is scientific knowledge.

References

Ali, P. A., & Watson, R. (2016). Peer review and the publication process. *Nursing Open, 3*(4), 193–202. https://doi.org/10.1002/nop2.51
Association for Psychological Science. (2021). Contributor FAQ. https://www.psychologicalscience.org/publications/psychological_science/contributor-faq
Castelló, M., McAlpine, L., & Pyhältö, K. (2017). Spanish and UK post-PhD researchers: Writing perceptions, well-being and productivity. *Higher Education Research & Development, 36*(6), 1108–1122. https://doi.org/10.1080/07294360.2017.1296412

Chan, H., Mazzucchelli, T. G., & Rees, C. S. (2021). The battle-hardened academic: An exploration of the resilience of university academics in the face of ongoing criticism and rejection of their research. *Higher Education Research & Development, 40*(3), 446–460. https://doi.org/10.1080/07294360.2020.1765743

Crome, E., Meyer, L., Bosanquet, A., & Hughes, L. (2019). Improving engagement in an early career academic setting: Can existing models guide early career academic support strategies? *Higher Education Research & Development, 38*(4), 717–732. https://doi.org/10.1080/07294360.2019.1576597

Deci, E. L., & Ryan, R. M. (1985). *Intrinsic motivation and self-determination in human behaviour*. Plenum.

Deci, E. L., & Ryan, R. M. (2000). The "what" and "why" of goal pursuits: Human needs and the self-determination of behavior. *Psychological Inquiry, 11*(4), 227–268. https://doi.org/10.1207/S15327965PLI1104_01

Denton, A. W. (2018). Improving the quality of constructive peer feedback. *College Teaching, 66*(1), 22–23. https://doi.org/10.1080/87567555.2017.1349075

Emerson, L. (2012). The life cycle of the scientific writer: An investigation of the senior academic scientist as writer in Australasian universities. In C. Bazerman, C. Dean, J. Early, K. Lunsford, S. Null, P. Rogers, & A. Stansell (Eds.), *International advances in writing research: Cultures, pleaces, measures*.

Ennis, R. H. (1991). Critical thinking: A streamlined conception. *Teaching Philosophy, 14*(1), 5–24.

Ennis, R. H. (2018). Critical thinking across the curriculum: A vision. *Topoi, 37*(1), 165–184. https://doi.org/10.1007/s11245-016-9401-4

Gálvez, R. H. (2017). Assessing author self-citation as a mechanism of relevant knowledge diffusion. *Scientometrics, 111*(3), 1801–1812.

Hagger, M. (2014). Avoiding the "déjà-variable" phenomenon: Social psychology needs more guides to constructs [general commentary]. *Frontiers in Psychology, 5*(52). https://doi.org/10.3389/fpsyg.2014.00052

Hollywood, A., McCarthy, D., Spencely, C., & Winstone, N. (2020). 'Overwhelmed at first': The experience of career development in early career academics. *Journal of Further and Higher Education, 44*(7), 998–1012. https://doi.org/10.1080/0309877X.2019.1636213

Hudson, T. D., Haley, K. J., Jaeger, A. J., Mitchall, A., Dinin, A., & Dunstan, S. B. (2018). Becoming a legitimate scientist: Science identity of postdocs in STEM fields. *The Review of Higher Education, 41*(4), 607–639. https://doi.org/10.1353/rhe.2018.0027

Hyland, K., & Jiang, F. (2020). "This work is antithetical to the spirit of research": An anatomy of harsh peer reviews. *Journal of English for Academic Purposes, 46*, 100867. https://doi.org/10.1016/j.jeap.2020.100867

Jefferson, T., Alderson, P., Wager, E., & Davidoff, F. (2002). Effects of editorial peer ReviewA systematic review. *JAMA, 287*(21), 2784–2786. https://doi.org/10.1001/jama.287.21.2784

Kelly, J., Sadeghieh, T., & Adeli, K. (2014). Peer review in scientific publications: Benefits, critiques, & a survival guide. *EJIFCC, 25*(3), 227–243. https://pubmed.ncbi.nlm.nih.gov/27683470

Kovanis, M., Porcher, R., Ravaud, P., & Trinquart, L. (2016). The global burden of journal peer review in the biomedical literature: Strong imbalance in the collective enterprise. *PLoS One, 11*(11), e0166387. https://doi.org/10.1371/journal.pone.0166387

Mur-Dueñas, P. (2012). Critical acts in published and unpublished research article introductions in English: A look into the writing for publication process. In C. Bazerman, C. Dean, J. Early, K. Lunsford, S. Null, P. Rogers, & A. Stansell (Eds.), *International advances in writing research: Cultures, places, measures* (pp. 403–420). Parlor Press.

Nature. (2021). *Editorial criteria and processes*. https://www.nature.com/nature/for-authors/editorial-criteria-and-processes

Peterson, D. A. (2020). Dear reviewer 2: Go f'yourself. *Social Science Quarterly, 101*(4), 1648–1652. https://doi.org/10.1111/ssqu.12824

Pyhältö, K., McAlpine, L., Peltonen, J., & Castello, M. (2017). How does social support contribute to engaging post-PhD experience? *European Journal of Higher Education, 7*(4), 373–387. https://doi.org/10.1080/21568235.2017.1348239

Rigby, J., Cox, D., & Julian, K. (2018). Journal peer review: A bar or bridge? An analysis of a paper's revision history and turnaround time, and the effect on citation. *Scientometrics, 114*(3), 1087–1105. https://doi.org/10.1007/s11192-017-2630-5

Shashok, K. (2008). Content and communication: How can peer review provide helpful feedback about the writing? *BMC Medical Research Methodology, 8*(1), 3. https://doi.org/10.1186/1471-2288-8-3

Signoret, C., Ng, E., Da Silva, S., Tack, A., Voss, U., Lidö, H. H., Patthey, C., Ericsson, M., Hadrévi, J., & Balachandran, C. (2019). Well-being of Early-career researchers: Insights from a Swedish survey. *Higher Education Policy, 32*(2), 273–296. https://doi.org/10.1057/s41307-018-0080-1

Sky News. (2016). Michael Gove – 'EU: In or out?'. [YouTube video]. https://www.youtube.com/watch?v=t8D8AoC-5i8

van der Weijden, I., Teelken, C., de Boer, M., & Drost, M. (2016). Career satisfaction of postdoctoral researchers in relation to their expectations for the future. *Higher Education, 72*(1), 25–40. https://doi.org/10.1007/s10734-015-9936-0

Vekkaila, J., Virtanen, V., Taina, J., & Pyhältö, K. (2018). The function of social support in engaging and disengaging experiences among post PhD researchers in STEM disciplines. *Studies in Higher Education, 43*(8), 1439–1453. https://doi.org/10.1080/03075079.2016.1259307

Chapter 14
Presenting and Speaking About Your Work

Silja-Riin Voolma

Abstract Effective communication means reaching a mutual understanding with your audience defined by empathy, interpersonal resonance, and storytelling. This chapter shares the three pillars of delivering effective communication in presentations and speeches: mind–body connection, celebrating your audience, and practice. As an early career researcher, initiate presenting opportunities wherever you can and aim to present to as varied of audiences as possible, academic, industry, and students alike. Design a prepresentation ritual to regulate your nervous system and sustain mind–body connection. Design an experience for your audience with an engaging frame and narrative for your presentation structure, placing your audience and their interests as the heroes of your storyline. Make sure your audience leaves the experience with something to keep thinking about and with knowledge of how to contact you in the future. Effective communication through presentations and speeches can create further professional and personal opportunities in any line of work. I'm excited to see the opportunities it creates for you!

Keywords Presenting · Public Speaking; Science Communication · Interpersonal resonance · Mind–body connection · Flow · Audience · Engagement; Science Dissemination

Introduction

What is the best presentation or speech you have ever seen or heard?
How did it make you feel?
Why did it matter to you?

Throughout history, the power of certain speeches has reverberated across multiple audiences, cultures, political movements, and generations. You might have

---

S.-R. Voolma (✉)
Behavioral Design Global, New York, NY, USA

© The Author(s), under exclusive license to Springer Nature Switzerland AG 2022
D. Kwasnicka, A. Y. Lai (eds.), *Survival Guide for Early Career Researchers*,
https://doi.org/10.1007/978-3-031-10754-2_14

grown up knowing Martin Luther King Jr.'s "I have a dream," Brene Brown's "The power of vulnerability," and Malala Yousafzai's speech to the United Nations on her 16th birthday. These renowned speeches have one important factor in common: They are presented with vulnerability and grounded in personal experience. I used to think speakers like these have nothing to do with me because they are not about sharing academic research. Brene Brown is, of course, an established and decorated academic researcher, but as someone who also consults for Fortune 500 companies and coaches executives, she seemed to exist in a different world from me. I believed, my mixed methods behavioral science research on healthy lifestyles spoke for itself to the audiences of academics and students I started presenting to as a graduate student. I wasn't trying to change the world, to create a human rights movement, and hadn't faced the kinds of personal struggles Malala had.

Then, a month before submitting my Ph.D. thesis, I was invited to give a talk about the role of intuition in behavior change to a community of female entrepreneurs. As an almost-graduate, I felt fairly confident about sharing the power of behavioral science in creating change in everyday life. I also felt excited to speak with a new kind of audience and see the real-life impact my science could have. The event took place in a small community space in Tallinn, Estonia. About 30 women attended, all eager to learn the exciting tools behavioral science could recommend for the benefit of their personal and professional lives. For the first time in my academic career, I was faced with an audience for whom what I said could really make a difference in life and work. They could actually implement my research insights. Being successful in that implementation might mean an improvement in their health and wellbeing or even their business outcomes. Unfortunately, this realization hit me just as I was about to step on the stage. It was unfortunate because it sent me down a debilitating spiral of stage fright. Instead of oozing charisma like I had intended to, my voice got stuck in my throat, I couldn't feel my body, and my carefully prepared research presentation generated no obvious "aha" moments in my audience. Now, 5 years later, having spoken at 600+ events, received coaching from leading public speakers and storytellers, and running my own behavioral design business, I know what was missing that day from my speech to create the kind of transformation Brene and Malala do when they share insights.

My audience of female entrepreneurs that day 5 years ago probably answered the questions of "How did it make you feel?" and "Why did it matter to you?" with "I don't know." When Brene speaks, chances are you are answering these questions with "I feel seen and recognize the potential for transformation" and "I understand how it relates to my own life." I know now the key to presenting transformative speeches is to prepare the three pillars of interpersonal resonance: mind–body connection, practice, and celebrating your audience. In this chapter, I want to share with you a process of preparing each of these three pillars based on my own experience of learning, practicing, and delivering presentations to achieve interpersonal resonance with any audience.

Interpersonal Resonance

"Why should I care about presenting to transform or create interpersonal resonance?", you might be asking yourself. There are several reasons to hone your presenting and speaking craft, whether you are in academic research, industry, policy, running your own company, or pursuing another exciting career. Even as graduate students, the importance of great communication skills is drilled into us when writing papers, funding applications, and academic conference presentations. Feliú-Mójer (2015) has said, "to be a successful scientist, you must be an effective communicator." Let's add interpersonal resonance to our definition of "effective communication" and we'll see much better results in any of the communication we do as scientists. Had I achieved this in my presentation to those female entrepreneurs 5 years ago, I might have succeeded in attracting a new client for my business, or another type of opportunity as has been the case after many of my presentations since then. For example, after a presentation at the 2020 Health Experience Design conference by Mad*Pow, attended by 200+ health researchers and designers, I had several audience members reach out for potential collaboration opportunities and closed one new client for my business. A conference organizer called my presentation "a clear highlight event." For me, as a business owner, "effective communication" means getting connected to new clients, projects, and potential opportunities to grow my team and company. What about you? What brings you the most opportunity in your line of work? These are the activities where you might want to pay particular attention to your communication and take the interpersonal resonance metric as a metric of success. I'd love to know what kind of impact it makes in your work!

Let's get into what interpersonal resonance is and why it is a useful metric for gauging the impact of your presentations. Interpersonal resonance is a term used in communication science and the public speaking industry. At its core, interpersonal resonance is the process by which we understand each other and what creates a foundation of empathy in our communication (Tennant et al., 2019). Do you know the feeling of talking to a very supportive and nonjudgmental friend, the feeling of physical comfort, not just resonating with the words you hear? This physical experience of engaging communication is at the heart of interpersonal resonance as it refers to the biofeedback mechanisms of emotion and psychophysical regulation that occur when we connect to each other empathetically. Biofeedback processes are activated in both parties involved in the communication and as such, are a useful metric to keep track of from both the speaker's and audience's perspective.

For me, interpersonal resonance is what I aim to achieve in every presentation or speech. I pay attention to the emotional activation and nervous system regulation in my own physical experience and my audience's. Once interpersonal resonance is achieved, in my experience, audiences start to open up about their personal experience or ask questions that might put them in a vulnerable situation. I'd invite you to reflect on this from your own experience. When you are in a communication space that makes you feel safe, seen, and empathized with, what is your response? Do you tend to open up more? Ask more daring questions? This is what I see happen in my audience members increasingly frequently. For example, I recently presented to 100+ alumnae from a well-known university in Europe on best practices of mentoring relationships. As usual, I turned my attention toward my own physical cues as a metronome for pacing the material I had prepared to share with this audience. Somewhere in the middle of the 2-h session, audience members started asking questions like "I feel a very big power dynamic with my mentor, what would you recommend?" or "I'm really not sure where I'm going in my career, does anyone else feel this way?" That's when I know interpersonal resonance has been achieved and the desired impact of my communication likewise. I'd argue this does not just happen because of the field I am in or the subject matter I present. Interpersonal resonance is present for example when a Ph.D. student feels safe enough to say at a department presentation they do not know how to proceed with a certain type of analysis.

These are just a few examples of the kind of impact creating interpersonal resonance can have in your work. I invite you to explore how to lean on the following three pillars of delivering effective communication to create interpersonal resonance in speaking engagements: mind–body connection, practice, and celebrating your audience.

Pillar I – Mind–Body Connection

Being connected to your physical self is critical when delivering presentations. Without that biofeedback from your emotions and nervous system, you are less likely to deliver and recognize in your audience when there is a space for vulnerability and empathy. Learning from what works in your presentation style is in this case also compromised, meaning you will take longer to learn what "effective communication" means for you with different audiences. I like to follow a two-step process to prepare myself for a continuous mind–body connection throughout my speaking engagements.

Prepare Your Nervous System

You might have heard of Amy Cuddy's highly-debated research on power posing before high-stakes social evaluation (Cuddy et al., 2012). The power-posing technique recommends taking up as much space physically, as you can, before a big presentation. For example, you might stand up and stretch your arms out like a starfish. Or you might just place your hands on your hips and keep your elbows out. It is definitely worth a try to see if it works for you. Be sure to explore other techniques also to create your own prepresentation ritual, akin to a professional athlete's pregame ritual. Those of you who are or have been athletes will already have a good idea of what this consists of. You might not be stepping onto a field with your research presentations, but the pregame ritual can remain as close to that as you want to have it, as it serves one function: getting your mind, body, and emotions connected.

Why is it important to create this kind of connection between your physical, emotional, and mental self before a speaking engagement or a presentation?

The goal of a presentation preparation ritual is to create an internal environment within you that supports your best performance as the speaker. Speaking and presenting activate your sympathetic nervous system, or the stress response system as these are environments that hold a lot of potential threats. Social exclusion is still a threat that directly targets the sympathetic nervous system and the fear of rejection most of us experience when entering such environments is a threat to our sense of self, our inclusion in our social group and can impact our performance as speakers. The presentation preparation ritual should soothe your sympathetic nervous system and take away the risk that your own body gives signals of threat while you are presenting, thus doing everything it can to get you out of this dangerous situation.

My presentation preparation ritual is simple but effective. Three anchor components create the foundation of the ritual that I always follow, and several others are in my bank of techniques to be pulled out when I happen to have more time to prepare or am particularly nervous. My anchor components are hot water, deep breathing, and *Gilmore Girls*.

Yep, you read that right. Let me tell you why this early 00's TV favorite made it into my prepresentation ritual as well as the first two components.

In my anchor components, I like to focus on intensive nervous system regulation. My default state in life is anxiety so it might take me more than others to achieve a state of relaxation in my nervous system, imperative for holding that mind–body connection. Hot running water has always been soothing to me for its warmth as well as sound. I will either take a hot shower before a presentation or drink a cup of hot tea. In presentations where it is appropriate and where I feel especially nervous, I will have tea in a thermos mug with me throughout the event. Deep breathing is another anchor component that I adjust to the time, space, and energy I have available before the speaking event. Before my Ph.D. viva, I woke up at 4 am due to anxiety and did a 2-h Ashtanga yoga practice in order to regulate my nervous system with this intense breathing practice. Before meetings at work today, I spend about 1-min breathing deeply to make sure I can maintain that mind–body connection and regulate my system. I like breathing as a ritual component because it is so malleable to each person's individual needs and context.

Why Gilmore Girls? Sometimes, I need to engage all of my senses in an immersion activity when prepping for a speaking engagement because deep breathing and the hot water will only get me so far into a relaxed state. Gilmore Girls is a very familiar show to me. I know every scene so there is nothing unexpected to jolt me out of this immersion, the aesthetic of this fictional world is colorful visually and tonally to engage my sight and hearing. The dialogue has a very unique tempo to it, which helps give me a beat to regulate my breathing and heartbeat around. So, sipping my hot tea, I immerse myself in this world for 5–10 min and it soothes me almost instantly. Sounds crazy, right? Trust me, the next time you are very nervous about a speaking engagement, watch 10 min of your favorite TV show or listen to your favorite song on repeat. It might not work for all, but it will work for many of you.

What would your ritual anchors be?

You can choose any activity you like as your presentation preparation ritual, just make sure it is somewhat "portable," meaning you can carry it out even if you are traveling or in rooms where you might not have a lot of privacy.

Deliver with Flow

Once you've identified or designed your presentation preparation ritual and will learn to rely on it to soothe your sympathetic nervous system before presentations and speaking engagements, all that is left to do is to deliver your prepared materials in a flow of engaging, involving, and interpersonally resonating with your audience. The flow state of presenting is just a sustained mind–body connection that allows you to pay attention to your physical experience and ensure you are creating that interpersonal resonance with your audience. Being in "flow" is a good way to check whether you are sustaining your mind–body connection. Usually, when the connection goes, so does the feeling of flow and you can course-correct in real-time. Once you have become a seasoned speaker and presenter, you will have to spend less and less time on your ritual and will find yourself in the flow state quite easily.

Pillar II – Celebrate Your Audience

The second pillar of delivering presentations and speeches that create interpersonal resonance is to celebrate your audience. This is a combination of empathizing with your audience's interests and challenges, accepting them without judgment, and seeing your audience's interests and challenges as an opportunity for growth and learning. It is a mutual process of creating a learning experience together, based on interpersonal resonance and a few foundational presenting techniques which we will dive into in this section of the chapter. Techniques to present your insights and material in parallel to creating interpersonal resonance include finding the frame for your insights, telling a story, and intentionally designing an experience as the container for your insights, your presence, and your audience. The frame and story of your insights create connections with your audience's own experiences. The intentional experience design connects this to the interpersonal resonance you are already paying attention to. Altogether, this is a comprehensive experience of learning and connecting, the kind that Malala and Brene created in their most famous speeches.

Find the Frame

Just as a photograph or a scene in a film, a presentation is only as engaging as the frame within which it is set is clear, relatable, and relevant to the audience. The frame of the story through which you choose to share your message is audience-dependent. Essentially, the frame is the larger context, topic area, or type of experience your audience is familiar with, hoping to learn about, or looking to apply. For example, in a recent webinar of mine titled "The Art of Mentorship," I knew I was speaking to college alumni interested in personal and professional development and they had signed up for a networking opportunity within the context of mentoring relationships. The *frame* I chose for the presentation slides I designed was the origin of the word mentor and how mentoring relationships were defined in Greek mythology. This frame allowed the webinar participants to engage in the story of the Odyssey, get involved in a discussion on what their own understanding of mentoring had been thus far, and have the opportunity to transform any myths and assumptions about mentoring relationships into something new. Your particular field of expertise might not directly lend itself to a human story, but I encourage you to find metaphors, analogies, and other creative ways to connect your material to a context your audience might recognize. It makes it easier for them to follow your story and therefore creates more impact from the insights you share.

Tell the Story

The frame of your presentation represents the world within which you tell the story of your research. The story itself delivers the engagement, involvement, and transformation to engage and celebrate your audience. A good foundational storytelling technique to start with is the narrative arc. Nancy Duarte, the founder of Duarte Inc and a communication powerhouse, recommends starting with a simple, three-step narrative arc in your presentations (Duarte, 2021). The narrative arc is essentially the structure of your insights, the order in which you share them in the context of your chosen frame. Duarte names them Act I, II, and III. Act I is where a "likeable, but flawed hero is faced with a new and challenging situation." Act II is where "the hero encounters roadblocks and setbacks that challenge them physically and emotionally." And Act III is where "because of all they went through in the messy middle, they're changed by it." In other sources, this same narrative arc or presentation structure is also named the hero's journey. The "hero" is just the main character, feature, theme, or focus of the story.

Why is this relevant to celebrating your audience?

Because in the story you share, your audience should be the hero, not your research methods, data analysis wizardry, or the level of statistical significance your impact analysis shows. The more you can bring the presentation structure to your audience's everyday experiences, the more seen, understood, and celebrated they will feel. An easy example is a story you tell to funding organizations that might be interested in supporting your research. You are likely to find out what their funding priorities are, which kinds of research projects they've funded before, and who will be on the funding proposal evaluation panel, if this is public information. In this case, the funding organization or the people on the evaluation panel are the heroes of your narrative arc, which centers their needs, experiences, and challenges and offers your research as a potential solution. You can apply the same logic to any presentation, but you might use different sources of information to understand and celebrate your audience.

Research insights are, of course, based on data and evidence. This is important to share in your presentations and speaking engagements as it is one of the things that sets your expertise apart from others speaking on similar topics. In sharing your insights and explaining how they are related to the data you work with, it is important to design the level of detail according to the specific audience you are speaking to. Academic audiences are most likely to want to know the details of your data analysis and the conclusions you reached; however, other audiences are more likely to be engaged and feel involved when you adopt an insight before analysis approach and share what the data suggests in the context of your frame and narrative arc. As a general rule of thumb, I invite you to use your data and its analysis as a way to accentuate your narrative arc, rather than make it the main character of the story, as it sometimes is presented in academic presentation structures.

Design an Experience

During your presentation or speaking engagement, your audience is a part of an experience. They experience your tone of voice, choice of words, the stories you share, and the insights you deliver, as well as the physical or virtual environment. Your responsibility and prerogative as the speaker are to create this environment as intentionally as possible, with the goal of celebrating your audience.

Before choosing the specific research studies, data analysis results, and conclusions you want to share, I encourage you to think of the end-to-end experience your audience will have and create your presentation materials using the 5E experience design model, created by the design and leadership school Kaospilot, in Aarhus, Denmark (Sontag, 2018). This experience design model presents a five-step journey to take your audience through in every speaking engagement: excitement, entry, engagement, exit, and extension.

1. *Excitement*: defined as the "awareness of and attraction to the experience," the excitement stage begins in the communication around your speech or presentation before you even meet your audience. Think through how you want to reach out to potentially interested audience members and what kind of an emotional experience you want to create for them even in the first interaction with you or your presentation theme.

2. *Entry*: defined as "entering into the designed experience," think of this stage as the doorway into your presentation. What do you want people to experience and know when they are standing at the door of your presentation. In the virtual world, this would be the Zoom waiting room for example. Here, we aim to remove as many barriers to entry as possible, such as unclear registration processes, or unclear directions for how to join your event.
3. *Engagement*: defined as "the main activity that captures the audience's attention," this part of the experience is essentially you giving your presentation and interacting with the audience. Engagement is a part of the interpersonal resonance equation for effective communication and is indicative of it being present. Engagement can show up in different ways in different audiences, and most often falls under the label of an "interactive audience." When your audience is asking questions, chatting to each other, or asking for further learning resources, you have an *engaged* audience.
4. *Exit*: defined as "the clear end of the experience," this stage of the experience is how your audience leaves the presentation. In a virtual space, this might include each audience member sharing what their main takeaway from the session was, or sharing contact details to be able to continue the conversation. For you as the presenter, this stage of the experience involves creating a clear ending in your narrative arc and in the event.
5. *Extension*: defined as "a physical or digital object to take home and remember the experience," this stage of the experience is equivalent to a "goodie-bag" you might receive as a takeaway gift at certain types of events. Essentially, your goal as a speaker is to do everything you can to make your audience members feel welcome and interested in coming back to your future presentations and events as well. The extension is a free resource they can already implement in their work or life, such as a toolkit, an article, worksheet, game, or anything else that connects their world to yours.

The model provides a high-level backbone for arranging your research insights for each specific audience and gives you a touch-base for evaluating the quality of the experience you provide for your audience. Throughout the preparation and even during the delivery of your presentation, you can come back to this framework and check which of the five steps you are on, ensuring you complete the journey and have a high chance of delivering your planned impact.

An important part of the experience you share might be presented on slides. Some speaking engagements are of the nature where slides, any written or visual material might not be necessary to prepare, such as fireside chats or more casual conversations. However, for many of us, creating slides to go with your presentation is likely to be needed in most speaking engagements. The slides you create and present are a critical part of the overall experience you design for your audience.

As researchers, we often shy away from the world of visual design and treat slides as a way to share bullet point versions of our much longer text-based articles, idea sharing, etc. I invite you to delve into the world of presentation templates and use the structures created for you to learn about and efficiently create presentation slides that not only engage but also teach you how to involve and transform your audience. Visual and experience designers have provided us with tools that go far beyond the traditional structure of research presentations and give us ideas of how to introduce ourselves, our topic, how to build the narrative arc as well as how to invite the audience into the world of your research in a compelling way. There are many examples of presentation template software, some of which include brands like Canva.com, beautiful.ai, wetransfer.com, and more.

Using presentation templates frees up your time to let your mind roam free in search of the narrative arc and distills your research insights into a compelling story. However, you do want to have a good basis in being able to decide which presentation template to use or how to edit one for your own presentation. To become a confident decision-maker in which presentation template to use, educate yourself on the latest visual design trends with reports from industry heavy-hitters such as IDEO (Sullivan, 2020), Frog Design, and 99designs (11 inspiring graphic trends for, 2021). Stay on top of such design trends to distinguish between outdated presentation templates and choose the template that might most resonate with each audience you present to.

Pillar III – Practice

Practice presenting and speaking about your work with as many people as possible. Watch out for those moments of interpersonal resonance, and notice, when does your audience start asking more personal questions? When do you notice their interest visibly peaking in their body language, tone of voice, eye gaze, etc.? This is the data you need to create a body of knowledge around which speaking points or insights are most meaningful to the audiences you speak to.

So, how can we get enough practice? While we might think of presenting our work as being something we are *invited* to do, I encourage you to proactively seek out as many speaking experiences as possible, across a variety of audiences. Think of every meeting in your day-to-day work as an opportunity to practice, seek out online communities who might be interested in your field of expertise, and test-drive your story and data highlights with friends and family. When it comes to public speaking, practice really does make perfect. In this section, we will consider three different audiences you can practice with and the pros and cons of doing so with each: academic, industry, and student audiences.

Academic Audiences

Academic audiences might be already fairly familiar to you. However, early career researchers' experiences vary immensely and many of us might not get the chance to present our research beyond the one or two required presentations to pass the degree. As we step into our careers, whether in an academic setting or not, our strong academic research background attracts speaking engagements likely to include those with similar skills of critiquing research methods and insights.

Reasons to Practice with Academic Audiences
- Low barrier to entry, as expected narrative arc of presentations and insight sharing likely to be somewhat familiar.
- Hones your research methods and data analysis critiquing skills.
- Likely to have a good idea of what brings value to the audience.

Reasons Against Practicing with Academic Audiences
- Keeps you in your comfort zone which can be detrimental to learning the most transformational narrative arcs to present your research.

Industry Audiences

Presenting in industry contexts can feel intimidating at first, but with the right preparation, it can be a highly fulfilling and rewarding experience. Industry settings relevant to your field of expertise are likely to connect you with organizations, leaders, and teams interested in your work which often propels you into innovative partnership projects. Industry audiences are also relatively accessible to experts of your caliber and are worthwhile practicing with whenever you get the chance.

Reasons to Practice with Industry Audiences
- Creates powerful context to identify the narrative arcs most likely to engage, involve and transform a wide range of audiences as industry events represent a diverse group of participants from a variety of backgrounds.
- The fastest way to learn about where your research could potentially provide value in industry contexts, thus making it easier to identify future collaboration opportunities.

Reasons Against Practicing with Industry Audiences
- Might require more extensive preparation and rehearsal than academic or student audiences.
- Might be more unpredictable in its response in the beginning, as you learn how to present your work to such an audience so it can cause some stress.

Students

As an early career researcher, you are likely to have access to some student audiences, even if you are not engaged in a teaching position per se. I highly recommend taking and seeking out opportunities to speak to a wide variety of student audiences, including school, undergraduate and postgraduate contexts. Students represent a unique opportunity to develop the narrative arcs of your research insights in a multitude of ways as they often have unique viewpoints and suggestions to share about how your material resonates with them.

Reasons to Practice with Student Audiences
- Low barrier to entry for early career researchers.
- Unique feedback on what works for your presentations and what does not.
- Likely to be a supportive audience to get your presenting feet wet.

Reasons Against Practicing with Student Audiences
- Presenting to students usually involves integrating tangible learning outcomes which adds complexity to developing your narrative arc.

Conclusions and Practical Recommendations

In conclusion, there are several ways to start on your journey of presenting and speaking about your work, and I encourage you wholeheartedly to do so. Choose the lowest barrier-to-entry audience to start practicing, take the experience design approach to proactively create the desired outcome for your presentations, and use framing and storytelling techniques to really captivate your audiences. Lastly, make sure to prepare yourself mentally, physically, and emotionally with a presentation preparation ritual to soothe your sympathetic nervous system response in stressful situations and find yourself flowing with your audience. The benefits of learning to share your work with diverse audiences are countless, starting with future collaboration opportunities, funding, to simply being able to share the joy in your work and expertise with others.

Here is a checklist to follow the next time you are getting ready to present:

1. Research your audience: what do they care about? What are they hoping to achieve with your insights? What are some of the challenges they are facing in work and life?
2. Find a frame for presentation that connects to your audience's interests.
3. Create a narrative arc showcasing your insights as the solution to your audience's challenges, placing your audience in the position of the hero in your hero's journey.
4. Design the end-to-end experience your audience will go through with you, including a giveaway they can take with them and continue thinking about your message.
5. Design a prepresentation ritual to regulate your nervous system and prepare yourself to sustain a mind–body connection when presenting. A toolbox of different preparation activities makes for the most versatile and adaptable ritual.
6. Deliver your presentation in a flow, endeavoring to maintain the mind–body connection and looking out for moments of interpersonal resonance to ensure you are communicating effectively.

7. When in doubt about anything, ask your audience directly: what does this mean to you? What makes this challenging for you? What is most important to you right now? What do you take away from my presentation?

   Happy presenting! I'm rooting for you.

References

99designs Team. (2021). *12 inspiring graphic design trends for 2022*. 99Designs Blog. https://99designs.com/blog/trends/graphic-design-trends

Cuddy, A. J. C., Wilmuth, C. A., & Carney, D. R. (2012, September). The benefit of power posing before a high-stakes social evaluation. *Harvard business school working paper*, No. 13-027.

Duarte, N. (2021). *How to move your presentation audience with this powerful story technique*. Duarte.com. https://www.duarte.com/presentation-skills-resources/move-presentation-audience-with-story-techniques-in-presentations/

Feliú-Mójer, M. I. (2015). *Effective communication, better science*. Scientific American. https://blogs.scientificamerican.com/guest-blog/effective-communication-better-science

Sontag, A. (2018). *The 5E experience model. Kaospilot*. UXBlog. https://medium.theuxblog.com/the-5e-experience-design-model-7852324d46c

Sullivan, M. (2020). *Here are the top tech trends of 2021, according to 30+ experts*. FastCompany. https://www.fastcompany.com/90588717/top-tech-trends-2021-post-pandemic-predictions-ai-fintech-health

Tennant, J. M., Cook, S., Moldoveanu, M. C., Peterson, J. B., & Cunningham, W. A. (2019). Interpersonal resonance: developing interpersonal biofeedback for the promotion of empathy and social entrainment. In T. Ahram (Eds.), *Advances in human factors in wearable technologies and game design*. AHFE 2018. Advances in Intelligent Systems and Computing, vol. 795. Springer. https://doi.org/10.1007/978-3-319-94619-1_20

Chapter 15
Engaging with the Press and Media

Nikki Stamp

Abstract I have been privileged to host TV shows and to engage with press and media to discuss scientific discoveries and to talk about heart disease, women's health and women in surgery. As ECRs and scientists we are often expected to work with media. To do so engagingly, we need to learn to distil our messages down to an effective message that may impact the wider public. The media can be a powerful tool and you have to learn how it works and how to make the most of it to ensure that your message is getting across. In this chapter, I give you actionable and practical recommendations for how to best engage with press and media to ensure that they portray you and your work exactly the way you want them to be framed. I also share several examples and recommendation for how to make the most from your media engagements – how to ensure that your message is clear and simple and that it has a potential to change the world by impacting listeners views and touching their hearts.

Keywords Press · Media · Engagement · Science Dissemination · Interviews · Media training · Communication

Introduction

In 2018, I was fortunate enough to be able to host two episodes of the Australian science show, *Catalyst*. In the episodes, we explored the intricacies of the heart and the burgeoning field of bionics. It was a far cry from my usual world of surgery and academia. Instead of being in the operating theatre, I was learning about framing shots, conducting interviews and walking in and out of doors so many times for that perfect scene. For both episodes, we followed some of the world's foremost

---

N. Stamp (✉)
Curtin School of Population Health, Bentley, WA, Australia

© The Author(s), under exclusive license to Springer Nature
Switzerland AG 2022
D. Kwasnicka, A. Y. Lai (eds.), *Survival Guide for Early Career Researchers*,
https://doi.org/10.1007/978-3-031-10754-2_15

researchers in these areas. As a doctor and a researcher, myself, I could have talked to each of our experts for hours, if not days on end. Their breakthroughs were so remarkable: finding ways to 3D print heart muscle to repair damaged hearts, preventing congenital heart defects or building mechanical limbs with extraordinary capabilities.

On this occasion though, I was not there to talk to these people as a colleague or an interested party. I was there to act as a conduit of information, to allow the world to see what they had achieved and what their discoveries could bring to the world. It is easy to see this is as an opportunity to raise awareness for chronically underfunded research institutes but it was also an outstanding opportunity for people to see the hope that science could bring to our lives.

The episodes were seen by over 500,000 people each. To put in perspective, as a cardiac surgeon, I can operate on two or three people per day. At a busy conference, I can share my research or expertise to a few hundred people. All of a sudden, hundreds of thousands of people were able to see what I do as well as the remarkable achievements of some of my medical research colleagues, for some, prompting them to speak to their doctors or donate to some of the research foundations we featured.

In addition to *Catalyst*, I have appeared on many media outlets around the world including hosting TV shows, or as guests on radio, podcasts or television, usually to talk about heart disease, women's health or women in surgery – my three big passions. Even though I am more comfortable around the camera than when I first started, each time I do something, I always learn more and know that my next appearance will be even better. But most importantly, as I get better at doing this, I know my important messages get across to more people and in a way that they can understand much more clearly. In addition, meeting other experts and academics in the course of doing this has led to some wonderful research collaborations, including my PhD.

In the face of COVID-19, scientists of all walks have been called upon to communicate their work and their expertise with the public, often on the daunting platform of the mass media. The importance of being able to do this well has been shown to be vital during the pandemic. In the media, we as experts must be able to effectively and engagingly distil our messages, sometimes our life's work, down to an effective message that may receive just a few seconds airtime but could have a profound impact on your institution, your career and, as we have seen, on the entire world. The media can be a powerful tool, but in order to get the best from it, you must understand how it works and how to make sure your message is getting across.

Why Go to the Media?

Traditionally, media such as television and newspapers would not be the first way we would look to disseminate our research. In the past, we may have relied upon conferences or other purely academic avenues to promote our research. Utilising the mass media not only allows widespread dissemination of your work, it has the ability to bring a number of advantages.

Citations remain an important metric in academia. If you and your work appear in the media, there is a potential to increase the impact of your work. It may seem as though press will only bring the lay public to your work, but it can also increase the reach among the scientific community. The press can include specialty publications such as *Psychology Online Australia*, read by people within your field. Several small studies have confirmed that media coverage increases citations when compared to studies that do not receive such coverage (Dumas-Mallet et al., 2020; Sage Anderson et al., 2020).

Seeing science and research in the media is also likely to increase the public's confidence in science (Feine & Jakubovics, 2021; Hilgard & Jamieson, 2017).

Whether it be in specialised science-related publications, or the lay media, widespread dissemination of new and important findings have the power to change practice. Even the intended users of your research will read the newspapers, or see your work on television, so that they can explore and put your hard work into practice.

Of course, in the highly competitive world of academia, funding is an ever-present consideration. Exposure in the media can open up avenues and connections that can lead to funding, sponsorships or other connections that can support your research and career progression.

While media exposure may seem gratuitous, in an ever-connected world, it may become more important in supporting your academic career. When opportunities arrive, embrace them rather than avoid them to further your work.

Common Pitfalls in the Media

While there may be some important benefits for using the media, this advantage can be tempered if we fall to some of the more common pitfalls when using the media. While many of us consume the media, the inner workings are a bit of a mystery. There are a number of common pitfalls that can attenuate the power of your message to be aware of.

One of the ways to avoid missteps is to firstly understand how the media works. Whether it be print, radio or television, journalists are usually given a brief that they need to fill. This brief is like a framework for a story where you may be the main feature or your work and expertise can be used to fill in the story and support the point that they are trying to make. Space in the media is at a premium; often what is a 20-minute discussion with a journalist can be distilled down to a single quote to meet constraints. Journalists may also have an angle for a piece in mind and, as such, can direct conversations to fit their needs which can be confusing as the person being interviewed, trying to get a totally different point across. It is important to have an awareness of that so that you can be mindful to keep your point at the forefront.

Nervousness or anxiety around being in the media is very common, after all for many, this can be very outside of your comfort zone. Unfortunately, being nervous can come across and impact the clarity of your message. One of the most effective ways that you can reduce your nervousness is to practice, whether it be to your mirror or on your phone so that when the real event comes up, you are much more comfortable with what you have to say and how you say it. And of course, if the media is going to feature strongly in your future, the more you do, the more relaxed and familiar with the environment you will become. Most of us have had to present our research on stages at conferences or in meetings; the first one you did was probably confusing or even terrifying! But with every other presentation that you do, the more comfortable you become. The exact same thing applies here.

Scientific jargon is another way that your message can be muddied in the media. While most of us are comfortable communicating with our colleagues using jargon, in the media especially if it is for the public, jargon makes your message confusing or at worst completely unintelligible. Your quotes may even be misused if the journalist does not understand what you are trying to say. Jargon is a habit but we also may use it because we do not know how to explain things another way, or because we want to sound knowledgeable in what we have to say.

A great fear of using the media is that your words will be misconstrued or misquoted. This is a lesson I have had to learn the hard way myself! In radio or television, it can be hard to get the right reply or final say; however, in print media there are ways to assure that your quotes are being used correctly. For instance, you can request to read and approve the transcript, quote or article before it goes online. There are some easy ways to guard against this and you certainly should not be afraid to get involved with the media because of this.

Making Your Message 'Media-Ready'

With the risks and benefits in mind, how can we make our message 'media-ready'? There are some very simple ways in which you can ensure your message comes across well, you are polished and prepared and to safeguard your message's integrity.

One of the first things to do before you even start an interview is to ask the journalist for the questions they are going to ask you. As experienced learners and teachers, we would never turn up to an exam unprepared and not knowing the material and a media interview is no different. It is entirely reasonable to be firm with this request, and it is unlikely that someone will decline to provide you with questions or at the very least topics, prior to the actual event. In addition to allowing preparation, if there are questions that you would rather not answer or fall outside of your expertise, do not be afraid to say that you cannot answer that question. A quick email or a phone call before you get started to get the questions is almost always met with happily providing you with some questions, after all the journalist wants the best out of you too.

Once you have some questions, you can practice your answers. Since everyone has a camera on their phones now, practicing your responses using this gives you a way to practice what you will be saying and see how it will come across. When you are answering a question, especially for radio or television, starting your answer by rephrasing the question gives the editors and journalists great sound bites that are easily edited in to make you look outstanding. For example, if the question is, 'what is the difference between men and women who have a heart attack?', your answer would start with 'The difference between men and women who have a heart attack is…'. Your answer should be short, sharp and to the point considering it can be edited down to a few seconds or a few sentences. Usually, if more detail is required, the journalist will ask for it.

Practice is also a way to stop jargon from creeping into your answers. Whether it be on the day or when your practicing, try to imagine you are explaining your concept to a school student if your message is for the mass media. As in our example above, a jargon-laden answer might include references to myocardial infarction or atherosclerosis which will not be understood by many people. If you need to refer to something in a technical term, be sure to explain it in everyday language so that your message is clear. Although it might feel like you are dumbing down your work, actually having as many people as possible understand and engage with your work is the ultimate goal here.

As with anything, the more you practice getting your message across succinctly, the better you will be equipped when the cameras are rolling to show off all of your hard work.

Media Training

Media training is an excellent way to improve your confidence and your skills when interacting with the mainstream media. Media training is most often offered by experienced journalists and encompasses practical and theoretical education. Media training can assist in helping researchers communicate their message in a clear and succinct fashion as well as improve familiarity with the sometimes-challenging environment of television, radio or print media.

Media training is often conducted for those in the medical or scientific fields. Courses can be done over a few hours where you are taught vocal warm-ups, where to look at the camera, how to stand and what to wear, along with the chance to practice your message with someone outside of your own field. A media trainer can look over what you are doing with an experienced, journalistic eye to help you polish your message and your delivery. If you are going to be interacting with the media on any regular basis, media training is a great way to make sure that your important work is effectively shared with the broader audience.

Practical Tips for Interacting with the Media

Now that we have covered some points that can make or break your media appearance, including how your message comes across, we need to know about the practicalities that make you feel prepared and your message look professional and polished.

One of the most important tips is to use your institution's public relations team. They will be able to provide you with support, including liaising with media outlets, sourcing opportunities and assisting your preparation. They are also experienced at interacting with journalists and can be useful when questions or segments need to be declined or modified to ensure that your interests and the interests of the institution are put first. They can also follow-up after the interview to make sure that the final version is an accurate representation of you and what you are doing. Many institutions' public relations teams will pitch your research to media outlets for stories, if your research is important or significant, which is a great way to get these opportunities in the first place.

Once your interview is booked and you have the questions and have practiced your answers, the next thing comes the actual interview. If the interview involves a camera crew or journalist attending your workplace, your PR team can help arrange a suitable venue and be present if you need. Do not be afraid to ask for an alternative if a crew wants to come to your office or occasionally your home if there is a personal angle to a story. These things can feel very invasive for some people, or disrupt important work, so make sure that you will be happy with any venue.

It is common to worry about what to wear for an interview when you will be on camera. Patterns should generally be avoided because they can cause the camera to strobe which looks distracting on screens. Plain colours are the safest bet, although black or white can be quite stark on screen or even see-through. If you are going to wear a pattern, be careful with really fine stripes. You want to look and feel like yourself, but still try and keep these tips in mind. As for hair and make-up, simple and neat is best. If you are going to be interviewed in a studio, be sure to confirm any wardrobe, hair and make-up requirements prior to going. As I have done more media over the years, I have definitely changed what I have worn so that I am comfortable and look confident and trustworthy. I used to want to be as fashionable as possible, but take a look at popular journalists. They often wear simple and timeless staples and provide a good yardstick of what might be expected.

Prior to the interview, it is a good idea to do some vocal warm-ups – I am a fan of using tongue twisters like 'red leather yellow leather' and getting a few big yawns to relax the face and get your mouth used to talking. If you are feeling a bit nervous, simple relaxation exercise can be useful to calm your nerves such as few deep breaths. Be aware that if you get a bit shaky or anxious after caffeine, try to avoid consuming too much before your interview. Anxiety or just lots of talking can dry your mouth so be sure to keep your mouth from getting to dry which can make you stumble over words with plenty of water.

To help with confidence as well as ensuring that you are looking your best on camera, avoid slumping in your chair. When I have seen clips where I have been slumping, it makes me cringe; I looked disinterested and too casual. In order to make sure my posture is at its best, I try to sit towards the edge of the chair so I cannot accidentally lean back in it. Depending on the interview setting, you might be required to look at an interviewer or straight down the barrel of the camera, as if you are talking to the audience directly. Whatever the setting, you will most likely be briefed as to your role but do not be afraid to ask questions.

Once the interview is over, the editing team will get to work. For print articles, you can request to see a final copy prior to it going live, which is useful to check for accuracy and any conflicts that you need to be aware of. It can be a bit harder with audio or television to get any right of edit, but your institution's PR team can assist you if this needs to be checked at all. While it may feel defensive, journalists want to put the best work out there so most are grateful for your feedback to make sure that the piece is as good as it can be.

One final word, it is always good to assume that everything you say will be heard and can be repeated. Be mindful not to talk even when you think a microphone is off because many people have been caught out! It is always a good idea to only say things that you would be happy or comfortable having them repeated.

Once your media is out in the world, do not forget to share it. It is also useful to keep a record of any media appearances, especially if you are going to be doing it more often, to build a kind of resume of all of your wonderful media appearances. That list can be useful for you to demonstrate the impact of your work and also it may come in handy when applying for promotion.

Broadcasting from Home

COVID-19 meant that many of us have been working remotely and interacting with the media has been no different. Even after the pandemic, we may still see some at home broadcasting continue. When you are in the comfort of your own home, putting your best foot forward in broadcasting is still important.

Whether it is for print or other media, it helps the journalist to do their job if you talk to them from a quiet room where you are not likely to be distracted. This can mean working out how to keep children, spouses and pets out of the room although kids on camera during COVID-19 have been great for some light-hearted relief. The room should also be quiet and sound quality tends to be better when you are in a room with soft furnishings, such as a carpet. Lighting is also an important consideration; if you are able to face a window for some natural light but if this is not possible, a ring light can help make you look your best and widely available at very reasonable prices. Make sure that you are not sitting with your back facing the window, as you will appear very dark on the screen.

Next comes positioning your device. Whether you are using a computer or a smartphone, always ensure that your camera sits at eye level to you. It is easy to put the device on your desk so that you are looking down on it but this gives a very unflattering view and undermines your message. Use a stack of textbooks, a stand or a tripod to elevate your device to a much more flattering angle.

Finally, in addition to a quiet room, sound tends to be best by using headphones with an built-in microphone. Plug in headphones or use Bluetooth headphones to make sure that you can hear the interviewer well and so that they can hear your voice much more crisply and cleanly. If you do a lot of broadcasting, a separate USB microphone can be a useful investment to really ensure your sound quality is outstanding.

Finally, especially if your camera is going to be on, still remember to dress appropriately. Even though you might only be seen from the waist up, if you happen to get up, you might give the camera a glimpse of an outfit you would rather not see recorded!

Conclusions and Practical Recommendations

The media can be utilised to benefit your academic work and a little bit of knowledge and ensure that your message is clear and well understood.

- Always prepare by getting a list of questions before your interview.
- Practice making your message succinct and understandable to a broad audience.
- Avoid using jargon.
- Engage your institution's public relations or media team for assistance.
- Prepare your wardrobe and be mindful of your posture.
- Warm up your mouth and voice before any interview.
- Where possible, try to get a review of the final piece before it goes live.
- Act like the microphone is always on and what you say will be repeated.
- Optimise your at-home broadcasting set-up with a quiet room, good lighting and good sound with your device at eye level.
- Strongly consider media training.
- Remember to enjoy yourself and imagine how your message is going to change the world.

References

Dumas-Mallet, E., Garenne, A., Boraud, T., & Gonon, F. (2020). Does newspapers coverage influence the citations count of scientific publications? An analysis of biomedical studies. *Scientometrics*,123(1) 413–427.
Feine, J., & Jakubovics, N. (2021). Science in the spotlight: A crisis of confidence?
Hilgard, J., & Jamieson, K. H. (2017). Does a scientific breakthrough increase confidence in science? News of a Zika vaccine and trust in science. *Science Communication, 39*(4), 548–560.

Sage Anderson, P., Odom, A. R., Gray, H. M., Jones, J. B., Christensen, W. F., Hollingshead, T., & Seeley, M. K. (2020). A case study exploring associations between popular media attention of scientific research and scientific citations. *PLoS One, 15*(7), e0234912. https://doi.org/10.1371/journal.pone.0234912

Chapter 16
Make Your Science Go Viral: How to Maximize the Impact of Your Research

Mike Morrison and Kelsey Merlo

Abstract Reaching even one additional person with your research can have an impact. This chapter maps a path from reaching one new person with your science to reaching one hundred thousand people, teaching you increasingly advanced design principles at each level. At minimum, boost your impact by posting the scientific products you are already creating on public, Open Access repositories (your papers on preprint websites, your posters on Figshare.com, and your talks/lectures on YouTube). Learn how to check your views to keep yourself motivated. Building an audience is easiest with social media, but also doable by attracting people organically to your articles and videos. Boost your engagement further by creating scientific products that are high value and low effort. Inspire people to share your science by adding emotion (i.e., do not neglect affective processing). Finally, you can maximize your impact by finding and communicating what you personally find most meaningful about your research, because meaning is attractive.

Keywords Impact · Research · Social media · Science dissemination · Knowledge translation · Science communication

Introduction

One phone call during my (Mike's) second year of graduate school changed the way I present science. Somewhat by luck, I was offered one of two "give a student a chance" spots in a new event at our field's annual conference where I, a lowly second-year grad student, would be presenting alongside 12 superstar professors and practitioners in my field – scientists known for both their scientific research and their exceptional presenting ability – in front of several hundred peers at a

---

M. Morrison (✉)
Researchable, Groningen, The Netherlands

K. Merlo
University of South Florida, Tampa, FL, USA

© The Author(s), under exclusive license to Springer Nature Switzerland AG 2022
D. Kwasnicka, A. Y. Lai (eds.), *Survival Guide for Early Career Researchers*,
https://doi.org/10.1007/978-3-031-10754-2_16

conference. Ever the neurotic grad student, I called the organizer and asked a million questions: How long do you want me to talk for, what do you want me to focus on, etc. Her response: "Talk about whatever you want. There are only two rules: First, it has to be shorter than 3 min. One second longer and I'll yank you off stage. Second, you have to try to disturb the audience. Blow their minds and make them feel something."

I could have spent a career in academia without anybody ever giving me permission to emotionally and intellectually disturb my fellow researchers, much less outright commanding me to. I gave her two topic ideas: a safe one about my current research and a crazy idea I was just passionate about. Without hesitation, she said "do the crazy one."

I took her advice. Getting everything under 3 min was physically painful. I had to scrutinize every single word. And the need to make it emotionally stirring meant I could not just throw in "relevant but bland" visuals; every graphic needed to be powerful. And it worked. My talk (on the future of work and work psychology, my field) had such an impact on the audience it was featured in articles and blogs from attendees and even inspired a whole session at my conference the next year. Legends in my field told me a year later they still remembered my imagery. And I was forever hooked on presenting to make an impact, rather than just presenting to dutifully report stuff.

A year later, I had a major health scare, and it weaponized my budding presenting skill. Even though I was becoming a skilled presenter, I was still preoccupied with how each presentation would affect my career. After my health scare, I stopped caring about anything besides actually creating change in the world. I wanted to save myself and all the people suffering like me. For my next major conference talk, I combined my new passion for impactful presenting with something unique: a worthy cause I deeply believed in. That presentation – on applying design principles to improve the dissemination of science between scientists – "Nearly started a nerd riot" in the words of a fellow graduate student. After it was posted on YouTube, it reached tens of thousands of people and led directly to my dream job reaching out and hiring me.

The following year, still driven to create more impact and change, I created a YouTube cartoon about redesigning the scientific poster, under the hashtag #betterposter. My cartoon went viral in the scientific community (with over 700,000 views and 250,000 template downloads as of this writing), was featured in national news, and endorsed by major academic conferences. But more importantly to me, I think it meaningfully influenced the way posters are designed across science. It put a chip in years of conformity and helped scientists feel the courage to experiment more boldly with their posters. A year after #betterposter, I created another cartoon (#TwitterPoster) that inspired scientists to create animated GIFs of their research, many of which have gone viral and reached tens of thousands of people on their own.

There are unifying design principles behind my work. But the greatest lesson I learned from all this was to drop all conventions, present what truly matters to you, and embrace the challenge of making it matter to other people as much as it matters to you. No advice I can give you, and no amount of communication skill, will catapult your impact as much as simply having a worthy cause that you believe in.

But if you have that and if you find yourself a worthy cause – a change you want to see your science make in the world – and you combine it with the skills in this chapter, I hope it brings you as much meaning as it has brought me. The feeling of making a big, positive difference with your work is profound, and after you experience it, you will never be the same.

How to Make Your Science Go Viral

Here is the short version: You can get somebody to engage with your science by making it (1) easy to process and (2) valuable. You can get people to *share* your content by also making it emotionally stimulating.

Level 1: Do It for the Love

Meaning Makes Ideas Contagious

There are at least two reasons to try to reach more people with your science. The first is because you "should" do it because it is better for your career. Getting your science out more widely on the Internet can bring you more collaborators (Jia et al., 2017), more name recognition, and more job opportunities and may even help you get tenure if you are an academic (Gruzd et al., 2011). Your first author (Mike) has personally experienced many of these. I found my favorite collaborators and my dream job thanks to posting just one of my conference talks on Twitter (or rather, *they found me* because of that talk). Your second author (Kelsey) has her best lectures in a public YouTube playlist so she can share them with students and prospective employers.

Sharing your work as part of a professional plan to better your career is smart. However, depending on that extrinsic motivation alone may limit your reach and the quality of what you do in this particular case. Emotional contagion is a key factor in sharing things online (Guadagno et al., 2013). People share stuff that makes them feel something, because they want to share that feeling. In order to make others feel something about your research, you may have to feel it first.

As a scientist, you have a small piece of humanity's bright future contained within you. If your work becomes more widely known, it will improve human's understanding of something that matters and will help us address societal problems and suffering, even in a little way. If you can emotionally invest in your work as meaningful (or switch to a topic you can feel that way about), it will help you communicate and spread your research. Because meaningful work is attractive to others (Stillman et al., 2011). The paradox may be that if you focus on reaching people with your research for its own scale, as if you do not care about career opportunities, you will likely get the career opportunities as a side effect.

If you do not know what your burning passion is, start with your favorite among what you have studied so far, like the idea you keep coming back to. Your second author (Kelsey) has given dozens of lectures on a myriad of topics, but she is most passionate about a single lecture she gives to students every year on professional skills, so she started with that.

Finding meaning in your science is on you. That is the hard part. The rest is just learning and practicing the design principles, which is what the remainder of this chapter will now focus on.

Every Extra Eyeball Counts

You do not have to go "full viral" and get zillions of views and become Internet-famous to make a personally and professionally meaningful impact with your research. Aim to just get your science out to a few more people. If you reach ten more people with your science than you otherwise would have, that matters. And if you keep trying to reach a few more people, trying to get more eyeballs on your science, then one day you will likely hit on something that succeeds beyond your dearest expectations.

Things Get Shared When They Are Easy to Process and Emotional

Guadagno et al. (2013) attempted to dissect the process by which content on the Internet "goes viral" in the sense of spreading widely and getting lots of shares. They arrived at the following viral cycle, which relies on emotional contagion:

1. A person notices your content.
2. They can grasp what you are saying quickly (note: this is challenging for us researchers).
3. They have an emotional reaction.
4. They want to share that emotion with others, so they share it.
5. Other people see your content as shared by somebody else, or having a higher share/like count, adding social validation to your content.
6. They have the same emotional reaction and want to share it.
7. Repeat.

In the rest of this chapter, you are about to learn the research and skills to help you nail each of the above steps, from getting your content noticed and understood to making it transmit emotion. Some steps require more advanced research concepts and more work on your part than others, so we will start with the easy stuff and work up from there.

Level 2: Get One View On Anything

How many people did your last research project reach? You likely do not know the answer to this. And given how outdated the scientific publishing system is, you could spend a career wondering whether *anybody* even reads what you are publishing. And that lack of feedback likely lowers your self-efficacy about having an impact, and a lower self-efficacy is likely associated with less interest in trying to make an impact in the future (Zimmerman & Wiernik, 2020). The first step in the "going viral" cycle is people seeing your science at all (Guadagno et al., 2013). So, your first assignment is to get yourself from "zero to one" eyeball (er, pair of eyeballs?). Getting even one stranger to see a piece of your science who would not have otherwise seen it is a good start.

For most scientists, getting a paper published is the only way you share your science with the broader world, and after your research is accepted for publication, that is the end. But that is not true online, where your work can have a much more fulfilling second life. Happily, there are lots of other ways to get your research out into the world online besides publication. And this applies to research at every stage. If you have ideas for future research, posting them online can help get early reactions to help you improve your idea. And if you have skills and understandings outside your core research area (like stats) that you would enjoy sharing and would benefit others, that works too!

So, let us get something online. Here is an incomplete list of ways you can post your scientific content online. If you have already done anything on this list, you can skip this step.

- Upload one of your past publications and/or class papers as a preprint (on sites like PsyArXiv, bioaRxiv, arXiv.org, Qeios, Researchers.One).
- Upload one of your recorded lectures or conference talks to YouTube.
- Upload one of your past posters or data visualizations to Figshare.com (it is like preprints for scientific figures, slides, and posters).
- Upload some of your past presentation slides to the Open Science Framework or Figshare.com.
- Upload an R function you wrote to GitHub.
- Post anything about your science on any social media (Twitter, Facebook, Instagram, TikTok). Even just a finding you thought was cool from somebody else's work. Talking about what you study at all can be as impactful as publishing.

Check Your Views

Once you get your content posted, wait a bit (a day, a week, whatever) and then go back and find out how many people have looked at it. This is different for every platform, and you may have to Google "how to see how many people have viewed my whatever on [platform]" to figure it out. On Twitter, you can click "View Tweet

Activity." On YouTube, you can click "Your Videos > Analytics." On PsyArXiv, you can view "My Preprints" and see a count of downloads beside them.

Incidentally, in preparing to write this section, I discovered that lots of people have downloaded the preprint I posted 2 years ago of my unpublished master's thesis! So cool. Those are people who benefited from my thesis work who would not have if I had waited to get it submitted to a journal before putting it somewhere. Note: If you are stuck at zero views for more than a month, post something else, maybe on a different platform, or try posting a link to the first thing you posted. Links to your content from other sites help Google see and promote your content in search results (these are called "backlinks").

Level 3: Get Ten Views on Something

If you have already gotten one view on something, getting to ten views is probably just going to be a matter of time. But here is a simple design tip on getting your content noticed.

A common wisdom in graphic design is that people's eyes will naturally go to the highest-contrast thing on a page first (Williams, 2014). Whatever platform you have chosen to post on, look at how your content appears in search results, or in the "feed" if you posted on social media. Think of that feed or those search results as a single design. Look away from the screen and then back to it. Where do your eyes go first, second, third? How much does your content stick out visually from the rest of what is on the page?

Generally, bigger things have higher contrast than smaller things. Dark colors are higher contrast on a light background; light colors are higher contrast on a dark background. But contrast is contextual. Making your YouTube thumbnail bright yellow will not make it stand out, if all the other thumbnails of similar videos are also bright yellow (in that case, a dark color might work better). So, the key is figuring out how to make your content look different from its "competitors." If everything is text, try an image or emoji. If most people are posting photographs, try an illustration. If all the titles make statements, try including a question mark in yours.

Online, People Skim-Read

Moran (2020) has done a number of studies on how people read online. Their overarching finding about how people read online is this: they do not. People do not read online. They skim and they scan and their eyes bounce around looking for something valuable. They also may skim in predictable patterns, such as the famous "F-pattern" for reading search results, where people read the entire first line, then the first bit of the second and third parts, and then skim down vertically (Moran, 2020). The takeaway for you here is that online (1) you have to design for skim-reading and (2) things on the left (e.g., the first few words of your headings) are particularly important (in cultures that read left-to-right, at least).

Here is a quick personal story from the first author (Mike): Before I launched the #betterposter YouTube cartoon, I took a screenshot of the YouTube search results page for the key term "research poster" and Photoshopped different titles and thumbnails for my video onto the screenshot of the other results, until I found one that looked different from all the others.

Experimenting with contrast and directing people's eye movements should easily get you to ten views or more. But to get to 100 views, you are likely going to have to build up your audience.

Level 4: Reach 100 People with Your Science

To increase your reach to the next level, you have to start being thoughtful about where you put your content and more persistent about building a foundational audience to everything you do.

Writing an Article for a Popular Outlet Is a Shortcut

If you write an article or blog post for an established online outlet (e.g., TheConversation.com, Medium.com), they have already done the hard work of building an audience for you. The Conversation in particular has a great track record of drawing attention to great research. The majority of researchers who write an article on The Conversation end up getting some attention from the popular press (The Conversation, 2020). And with a monthly readership in the millions of people, reaching 100 people will be almost automatic.

Similarly, asking the organizations you are connected with (e.g., your department, your annual conference) to share your science on their social media accounts lets you reach people on social media without having to join social media. Plus, your professional organization's social media team is always hungry for content to post, so you are helping them in addition to them helping you.

Building Your Own Audience Gradually Takes Times

Whatever platform you choose for getting your science out, remember that it takes time to get traction and visitors. For example, if you are going to start your own blog (even on your own lab website or something), and you have a lot of passion for your topic, and you are the kind of person who likes to write often, you can reach a lot of people, and it can bring a lot of good attention to you and your work. But it takes time. It can take a year or more of persistent, semiregular effort to build a steady flow of what is called organic traffic (which is people finding your blog from search engines like Google).

If you are going to create a personal science blog, or if you already have a lab website, I highly recommend asking your website host (e.g., Squarespace, your IT department, that kid in your lab who can do website stuff) to install the free package Google Analytics. This will help you track your views and reach as you continue to write articles and post content. Especially, Google Analytics helps you see which of your writings are hitting and which are missing, so you can calibrate.

And remember, you do not have to write every article on your own science blog; let your research assistants and students get some experience!

Unfortunately, It Is Much Easier to Increase Your Impact If You Post on Social Media

Many scientists are hesitant to start participating in social media, even though they have heard all the benefits. However, building a network on any social media platform (e.g., Twitter, LinkedIn) is likely the highest-potential path to reaching more people with your science. Every additional "follower" on social media exponentially increases your reach, especially after 1,000 (Cote & Darling, 2018). On Twitter, a commonly reported heuristic is that you will reach about 20% of whatever your follower count is with any given Tweet.

If you joined Twitter today, followed people in your field, and announced yourself, you would probably get approximately 30 followers pretty quickly (note: people will follow you back if you follow them). So that is 6 extra people *probably in your field* you can get every single thing you do in front of (which may already exceed the average readership of a scientific article). And that is six extra people you can potentially get to look at your blog posts, YouTube videos, R code, etc. If you build up to 500 followers, you will reach at least 100 people with everything you do. And even if you come back after time away from social media, many of your followers will still be there! It is a permanent platform.

Next, we will try to make getting started and getting followers as painless as possible.

You Already Have a Network!

Many of your colleagues are already on social media. Cote and Darling (2018) suggested that on Twitter in particular, most of your initial followers will be other researchers in your field. What this means is that you are really doing "in reach" more than "outreach" on social media at first.

After you join a social media platform, just make sure you have a profile picture, a couple sentences about what you study, and maybe one awkward "Hey I'm new here. Woo!" tweet/post/whatever. Then, you can start by simply finding your colleagues, friends, and heroes and following them and then just lurk and read what they post and start liking, sharing, and replying to what your friends post about their research. It is totally fine to start by being a good friend and boosting your colleagues' work. Eventually, you will get the urge to post something about your own or somebody else's research, and it will just come naturally. And your colleagues who you have boosted will all be eager to help boost you.

Keep in mind also that social media is a great leveler. Even as a grad student, I regularly get to participate in conversations with big names in my field (even past and current presidents), who then recognize me when I bump into them at conferences. Everybody is a person, and the level of access you have to major names in your field on social media is incredible.

Level 5: Reach 1,000 People with Your Science

Ok, now it is time to get advanced. You have already started building a platform, either on YouTube or social media or a blog or an outlet like TheConversation.com. You have got some followers/regular commenters. You know how to get noticed through visual contrast and try to help people skim, and reaching 100 extra people with your science is commonplace. Now it is time to start increasing the value and reach of what you are putting out there.

To boost your reach, think about creating mini "products" related to your research that are both useful/informative and low effort (to consume). To this end, let us advance your understanding of the science behind how people engage with content.

People Forage for Information Like They Forage for Food...Lazily

The bedrock theory of human behavior on the Internet is Pirolli and Card's (1995) information foraging theory. Professional web designers and content marketers all tacitly rely on the information foraging theory, even if they do so without knowing it. The basic idea is that humans forage for information on the Internet using similar cognitive systems and heuristics that they used to use to forage for food in the wild when we were cave people (Pirolli & Card, 1995).

Generally, people are lazy about how they forage. In science, calling something "lazy" is a huge insult. But in the foraging theory, laziness is seen as efficiency. People want the maximum possible reward for the least possible effort. Think about this in context of food foraging: In order to survive, you must find food that contains more calories than the energy you spent finding the food. In the same way, we engage with content online that is more interesting than it is effortful.

This means when people browse content online, they are making quick judgments about how much effort things will take to interact with (called the "interaction cost") and how valuable it "smells" (called "information scent").

Your goal is to create content that is perceived as more valuable than it is effortful, or in the foraging theory terms, has a strong information scent (to your target audience, like fellow researchers) and a low interaction cost. Creating a strong information scent starts with creating something useful and/or interesting to most researchers and including quick cues in your post as to its topic and value. But if it is too much effort to engage with your content, it does not matter how valuable it is. So let us help you lower your interaction cost.

Lower Interaction Cost

Any effort – physical, cognitive, or emotional – that a person has to expend getting value out of your content is considered interaction cost (Pirolli et al., 2005). A short article that is also designed for skimming (lots of bullet points) has lower interaction cost than an essay or a book chapter (heh). Reading a Tweet is a lower interaction cost than clicking through to an article. Glancing at a meaningful image is less effort than reading a Tweet's text. But the format of images matters too (something to keep in mind if you are sharing data visualizations, posters, etc.). For example, Lam (2008) treats visual clutter as its own form of interaction cost, because visual clutter requires you to dedicate mental effort orienting yourself to the content, which increases the cognitive load (Mayer & Moreno, 2003).

Minimize Cognitive Load

Cognitive load is how much mental burden it requires to understand a scientific product you share (Mayer & Moreno, 2003). In terms of the going viral cycle, it is a factor that both determines whether people will grasp what you post, and it is also a form of interaction cost. There are two types of cognitive load: The first is intrinsic cognitive load, which comes from the material itself. Sadly for you, since it is science you are trying to reach people with, the intrinsic cognitive load of your content is likely pretty high. That makes it extra important for you to focus on reducing the second, controllable type of cognitive load: extraneous cognitive load (which comes from how the material is presented).

Mayer and Moreno (2003) summarized nine evidence-based strategies for lowering the extraneous cognitive load of any design. Here are two particularly relevant ones:

1. *Eliminate redundancy* – You are trained in science to repeat yourself often (e.g., restating something in your intro, hypotheses, and results). But showing people something they have already seen wastes cognitive load on filtering out redundant content. Combine it.
2. *Weeding* – Eliminate interesting but nonessential information. This is particularly hard for scientists. Researchers are rewarded for thinking of and including every nuanced detail you can think of. And leaving something out is punished, like you are lying by omission. But online, you want to convey one point quickly and then maybe link them to all the secondary stuff.

Some Examples of Low Interaction Cost, High-Value Products

There are many scientific communications that meet the "lazy-valuable" ideal. The simplest example is just a Tweet or post that shares a short takeaway about some research you like, or a tip you learned about some method. Here are some more: The YouTube channel Two Minute Papers summarizes new research papers as short animations or presentations. Another example is a "flipbook" science GIF, which our first author Mike helped popularize in the #TwitterPoster YouTube cartoon (Morrison et al., 2020). You can see examples under the hashtag #TwitterPoster on Twitter.

The basic idea behind a #TwitterPoster is that you create five slides about your research in PowerPoint with big images and big takeaway statements (big enough to read on a mobile phone). You can save this as an animated GIF and post it on Twitter, and people just have to stare at it and watch the few slides advance to learn a little bit about your science. You can also save the same presentation slides as separate images and put them on Instagram as an album post, and users can swipe through your five research slides. Or put them on both Twitter and Instagram!

Even better than a five-slide explainer about your research is a one-slide explainer. If you can summarize a key scientific idea in a single, powerful image, that can spread like wildfire. For example, one medical doctor posted a side-by-side X-ray image of a healthy lung beside one infected with COVID-19. I have also seen scientists summarize a method by creating a looping GIF animation of a process.

As a final note, your science products do not have to be low interaction cost if they maintain a high rate of return for attention. A clear, engaging, 45-min tutorial video about a statistical method that lots of people struggle with can outperform a boring or confusing shorter video. And you do not have to just summarize findings. You can create resources, lists, archives, code, and tutorials – if it helps you, it can help somebody else too!

Level 6: Reach 10,000 People with Your Science

Reaching more people will require you to produce content that other people share with each other, versus you having to attract each person individually. And that likely means transmitting emotion with your content. As scientists we are cultured to think that making our science emotional is beneath us and belongs only to the realm of marketing and pseudo-science. This kind of thinking hinders science communication.

First, Guadagno et al. (2013) suggested that the emotion conveyed by content on the Internet is what initiates and perpetuates the viral sharing cycles. That is, when people share content on the Internet, it is a feeling they are trying to share. So, if you want to get the shares, you got to hit the feels.

Second, communicating emotion supports learning and engagement (Tyng et al., 2017). Several fields have found evidence that people receive communications on multiple, separate "channels." You have a visual channel, where you process the imagery of a post or video, and a verbal channel, where you process spoken words (and written words, to the extent that the voice in your head verbalizes them to you). And you have an emotional channel, which Mikels and Reuter-Lorenz (2019) refer to as an affective working memory. As a science communicator, you can maximize your impact by making all these channels sing together.

For example, let us say that you have found that a certain chemical gets released when a mouse learns a behavior. So, you create a #TwitterPoster with a text statement explaining the effect (verbal channel) and an image of a mouse (visual channel). It sounds like a fine science communication product. But you are missing the emotional channel! In a tangible way, many science communications neglect the emotional processing channel, which likely results in them being less learnable and less shared.

There are a bunch of ways you could fix this: Is the mouse happy to learn? Is this chemical being released helpful, or harmful? Any science can be made emotional. Even if you are a material scientist studying a new kind of rigid fiber, "rigid" can be the feeling you transmit. Color, font, imagery, and word choice all affect the emotion. When in doubt, try a Google Images search for the emotion you want to target. You will get lots of color and imagery ideas.

As a final note, if you can make your science funny, do that.

Level 7: Reaching 100,000 People and Beyond

> If you were hit by a truck and you were lying out there in that gutter dying, and you had one time to sing one song...One song that people would remember before you're dirt.... –Walk the Line

You can maximize the reach of your science by associating it with high-arousal emotions (e.g., humor, anger, excitement, distress, elation, fear), perhaps especially anger (Guadagno et al., 2013). Paradoxically, in order to do this, you may have to stop "caring" about reach and communicate an aspect of your work that *you* feel high arousal emotions about. This may not be your primary research interest. In Mike's case (first author), a major health scare made me feel desperate for the entire system of science to speed up and save me. That is what lead to the talk Let's Make Science User-Friendly (Morrison, 2018) and then to #betterposter (Morrison, 2019). I went viral the instant I stopped trying to go viral and started trying to improve lives (including my own) with my science communications. If you want to maximize your reach, do not just aim for meaning. Aim for change.

Conclusions and Practical Recommendations

At minimum, try to make sure that most scientific products you produce in your career (posters, publications, presentations, classes you teach) exist online somewhere in free-to-access form (link to Open Science Chapter 9). If you habitually upload a preprint for every paper you write, post the PDF on Figshare.com for every poster you make, and get a friend in the audience to record your conference talks so you can put them on YouTube – you will likely reach far more people with your science than the average researcher. And most of those actions take less than 5 min each.

If you want to boost your reach a little, start consciously communicating your research interests online somehow. Write blogs or articles – anything, or make a Buzzfeed.com listicle out of your science if you want – or post some videos on YouTube or post some pictures from your field work on Instagram. If you want to boost your reach a lot, find other researchers in your area on some social media platform (academic Twitter is particularly strong), and join the broader conversation in your field. Eventually, you will start figuring out how to package and communicate your science so it is easy to learn and interesting and has a feeling to it. If you are lucky enough to find a scientific topic that you personally care about – a change you want to make in the world with your science – then you will likely end up hitting a home run (reaching tons of people and making a difference) eventually.

You can learn more about many of the principles and theories referenced in this chapter (e.g., information foraging theory) way by watching the #betterposter Generation 2 cartoon, which illustrates many of them (applied to scientific posters, but the principles generalize) (Morrison, 2020). Templates for the #TwitterPoster-animated GIF posters can be downloaded from the Open Science Framework at https://osf.io/6ua4k/, and examples can be seen on Twitter under the hashtag #TwitterPoster. All these resources are under a Creative Commons–universal license, which means you, your organization, and/or your students can use and modify them freely without crediting the author or asking permission.

Remember, whatever science you do, it matters a lot to somebody. And that person hopes you are wildly successful in spreading what you are learning. Try to keep sight of that and draw meaning from it, because meaning is contagious (and addictive!).

References

Côté, I. M., & Darling, E. S. (2018). Scientists on Twitter: Preaching to the choir or singing from the rooftops? *Facets, 3*(1), 682–694.

Gruzd, A., Staves, K., & Wilk, A. (2011). Tenure and promotion in the age of online social media. *Proceedings of the American Society for Information Science and Technology, 48*(1), 1–9.

Guadagno, R. E., Rempala, D. M., Murphy, S., & Okdie, B. M. (2013). What makes a video go viral? An analysis of emotional contagion and Internet memes. *Computers in Human Behavior, 29*(6), 2312–2319.

Jia, H., Wang, D., Miao, W., & Zhu, H. (2017). Encountered but not engaged: Examining the use of social media for science communication by Chinese scientists. *Science Communication, 39*(5), 646–672.

Lam, H. (2008). A framework of interaction costs in information visualization. *IEEE Transactions on Visualization and Computer Graphics, 14*(6), 1149–1156.

Mayer, R. E., & Moreno, R. (2003). Nine ways to reduce cognitive load in multimedia learning. *Educational Psychologist, 38*(1), 43–52.

Mikels, J. A., & Reuter-Lorenz, P. A. (2019). Affective working memory: An integrative psychological construct. *Perspectives on Psychological Science, 14*(4), 543–559.

Moran, K. (2020, April 5). *How people read online: New and old findings*. Nielsen Norman Group. https://www.nngroup.com/articles/how-people-read-online/

Morrison, M. (2018, May 29). Let's make science user-friendly|Mike Morrison. [Video]. YouTube. https://www.youtube.com/watch?v=WBjhxjWDiHw

Morrison, M. (2019, March 25). How to create a better research poster in less time (#betterposter Generation 1)|Mike Morrison. [Video]. YouTube. https://www.youtube.com/watch?v=1RwJbhkCA58

Morrison, M. (2020, July 13). How to create a better research poster in less time (#betterposter Generation 2). [Video]. YouTube. https://www.youtube.com/watch?v=SYk29tnxASs

Morrison, M., Merlo, K., & Woessner, Z. (2020). How to boost the impact of scientific conferences. *Cell, 182*(5), 1067–1071.

Pirolli, P., & Card, S. (1995, May). Information foraging in information access environments. In *Proceedings of the SIGCHI conference on Human factors in computing systems* (pp. 51–58).

Pirolli, P., Fu, W. T., Chi, E., & Farahat, A. (2005, July). Information scent and web navigation: Theory, models and automated usability evaluation. In Proc. HCI International.

Stillman, T. F., Lambert, N. M., Fincham, F. D., & Baumeister, R. F. (2011). Meaning as magnetic force: Evidence that meaning in life promotes interpersonal appeal. *Social Psychological and Personality Science, 2*(1), 13–20.

The Conversation. (2020). *Our audience – The conversation*. https://theconversation.com/au/audience#:%7E:text=The%20monthly%20audience%20across%20all,%25)%20and%20female%20(53%25).&text=91%25%20of%20readers%20would%20recommend%20The%20Conversation.

Tyng, C. M., Amin, H. U., Saad, M. N., & Malik, A. S. (2017). The influences of emotion on learning and memory. *Frontiers in Psychology, 8*, 1454.

Williams, R. (2014). *The non-designer's design book* (4th ed.). Peachpit Press.

Zimmerman, M. D., & Wiernik, B. M. (2020, April 25). Interests and self-efficacy: One construct or "Related but distinct"? [Poster Presentation]. *Society for industrial and organizational psychology conference*.

Part IV
Research Outside of Academia

Chapter 17
Exploring the Horizon: Navigating Research Careers Outside of Academia

Rachel Carey

Abstract Given the growing number of PhD graduates and the breadth of research opportunities that exist beyond academia, there is no singular, linear path to a successful research career. Researchers are applying and enhancing their skills in charities, corporations, consultancies, local authorities, health services, start-ups, and a variety of other settings. For researchers who are curious about their options, there is a dizzying maze of pathways to consider. This chapter aims to shine a light on what non-academic research careers can look like, including some of the opportunities and challenges involved. It explores the reasons researchers might choose to pursue applied research roles, the steps we can take towards finding them, and the parts of the learning curve that can feel particularly steep. Focusing on the environment of new start-ups, it discusses the ways in which early-stage innovation can foster collaboration and creativity and its role in advancing scientific knowledge. It ends with a few final reflections and recommendations, including a discussion of the need for greater permeability between different research settings, and visibility of the opportunities and impact created by applied research.

Keywords Applied research · Start-up businesses · Innovation · Impact · Transferable skills · Collaboration

The Stories We Tell Ourselves

A few years ago, I was delivering a talk about my career journey so far to an audience of undergraduates. It struck me, hearing it out loud, how straightforward and coherent a narrative there appeared to be – as though my career movements had been following

---

R. Carey (✉)
Zinc, London, UK

Department of Clinical, Educational and Health Psychology, University College London, London, UK

© The Author(s), under exclusive license to Springer Nature Switzerland AG 2022
D. Kwasnicka, A. Y. Lai (eds.), *Survival Guide for Early Career Researchers*, https://doi.org/10.1007/978-3-031-10754-2_17

the flow of a river whose path had gently and uneventfully guided me along. It was strange to think of it this way, because of course, at the time, most of the journey had felt more like navigating choppy waters, squinting into the distance, surrounded by fog.

The stories we tell ourselves, and those we tell others, are powerful. They play an important role in helping us to make sense of our decisions, our identities, our life purpose and our careers (Cohen & Mallon, 2001). They allow us to connect our experiences to our current and future self-concept (Ibarra & Barbulescu, 2010), constructing a kind of causality, coherence and continuity that helps us to derive meaning from our experiences. Through stories and narratives, we engage in a 'dynamic process of career narrative construction' (LaPointe, 2010). This storied way we approach our careers helps us to find common threads. But the real-time experience is usually very different from the overarching rationale we create later. When we approach a fork in the road and have to decide, there is rarely any way of knowing if we are getting it right.

When I left academia, I first joined a newly formed behavioural science team in a large corporate setting. A year or so later, I joined the small team of a brand-new organisation called Zinc, as Chief Scientist. Over the last 5 years, I have spoken to and worked with dozens of PhD graduates who went on to pursue non-academic jobs. They are working in charities and corporations, consultancies and local authorities, health services and start-ups. One or two are clear on where they want to get to; most are on a journey of experimentation and exploration.

We are a growing community. Exact figures vary, but data from the UK, US and elsewhere suggest that it is a minority of PhDs across the sciences who secure tenured faculty positions in academia. The UK's Higher Education Policy Institute, for example, suggests that somewhere over 70% of PhD graduates are working outside of academia after three and half years (HEPI, 2020). Businesses and not-for-profits now employ as many PhDs as universities do (National Science Foundation, 2017).

Despite this, to a lot of PhD graduates, perhaps especially in the arts, humanities and social sciences, the world outside of academia can seem opaque. This chapter summarises some of my reflections on the opportunities and challenges for scientists working outside of traditional research settings. One obvious caveat is that I am coming at this from a specific perspective – much of the content below is based on my own and colleagues' experiences; it is not intended to be representative of the different pathways that exist, or the different experiences that researchers can have. My aim is to shine a light on what pursuing research roles outside of traditional academic settings can look like and to share recommendations for researchers who are curious about their options.

Forks in the Road

I did not start my PhD with the intention of pursuing an academic career. It is not that I explicitly *did not* want to be an academic; I just did not set out with that end goal in mind. I did my PhD straight after my undergraduate degree, primarily out of an interest and curiosity in my area of science and – honestly – the appeal of having a few more years of university life and research training before deciding what to do next.

It is easy to assume that most people do PhDs in order to pursue an academic career. While there are data to suggest that a majority of postdocs do want to stay in academia (Van der Weijden et al., 2016; Aarnikoivu et al., 2019), this unsurprisingly varies across individuals, disciplines and contexts. One paper suggests that, in Germany, PhDs are not as directly associated with pursuing a career in academia, compared to contexts like the US (Mueller et al., 2015). There are certain disciplines, like computer science or engineering, where the roads towards non-academic jobs are well-developed and well-worn. Others are more nascent.

Towards the end of my PhD, I started thinking seriously about an academic career. Colleagues around me were applying for postdocs and lectureships, and those paths – while tough – at least seemed clear. I understood what they involved and how my skills would translate. I took a role as a postdoctoral researcher in University College London, working with Professor Susan Michie, and spent a couple of years leading a fascinating and challenging project exploring how behaviour change interventions work (e.g. see Carey et al., 2019; Michie et al., 2021).

It was an extraordinarily valuable experience, and the connections and knowledge I gained opened up exciting opportunities. Coming into the project's final stages, though, I found myself curious about non-academic roles. The clarity and structure associated with the typical academic career path, that clarity that had once been attractive, were beginning to feel slightly oppressive. I felt I knew exactly what it would take to be a successful academic in today's context, and I found it hard to reconcile with the kind of work and life I cared about. I wrote about this at the time in a piece for the *Times Higher Education* (Carey, 2015).

Although I was curious, the world of research outside of higher education was a blur. I knew people who had made the move, but I found it almost impossible to imagine their day-to-day role. Moreover, being an academic had increasingly become a part of my identity, and I worried leaving it behind would feel like failure.

Push or Pull?

There is a lot of debate and discussion about why researchers, particularly early career researchers (ECRs), leave academia. Much of the discussion centres on what we might call 'push' factors: for example, the more negative aspects of the academic culture and structure. A recent report, drawing on survey results from 4000 respondents, found that research culture is leading to unhealthy competition, bullying and harassment and mental ill-health (Wellcome Trust, 2020). Postdocs are often subjected to stressful and taxing working environments and experience high levels of anxiety. One study found that work stress directly and indirectly related to postdocs' intention to leave academia (Dorenkamp & Weiß, 2018). This stress is likely to be at least partly driven by precarious, fixed-term research contracts – creating what has been referred to as 'postdoc purgatory'.

But job precarity and work stress are not the full story. Many researchers choose to leave academia not because they are driven out, but because they are attracted to what is on the outside. There is a perception that the best ECRs pursue academic careers and that those careers present the best opportunities for job satisfaction (Sinche et al., 2017). This assumption that the default, optimal path is the academic one and that moving into a more applied setting must be, at best, 'Plan B' does a disservice to the breadth of opportunities that exist elsewhere. As one *Nature* careers commentary (Kruger, 2018, p. 133) puts it: '...*scientists can start by appreciating a simple truth: researchers who leave academia are not failed academics [...] Students and their supervisors must begin to regard a PhD programme as a traineeship in scientific thinking and an invaluable qualification for a diverse range of careers. If everyone involved in academic science could accept a variety of roles as the default outcome, we could change our flawed definition of success*'.

The language of these discussions matters. After deciding to leave academia, it took me a long time to shake off the singular image that I had internalised about what a successful research career looks like. The shift in identity and purpose was, at times, painful and isolating. Reframing these narratives is becoming even more important and urgent, as we are producing more PhDs than ever before (Cyranoski et al., 2011) – OECD data (2013) show a 38% increase in the number of PhDs awarded between 2000 and 2009. We can advocate for change within academia while at the same time supporting and valuing researchers' decisions to work in other settings.

Navigating the Maze of Options

For ECRs who have decided, for whatever reasons, that they are interested in finding a job outside of academia, the first steps can seem overwhelming. Most of us do not prepare for non-academic jobs during our doctoral training (Morrison et al., 2011; Van der Weijden et al., 2016), and we feel ill-equipped to navigate the search: the number and range of options, the terminology and the application process. In particular, understanding the extent to which our skills translate to new roles and organisations can be daunting.

One report from Eurodoc (Weber et al., 2018) provides a useful summary of broad skills that are relevant to increasing the employability of ECRs (e.g. critical thinking, presenting, teamwork and collaboration). However, some research has highlighted mismatched expectations between the skills ECRs *think* are important and those that non-academic employers are actually looking for (e.g. see De Grande et al., 2014). Companies will often value general scientific research skills more than highly specialised but narrow 'topic knowledge' (Blomfield, 2020). Looking back, this tallies with my own misperceptions – I underestimated the value in more general research skills (e.g. survey design, experimental methods, literature reviewing, qualitative research, intervention development, data analysis) while probably overestimating the attention that would be paid to specific subject matter expertise. This prevalent narrative persists, despite evidence that a majority of broad skills developed and honed through PhD training are versatile and transferable to research and non-research careers outside of academia (Sinche et al., 2017).

Hiring social and behavioural scientists in businesses, governments, health services, charities and elsewhere is not a new phenomenon, and many organisations have growing research teams. Former academic colleagues of mine who have gone on to work in big tech companies are working in research teams the size of small universities. Many large, international companies are recognising the value of scientists who have the tools to understand human behaviour, a skillset that is at the heart of good product development, employee engagement and customer satisfaction. For some organisations, though, this is a newer capability they are looking to build, and there will not always be ready-made roles to step into. In many organisations, there is scope to 'job craft': to tailor or change the structure and content of the role (Lichtenthaler & Fischbach, 2019) depending on what is needed or what you are interested in.

There are a lot of events and courses designed to support ECRs who want to upskill in a particular area (e.g. in business, technology, policy). In my view, while these can be helpful, getting hands-on experience will often be a better use of time – for example, through internships, consulting, collaboration or job shadowing. This on-the-job learning strengthens job applications and also helps to paint a more granular picture of what applied research roles look like in practice.

There is no silver bullet, and different approaches will work for different individuals and organisations. Although time consuming, searching and applying for jobs, and getting experience working on applied projects, can demystify the types of research roles that exist, the language that is used and the skills required.

Learning and Unlearning

The first phase of any new job is tough. We are taking in lots of new information, and everything feels effortful. It is a steep learning curve, and it involves a period of acclimatisation and ambiguity. Many of the challenges I highlight below are not unique to the move from academia to industry; adapting to the demands of any new workplace is a stressful process (Ellis et al., 2015). Becoming familiar with a new culture, structure, values and working practices takes time, and the nuances of 'organisational socialisation' (see Klein et al., 2015) and onboarding will vary. Much of this requires a certain amount of unlearning – for example, leaving behind previous behaviours and ways of working (Becker & Bish, 2021).

For most new employees, adapting and assimilating requires us to adopt, to some extent, a new language. Businesses are full of jargon and baffling buzzwords. You do not need to go to business school to understand them, and the underlying concepts are often more familiar than the language used to describe them, but it does take a while. I spent a lot of time, during my first year or so in industry, writing down lists of acronyms to look up later, or looking quizzically at colleagues for a translation. It took even longer to get used to the bewildering assortment of metaphors – moving needles, boiling oceans, taking things offline, closing loops, pushing back, diving deep, etc. (the list is endless) – that seemed to be taken for granted as common parlance. These initial, inevitable hurdles can make an already unfamiliar environment seem even more alien, particularly when moving across sectors.

Another challenge many scientists face, where research is less well-established within the organisational culture or structure, is the need to act as an internal champion for science. For most of us, this means finding a balance: advocating for the value of research and evidence while also managing expectations about what can and cannot be achieved. For social and behavioural scientists, this can be particularly tough – the rising profile of behavioural science means that misperceptions about its nature and potential impact are rife.

Many of the behavioural scientists I know who have worked in businesses have been asked to produce a business case for their work, or to show its return on investment. These are not easy tasks (particularly considering that measuring the impact of social science research has always been a challenge; see Marar, 2019). Some of them have felt they were expending more effort justifying their theoretical existence than demonstrating their value. At the same time, these exercises can give us a worthwhile opportunity to redefine what research excellence and research impact really mean in our specific context – free from the traditional structures to which they are usually tied.

In a broader sense, assimilating as a scientist in industry can feel like trying to reconcile two dramatically different cultures. Uncertainty is core to good science. In business (and in other settings, like government), communication of uncertainty can be complicated. In the early days of one of my jobs, I was asked to share my views on an emerging area of technology that I did not know a lot about. After overcoming my first instinct, which was to respond with some version of 'I couldn't possibly comment', I spent some time reviewing the published literature, speaking to experts and synthesising evidence. Over time, I have become more comfortable responding to these questions with something along the lines of 'I have no idea, but give me a few hours and I'll see what I can find out'. I hope it goes without saying that I am not advocating for researchers advising off the cuff on areas that fall outside of their expertise, which clearly poses a range of risks. Many of us in applied research roles, however, do need to get more comfortable offering input based on a relatively quick bit of desktop research while making clear to highlight relevant caveats. This move to being more of a generalist is a strange and difficult part of the journey, but it has meant, for me, learning about many interesting areas and reading a *lot* of scientific literature – even more, perhaps, than I did when I was in academia.

Collaboration and Creativity

I have highlighted some of the challenges ECRs might experience when transitioning across different research roles. In the next two sections, I want to highlight a couple of the most exciting opportunities. One study exploring scientists' experiences in Austrian biotechnology companies (Fochler, 2016) described a selection of the positive aspects of working in science-rich, high-growth companies. Researchers in this study reported more control and collaboration in their industry role, compared to the kind of individualised and competitive culture they experienced in academia. They described the context in which they now work as rewarding new spaces 'in which they could engage in research differently' (p. 276).

The opportunities for autonomy and collaboration that these scientists found in their industry roles, which mirror my own experience, demonstrate the potential for these types of companies to foster good science and attract good scientists. The pace, of course, takes some getting used to. Business priorities change rapidly and often, and we need to get used to the ground constantly shifting beneath our feet. At the same time, seeing a project underway, and its learning implemented, within days or weeks rather than months or years can be rewarding and refreshing.

Collaboration with people from other disciplines and sectors was always a particularly enjoyable aspect of my academic work, and I have found this to be an even greater priority in the business roles I have had. Working in early-stage innovation means working not just with scientists from different disciplines, but with technologists, creative designers, marketers, product managers and others. Bringing divergent perspectives around the table and trying to align on priorities and plans is not always easy and can feel like everyone is pulling in different directions. But, when done well, this complementary teamwork can facilitate cross-pollination of ideas and produce higher-quality decisions and innovations (Loving, 2020).

A lot of the frameworks that businesses, particularly start-ups, are familiar with align well with social science approaches. An example is *design thinking*, a process used by entrepreneurs, innovators, designers and researchers to find solutions to complex problems. A lot of the components of design thinking, such as observation, synthesis, critical thinking, user research and testing (Black et al., 2019), are synergistic with theories and principles from behavioural science and health psychology. Researchers recognise the importance of these kinds of tools in developing usable and engaging products (Ben-Zeev & Atkins, 2017), and several studies have integrated these approaches to design interventions (e.g. see Mummah et al., 2016; Scholten & Granic, 2019). The complementarity between these approaches can also be seen in the number of social scientists, like anthropologists, moving into *user experience* (UX) research roles.

One of my favourite books, *The Emperor of All Maladies* (Mukherjee, 2010), talks about how great science emerges out of great contradiction; it often takes working with people who have different, even opposing, perspectives to create fresh ways of thinking and meaningful change. This is a particularly exciting time for inherently interdisciplinary fields (such as computational social science; see the recent editorial in *Nature*, 2016) to contribute to societal challenges and advance empirical knowledge.

Start-Ups as Centres of Knowledge Production

The reflections above come from my experience working in a very particular applied setting: the world of innovation and start-ups (for more details, see Carey, 2020). The early stages of innovation involve a series of experiments and research projects, and there are a range of opportunities for social scientists to derive benefit and add value. The lean, agile and design-led approaches in start-ups mean that they are continually testing, iterating and adapting. These processes can be made more robust, and their outcomes more valuable, through in-house scientific talent working side by side with technological, creative and commercial leads. While the pace is a step change from academic research, and there will inevitably be trade-offs in rigour and control; the kind of rapid research opportunities provided by start-ups can make important contributions to science.

The role of start-ups as knowledge creators is not new, but the role of scientists in service sector innovation in general has not always been visible – compared to, for example, the contribution of science to innovation in the world of manufacturing (Wealth, 2009). These days, innovation is being driven by in-house social scientists in big tech, financial services, digital health companies, insurance industries and beyond. Commercial science in biotechnology companies has adopted many of the conventions associated with academic research – in some cases accommodating academic norms better 'than does the academy itself' (Vallas & Kleinman, 2008, p. 302).

If designed in the right way and by facilitating 'new cultures of knowledge production' (Fochler, 2016, p. 260), companies can attract and retain top scientific talent who can, in turn, facilitate collaborations with other researchers and scientists – within and outside of academia. As our applied science community continues to grow and diversify, we have an opportunity to build new and better bridges with each other and with academia.

Conclusions and Recommendations

The best advice I got, when I was starting out on this journey, was to invest in building relationships and growing my network (see Chap. 8). Having this community is important not just in finding new jobs, but in supporting us through those jobs too. One of the things I miss about academia is the availability and proximity of researchers whose brains you can pick and whose support you can rely on. Recreating these kinds of networks in applied roles is important. These days, I am part of several groups, networks and communities (for example, on Slack, WhatsApp and LinkedIn) where applied scientists come together and exchange learnings.

I do not know anyone who has seamlessly transitioned into different roles without second-guessing themselves. As highlighted by Locke et al. (2018), there is rarely one traditional, linear path in any career. In their words (p. 55):

> Perhaps we should avoid thinking of early career researchers as a homogenous group pursuing a traditional linear path from undergraduate and masters study through postgraduate research, a post-doctoral position and into full-time permanent employment as a lecturer in higher education.

Careers involve a patchwork of experiences and experiments, and we make the best decisions we can with the knowledge available to us at the time. Contrary to what we might think, these decisions are not irreversible. Moving into a non-academic job should not be a one-way street, nor should it necessarily mean leaving everything about our academic roles behind. I have an honorary university contract and still teach on a couple of undergraduate and postgraduate modules. Many people have spent time outside academia after their PhDs and then come back to academic jobs. Research funders are increasingly supportive of this permeability and mobility.

In my experience of speaking to scientists working outside of academia and in much of the research I have read (e.g. Morrison et al., 2011), PhD graduates report high levels of engagement and job satisfaction in their roles and maintain their identity as scientists and researchers, regardless of their settings. As scientists, we often approach big career decisions in the way we would other tasks: systematically weighing up the pros and cons, doing our research, analysing and optimising. But this is not a perfect science. There is always uncertainty; there are always leaps of faith. And, despite the tales we might tell afterwards, it rarely feels like smooth sailing at the time.

References

Aarnikoivu, M., Nokkala, T., Siekkinen, T., Kuoppala, K., & Pekkola, E. (2019). Working outside academia? Perceptions of early-career, fixed-term researchers on changing careers. *European Journal of Higher Education, 9*(2), 172–189. https://doi.org/10.1080/21568235.2018.1548941

Auriol, L., Misu, M., & Freeman, R. (2013). *Careers of doctorate holders: Analysis of labour market and mobility indicators*. OECD Science, Technology and Industry Working Papers, No. 2013/4, OECD Publishing. https://www.oecd-ilibrary.org/science-and-technology/careers-of-doctorate-holders_5k43nxgs289w-en

Becker, K., & Bish, A. (2021). A framework for understanding the role of unlearning in onboarding. *Human Resource Management Review, 31*(1), 100730. https://doi.org/10.1016/j.hrmr.2019.100730

Ben-Zeev, D., & Atkins, D. C. (2017). Bringing digital mental health to where it is needed most. *Nature Human Behaviour, 1*, 849–851. https://doi.org/10.1038/s41562-017-0232-0

Black, S., Gardner, D. G., Pierce, J. L., & Steers, R. (2019). Design thinking. *Organizational Behavior*. https://opentextbc.ca/organizationalbehavioropenstax/chapter/design-thinking/

Blomfield, M. (2020). Hiring for knowledge or skills: How do firms use scientific human capital acquired from academia? In *Academy of management proceedings* (Vol. 2020, No. 1, p. 21305). Academy of Management.

Carey, R. N. (2015, April 30). *Would John Williams' stoner survive today?* Times Higher Education Supplement. https://www.timeshighereducation.com/comment/opinion/would-john-williams-stoner-survive-today/2019905.article

Carey, R. N. (2020, July 27). *Connecting social science and start-ups to tackle important problems*. LSE Blog, https://blogs.lse.ac.uk/businessreview/2020/07/27/connecting-social-science-and-start-ups-to-tackle-important-problems/.

Carey, R. N., Connell, L. E., Johnston, M., Rothman, A. J., de Bruin, M., Kelly, M. P., & Michie, S. (2019). Behavior change techniques and their mechanisms of action: A synthesis of links described in published intervention literature. *Annals of Behavioral Medicine, 53*, 693–707. https://doi.org/10.1093/abm/kay078

Cohen, L., & Mallon, M. (2001). My brilliant career? Using stories as a methodological tool in careers research. *International Studies of Management & Organization, 31*(3), 48–68.

Cyranoski, D., Gilbert, N., Ledford, H., Nayar, A., & Yahia, M. (2011). Education: The PhD factory. *Nature News, 472*(7343), 276–279. https://doi.org/10.1038/472276a

De Grande, H., De Boyser, K., Vandevelde, K., & Van Rossem, R. (2014). From academia to industry: Are doctorate holders ready? *Journal of the Knowledge Economy, 5*(3), 538–561. https://doi.org/10.1007/s13132-014-0192-9

Dorenkamp, I., & Weiß, E. E. (2018). What makes them leave? A path model of postdocs' intentions to leave academia. *Higher Education, 75*(5), 747–767. https://doi.org/10.1007/s10734-017-0164-7

Editorial. (2016). Young researchers thrive in life after academia. *Nature, 537*(7622), 585. https://doi.org/10.1038/537585a

Editorial. (2021, July 01). The powers and perils of using digital data to understand human behaviour. *Nature*. https://www.nature.com/articles/d41586-021-01736-y

Ellis, A. M., Bauer, T. N., Mansfield, L. R., Erdogan, B., Truxillo, D. M., & Simon, L. S. (2015). Navigating uncharted waters: Newcomer socialization through the lens of stress theory. *Journal of Management, 41*(1), 203–235. https://doi.org/10.1177/0149206314557525

Fochler, M. (2016). Beyond and between academia and business: How Austrian biotechnology researchers describe high-tech start-up companies as spaces of knowledge production. *Social Studies of Science, 46*(2), 259–281. https://doi.org/10.1177/0306312716629831

Higher Education Policy Institute. (2020). *The employment of PhD graduates in the UK: What do we know?* Retrieved from https://www.hepi.ac.uk/2020/02/17/the-employment-of-phd-graduates-in-the-uk-what-do-we-know/

Ibarra, H., & Barbulescu, R. (2010). Identity as narrative: Prevalence, effectiveness, and consequences of narrative identity work in macro work role transitions. *Academy of Management Review, 35*(1), 135–154. https://doi.org/10.5465/AMR.2010.45577925

Klein, H. J., Polin, B., & Leigh Sutton, K. (2015). Specific onboarding practices for the socialization of new employees. *International Journal of Selection and Assessment, 23*(3), 263–283. https://doi.org/10.1111/ijsa.12113

Kruger, P. (2018). Why it is not a 'failure' to leave academia. *Nature Commentary, 560*(7716), 133–135. https://doi.org/10.1038/d41586-018-05838-y

LaPointe, K. (2010). Narrating career, positioning identity: Career identity as a narrative practice. *Journal of Vocational Behavior, 77*(1), 1–9. https://doi.org/10.1016/j.jvb.2010.04.003

Lichtenthaler, P. W., & Fischbach, A. (2019). A meta-analysis on promotion-and prevention-focused job crafting. *European Journal of Work and Organizational Psychology, 28*(1), 30–50. https://doi.org/10.1080/1359432X.2018.1527767

Locke, W., Freeman, R., & Rose, A. (2018). *Early career social science researchers: Experiences and support needs*. Centre for Global Higher Education, UCL Institute of Education. https://www.researchcghe.org/perch/resources/publications/ecrreport.pdf

Loving, V. A. (2020). Collaborative interdepartmental teams: Benefits, challenges, alternatives, and the ingredients for team success. *Clinical Imaging, 69*, 301–304. https://doi.org/10.1016/j.clinimag.2020.10.003

Marar. (2019, May 29). The changing imperative to demonstrate social science impact. LSE Blog. https://blogs.lse.ac.uk/impactofsocialsciences/2019/05/29/the-changing-imperative-to-demonstrate-social-science-impact/

Michie, S., Johnston, M., Rothman, A. J., de Bruin, M., Kelly, M. P., Carey, R. N., et al. (2021). Developing an evidence-based online method of linking behaviour change techniques and theoretical mechanisms of action: A multiple methods study. *Health Services and Delivery Research, 9*(1), 1–168. https://doi.org/10.3310/hsdr09010

Morrison, E., Rudd, E., & Nerad, M. (2011). Early careers of recent US social science PhDs. *Learning and Teaching, 4*(2), 6–29. https://doi.org/10.3167/latiss.2011.040202

Mueller, E. F., Flickinger, M., & Dorner, V. (2015). Knowledge junkies or career builders? A mixed-methods approach to exploring the determinants of students' intention to earn a PhD. *Journal of Vocational Behavior, 90*, 75–89. https://doi.org/10.1016/j.jvb.2015.07.001

Mukherjee, S. (2010). *The emperor of all maladies: A biography of cancer*. Simon and Schuster.

Mummah, S. A., King, A. C., Gardner, C. D., & Sutton, S. (2016). Iterative development of Vegethon: A theory-based mobile app intervention to increase vegetable consumption. *International Journal of Behavioral Nutrition and Physical Activity, 13*(1), 1–12. https://doi.org/10.1186/s12966-016-0400-z

National Science Foundation. (2017). *Survey of doctorate recipients, survey year 2017*. https://ncsesdata.nsf.gov/doctoratework/2017/index.html

Scholten, H., & Granic, I. (2019). Use of the principles of design thinking to address limitations of digital mental health interventions for youth. *Journal of Medical Internet Research, 21*(1), e11528. https://doi.org/10.2196/11528

Sinche, M., Layton, R. L., Brandt, P. D., O'Connell, A. B., Hall, J. D., Freeman, A. M., et al. (2017). An evidence-based evaluation of transferrable skills and job satisfaction for science PhDs. *PLoS One, 12*(9), e0185023. https://doi.org/10.1371/journal.pone.0185023

Vallas, S. P., & Kleinman, D. L. (2008). Contradiction, convergence and the knowledge economy: The confluence of academic and commercial biotechnology. *Socio-Economic Review, 6*(2), 283–311. https://doi.org/10.1093/ser/mwl035

Van der Weijden, I., Teelken, C., de Boer, M., & Drost, M. (2016). Career satisfaction of post-doctoral researchers in relation to their expectations for the future. *Higher Education, 72*(1), 25–40. https://doi.org/10.1007/s10734-015-9936-0

Wealth, H. (2009). The contribution of science to service sector innovation. *The Royal Society Science Policy Centre*. https://royalsociety.org/~/media/royal_society_content/policy/publications/2009/7863.pdf

Weber, C. T., Borit, M., Canolle, F., Hnatkova, E., Pacitti, D., Parada, F., & O'Neill, G. (2018). *Identifying and documenting transferable skills and competences to enhance early-career researchers employability and competitiveness*. Eurodoc. https://munin.uit.no/handle/10037/19744?show=full

Wellcome Trust. (2020). *What researchers think about the culture they work in*. https://wellcome.org/reports/what-researchers-think-about-research-culture.

Chapter 18
An Alternative Career Path: Research and Evaluation in the Health Service and Not-for-Profit Sectors

Jenny Olson

Abstract Research and evaluation work in the not-for-profit and/or health service sector offers an alternative and potentially rewarding career path for early career researchers. Funding bodies are moving towards outcomes-based funding models, with an increasing onus on recipients to demonstrate the impact of programs and services. Thus, demand for individuals with the capacity to coordinate program evaluation will likely continue to grow. The skills typically attained through doctoral research are relevant to this type of work. Data management in real-world settings requires a flexible, pragmatic approach. Communication, advocacy and negotiation are essential to ensure stakeholders are engaged in evaluation processes. Depending on the organisation, opportunities may exist to contribute to knowledge translation, lead the production of manuscripts for peer review or be involved with grant writing and other research-related activities. Salaries in this sector may not be competitive and fixed-term employment contracts linked to 'soft money' funding arrangements are common; however, in my situation work-life balance seemed far more attainable. This chapter describes my experience as a Research and Evaluation Coordinator working for a not-for-profit health service provider in Australia over 12 months during the COVID-19 pandemic. If you are considering this type of work, I hope you find it enlightening.

Keywords Career path · Research · Evaluation · Health services · Not-for-profit · Knowledge translation · Industry

Introduction

Working in health services or the not-for-profit sector was not part of my plan. I graduated with a PhD in Psychology in September 2019 and was keen to progress my career as a research academic in behavioural science. I was doing part-time

J. Olson (✉)
Penn State University, University Park, PA, USA

© The Author(s), under exclusive license to Springer Nature Switzerland AG 2022
D. Kwasnicka, A. Y. Lai (eds.), *Survival Guide for Early Career Researchers*,
https://doi.org/10.1007/978-3-031-10754-2_18

research at an Australian university and searching nationally and internationally for a postdoctoral position. I was shortlisted for several jobs, and in February 2020, I accepted a role as Research Fellow at an R1 university (i.e. doctoral university – very high research activity) in the United States. Yep – you know what happened next! Cue – the global pandemic. I had finished up at my previous job and had no idea when, or even if, I would be able to start my new position. Luckily, a colleague recommended me for a short-term contract as a Research and Evaluation Coordinator at a local not-for-profit health service organisation. It seemed like a great stopgap to keep the money flowing in while I waited a couple of months for things to get back to normal.

Err ... I may have underestimated that one! I ended up staying in the position for almost a year. At first, I was worried that I would lose my shot at an academic research career. Academia is so competitive (Larson et al., 2014), and as many women unfortunately know, career disruption can be a real disadvantage (Klocker & Drozdzewski, 2012). In this case, it worked out ok for me. I learnt a lot – about working with clinical populations, chronic disease and the challenges of evaluating health programs and services in the real world, and importantly, I grew to understand the perspectives of health service providers. I also managed to write several first author publications, collaborate on a couple of funding applications, establish industry connections and build some fabulous friendships.

My fellowship eventually did go ahead, and my husband and I moved our life to the other side of the world in the middle of the pandemic. I could write a whole other chapter on that – but I will save that story for another day! As a result of my experience outside of academia, I have adopted a more pragmatic approach to my research – which I hope will translate to real-world impact as I develop as an independent researcher.

Overall, my time working for a health service provider in the not-for-profit sector was great, but like any job, it was not without challenges and frustrations. In this chapter will try to give a balanced overview of what it was like – the opportunities, the benefits and the challenges. These are my personal reflections of working for a not-for-profit health service organisation in Australia. Not everyone's experiences or interpretations will be the same. Nevertheless, if you are considering a career outside academia, I hope you find this chapter useful (also see Chap. 17 – on working in industry by Rachel Carey).

The Job, the Skills Required and a Note on Mentorship

The primary purpose of my position was to coordinate the evaluation of government-funded diabetes self-management education and support programs delivered by independent service providers in each state and territory of Australia. Evaluation was guided by a National Evaluation Framework (Olson et al., 2021) and involved work at all stages of the evaluation cycle, including: (a) identification of program aims, outcomes and objectives; (b) development, implementation, assessment and adaptation of evaluation plans; (c) coordination of data collection across settings, matching participants across multiple time points and managing large datasets; (d) data analysis; (e) reporting; and (f) making recommendations for quality improvement and future evaluations.

An example may help to illustrate the type of work involved in planning, implementing and assessing program evaluations. Imagine a new program is being implemented for people with type 2 diabetes. First, you would work with the program developers, administrators and funders to articulate the program aims. Let us say the main objective is to reduce diabetes distress. You will need to decide how to operationalise and measure diabetes distress. Ideally, you will use a measure where scores have previously been validated in a similar population. You will need to determine when and how the outcome and other variables, like demographics, will be measured (e.g. with an electronic survey at baseline, on program completion and 3 months post program). You will plan how the evaluation will be implemented (e.g. who is responsible for identifying participants, sending surveys, collecting and reporting data; what checks and balances will be incorporated to ensure data collection is occurring as planned; how participant data will be merged and matched across time points). You will also need to develop a plan for how the data will be cleaned and analysed. You will need to identify key stakeholders for reporting program outcomes and understand their requirements and preferences for reporting.

Finally, you will conduct statistical analyses, interpret findings and consider your recommendations for quality improvement for inclusion in a written report to be disseminated to stakeholders. You may also need to present findings orally to stakeholders. You should be able to clearly articulate whether the program reduced diabetes distress and, if so, to what extent (hint – clinical significance may be more important than statistical significance here). As a result of your work, the leadership of the not-for-profit sector and representatives of funding bodies will make decisions about the feasibility of continuing to offer the program, by carefully weighing costs and benefits. Stakeholders may also make decisions to change the program based on your recommendations, in the hope of achieving more impactful outcomes in the future. And then, the whole cycle of evaluation starts again!

I was able to apply many of the skills I had gained through my academic training. A solid understanding of quantitative and qualitative research methods was important, along with highly developed oral and written communication skills and the capability to manage projects involving multiple stakeholders. The ability to wrangle large and unwieldy datasets, match data collected across multiple time points and perform fundamental statistical analyses was also necessary. Think frequencies, descriptives, t-tests, chi-squared tests and content analysis. Nothing particularly challenging, but competency and confidence to independently conduct basic statistical analysis without guidance from an in-house stats expert were essential.

As a postdoc in a lab or research group, you will usually receive mentorship from a professor and/or other experienced researchers. You may even receive support from a biostatistician or an institution's methodological resource centre. This kind of support and access to resources and mentors provides an excellent opportunity to continue to grow your skills and knowledge, building on what you learned as a grad student (Faupel-Badger et al., 2015). Depending on the organisational structure of the non-profit or health service organisation, you may not have proximal access to mentors with knowledge of cutting-edge research methodology or advanced statistical analyses when working in this type of setting. I spent a lot of time troubleshooting problems online and teaching myself new skills and methods (also see Chap. 10 on being agile and gaining new skills by Olga Perski). You will certainly receive mentorship in other areas. For instance, I had little knowledge of diabetes, diabetes self-management education and support programs or challenges of service provision and evaluation in real-world settings when I first started. Nor did I have experience working in a not-for-profit setting, within an organisation reliant on external funding for survival, as most not-for-profit and some research institutes are. I worked with a multidisciplinary team of health professionals and administrators with a wealth of expertise and knowledge. My colleagues generously shared their time, knowledge and expertise with me. We were all working with the same goal in mind – providing optimal support to people with diabetes. I also sought mentorship from colleagues outside of the organisation when needed. My colleagues in the university sector were also generous with their time and advice.

The Challenges

Program evaluation in real-world settings can be challenging (Funderburk & Shepardson, 2017). Managing data collected without the resources, expertise and controls typically observed in an academic research setting can be frustrating, confusing and downright annoying. There may be missing, duplicate or indecipherable data, data-entry errors, datasets received from stakeholders well after the deadline and not in the format you asked for, missing participant identifiers making matching participants across time points impossible and more (Bamberger & Mabry, 2019). It will probably take more time than you ever imagined possible to clean, verify and match data. I do not know about you, but this is not my idea of a fun time at work!

In addition to having great problem-solving skills and patience for the more mundane tasks, strong stakeholder engagement skills are key. The benefits and nuances of evaluation are not always clear to health practitioners and administrators, but the engagement of these individuals is critical across every stage of the evaluation cycle (Bamberger & Mabry, 2019). For instance, when planning an evaluation, it may be difficult for health practitioners and administrators to identify, articulate or operationalise the specific outcomes and objectives of programs and services. Health professionals may be understandably reluctant to interrupt or extend consultations or educational programs to collect evaluation data. Employees and volunteers in the field may not understand the importance of collecting identifying information that makes it possible to match participants in pre-, post- and follow-up analyses. Resources for data entry may be limited in some organisations or may be performed by volunteers or workers who are not experienced in database management and may not attend to the task with the attention to detail that is needed. These factors can impact the quality of the data you are tasked with analysing. Advocating for the importance of evaluation and coaching, mentoring and encouraging stakeholders so that they are willing and able to support evaluation procedures is probably the most important part of the job. A little empathy can go a long way in these situations. It is important to take the time to understand the priorities and challenges faced by the stakeholders you are engaging with. Then work with them to find mutually beneficial solutions that minimise burden.

Moreover, unbiased reporting of evaluation findings can be challenging (Bamberger & Mabry, 2019). There may be tension between the desire for continuous quality improvement and the need to highlight programs that are less effective than others, particularly in the context of competitive outcomes-based funding upon which organisations are reliant for survival. Individual service providers may have competing agendas and priorities which impact their preferences for the way evaluation findings are presented and emphasised. In reality, these service providers are likely competing with each other for a limited pool of funding. Likewise, funding bodies and administrators will have their own agendas, which will influence requirements for reporting, communicating and acting on the findings of program and service evaluation. These challenges warrant effective communication and negotiation to ensure everyone understands the protocols for reporting and disseminating evaluation findings and engages with recommendations for quality improvement.

The Extra Stuff

Once I had learned how to do the fundamentals of my job, I was ready and willing to contribute more. I am passionate about health psychology and behavioural science and was keen to use my skills to benefit the community my organisation served. So, I started to look for opportunities to do so. By engaging with my colleagues throughout the organisation, I identified several opportunities to put my skills and expertise to good use.

Knowledge Translation

After talking with my colleagues, I realised that my ability to identify and interpret scientific research could support knowledge translation for the treatment and self-management of diabetes within the community we were serving. Effective knowledge translation is key to ensuring optimal clinical care and service delivery (Eljiz et al., 2020). Knowledge translation targeted to patient populations can support education, communication and decision-making, skill acquisition, behaviour change and participation in the consumer system and provide personal support (Chapman et al., 2020). However, the communication of research to diverse audiences can present a challenge for early career researchers; such challenges can be overcome with hands-on experience, thereby enhancing self-efficacy (i.e. belief in one's capability to perform the task) and building expertise in research communication (Mason & Merga, 2021). By nature, not-for-profits and health service providers have direct access to consumers and patients, those that provide them with physical and emotional support and their health care practitioners. Thus, I had an excellent opportunity to build my own skills in research communication while facilitating enhanced knowledge translation within the community in which I was working.

I volunteered to write a column in a quarterly glossy-print magazine distributed to people with diabetes throughout Western Australia (Olson, 2020a, b). The column, written in everyday language, focused on communicating established behavioural and cognitive approaches to supporting the adoption and maintenance of health behaviours conducive to optimal diabetes self-management, such as healthy eating, physical activity, medication adherence, self-monitoring, problem-solving, healthy coping and behaviours to mitigate risks of complications (e.g. foot care). Topics for the column included tactics to improve coping and reduce distress and tips for establishing healthy habits. I also identified relevant literature, summarising it in lay language for inclusion in a range of electronic and print publications distributed directly to people with diabetes. This work required staying up to date with the latest evidence on diabetes, self-management education and support and evaluation practise. However, this can be challenging with much medical research hidden behind paywalls, rendering it inaccessible without paid subscription (Day et al., 2020). Not-for-profit organisations and health service providers may be unable or unwilling to spend limited funds on providing access to expensive scholarly databases (which again emphasises the need for Open Science; see Chap. 9 by Emma Norris).

I also had the opportunity to contribute to knowledge translation targeted to health practitioners. For instance, I worked with a colleague to develop and present a webinar for health professionals, advising them on how to provide support to their patients to discern the quality of health information (and identify misinformation) accessible online and through the popular press. I also had the opportunity to write content for an online education program for general practitioners (primary care practitioners) on how to have conversations with patients about weight management, grounded in principles of behavioural science, patient-centred care and avoidance of language and actions that contribute to weight stigma.

Even though my focus was not necessarily on generating new scientific knowledge, the opportunity to facilitate knowledge translation to people with diabetes and to health practitioners was personally and professionally satisfying, aligned well with the 'why' for choosing my research pathway (see Chap. 19 by Amy Chan) and comes with the bonus of looking great on my resume.

Publishing and Grants

Even though I was enjoying the work I was doing, I was still holding out hope of returning to my academic career. This fuelled a desire to continue publishing, in addition to looking for research funding opportunities. Publishing in high-impact factor journals is a key goal for early career researchers, particularly in the context of the precarious employment status we typically face at this stage of our career (Nicholas et al., 2017). In my situation, the desire to publish was well received by members of the senior management team. Governments and funding agencies or commissioning bodies are increasingly adopting outcomes-based models of funding, and ongoing contracting for services may depend on health service providers demonstrating program impact (Gold & Mendelsohn, 2014). In this context it is critical that organisations can clearly demonstrate the outcomes and impact of programs and services they provide. Peer-reviewed publications provide an excellent way to present evidence of the impact of health programs and services to funding bodies. Peer-reviewed literature produced by health practitioners can also provide a valuable source of evidence for improving treatment methods and patient outcomes; however, there are numerous barriers that may preclude practitioners from contributing to scientific publications (Harvey et al., 2020).

Writing for scientific journals requires unique skills that may be developed through doctoral studies (Jalongo et al., 2014), whereas health professionals and administrators working for not-for-profits or health service providers may not typically hold these skills. Thus, the skills and experience I had in this area were relatively novel (there was another recent PhD graduate in my department, also on a short-term contract) and provided an opportunity to document some of the great work being undertaken within the organisation. After 12 months, together we had submitted five papers to scientific journals for peer review, including manuscripts detailing the development of a National Evaluation Framework (Olson et al., 2021), the process undertaken to adapt an online self-management program for type 2 diabetes for the Australian context (Olson et al., 2020), the impact of the COVID-19 pandemic on Western Australians with diabetes and on health service utilisation (Olson et al., in press), the results of 4 years of evaluation of a program designed to support self-management of carbohydrate intake (Mergelsberg et al., 2021b) and another describing the experiences of people with diabetes when admitted to hospitals as in-patients (Mergelsberg et al., 2021a).

I also identified relevant research-related funding opportunities and collaborated with my colleagues to write grant applications. This also required networking and collaborating with research academics and local, national and international institutions to advise and partner on funding applications. I found this work to be a little more challenging than leading and contributing to peer-reviewed publications, and unfortunately, none of the applications were successful. Research funding is extremely competitive, and in some circumstances, the track record of investigators can be heavily weighted in funding decisions (Reed, 2019). Unfortunately, as with most early career researchers, my track record was in its early stages. One option was to collaborate with one or more senior investigators from academic institutions. This can raise complex issues related to where the funding will be directed, contractual arrangements for services, ownership of intellectual property and who will own the program or service that is developed because of the work. An alternative is to apply for program or service funding, rather than research funding. This can allow the development and implementation of new and exciting programs and services, yet rarely provides accompanying resources for extensive research activity.

If you are interested in pursuing funding in the not-for-profit or health service sectors, seek mentorship for colleagues inside and outside of your organisation, and think carefully about what you want to achieve. Will you be satisfied with funding that allows for the implementation or development of new programs, but does not provide resourcing for research? Can you establish mutually beneficial partnerships with academic colleagues with transparent and documented agreements on issues like intellectual property and ownership of programs and resources? It is also important to consider whether administrators within your organisation and the academic institution would accept the terms of such agreements.

Opportunities for Doctoral Graduates in Industry

The numbers of doctoral-level graduates are increasing worldwide. High proportions of those graduates may wish to pursue careers in academia; however, opportunities are extremely limited, and the selection process is highly competitive. Only a very small proportion will attain job security (a.k.a. tenure), and fewer still will rise to the rank of professor. There are also numerous doctoral graduates that have no intention of ever pursuing a career in academia (see Chap. 17 on working in industry by Rachel Carey). Working for non-profit organisations or health service providers is an alternative career path for those not interested in pursuing an academic career.

Governments and funding or commissioning bodies are increasingly adopting outcomes-based models of funding. This necessitates that not-for-profits and other organisations vying for this type of funding need to be able to demonstrate the outcomes of the services and programs that they provide. Thus, there is likely to be continuing growing demand for program evaluation specialists, with the skills and expertise to develop and implement evaluation frameworks, evaluate programs and services through quantitative and qualitative methods, report evaluative findings and make recommendations to ensure continuous quality improvement. The increasing availability of jobs in program evaluation represents additional opportunities for people with the type of skills acquired when completing a higher research degree. However, given the reliance of external sources of funding in these sectors, many opportunities are likely to be in the form of fixed-term contracts. Salaries may not be particularly competitive, although in many countries, there are unique benefits available to those who work in the non-profit sector (e.g. salary packaging to reduce tax liability). Thus, those looking to avoid the job uncertainty that is ubiquitous within academia may be disappointed to learn that the stress and anxiety of 'soft-money' appointments can also be an issue in the not-for-profit sector.

On the flip side of less-than-competitive salaries and employment insecurity, work-life balance might be more attainable outside of academia. For nearly a year, I never received out-of-hours emails, messages, or phone calls (after the first couple of weeks, I actually checked if there was something wrong with the mail app on my phone, not believing that there were actually no emails). Over that year, I worked additional hours on only one occasion. This was to finalise an annual report due to the funding body. Even then, there was no pressure to stay back, and my additional efforts were recognised and appreciated. The pace of daily work was also more relaxed. I took lunch away from my desk every day. I also went for a 20-min walk on most days. Of course, this was my experience working for one organisation within this sector – I cannot speak to the generalisability of my experience! I was truly part of a team of wonderful and supportive people. They were friendly and caring (and had jigsaw puzzles in the lunchroom and 'bring your dog to work days'). We had diverse skills and took the time to share our skills with one another. We had each other's backs. If one person was struggling, for whatever reason, we all pitched in. From that standpoint, it was one of the best jobs I have ever had.

Conclusions and Practical Recommendations

Doctoral graduates have skills and expertise that can be adapted for the world outside of academia. This type of work can be extremely rewarding, providing an opportunity for more direct impact with consumers, health professionals and policymakers. In my case it also provided the opportunity to attain a healthy work-life balance. This may be offset by non-competitive salaries and precarious employment arrangements (i.e. repeated, short-term contracts that are dependent on the attainment of extramural funding).

Based on my experience, my tips and advice for graduates and early career researchers considering a move to research and evaluation in health services or the not-for-profit sector include:

- Do not underestimate the utility of the skills you gained throughout your academic training. Many of these skills will be highly relevant and valued in research and evaluation roles. You will also possess skills that are novel in this type of setting. This expertise can be leveraged for the benefit of your organisation and others while giving you an opportunity to contribute more to your particular area of interest.
- Find ways to build on your existing skills. Spend time talking with others in your organisation and learning about what they do. There are often opportunities to attend courses and seminars facilitated by external providers. Seek external mentors to augment the support and mentorship you receive from within the organ-

isation. It is useful to maintain contact with academic colleagues and collaborators at local, national and international institutions.
- Be prepared to adopt a more pragmatic and flexible approach to your work outside of highly controlled research settings. Data collection, dataset management, analysis and reporting in real-world settings can be messy and there is no place for dogmatic or rigid methodological approaches.
- If you are passionate about impact, look for opportunities to use your specialist skills and expertise to facilitate knowledge translation to consumers, patients, health practitioners and policymakers. You can contribute to bridging the gap between research and practice!
- If you are keen to keep ties with academia, look for opportunities to collaborate. This might include producing peer-reviewed publications or applications for grant funding. Beware, research-related funding may be challenging without the leadership of an experienced investigator with a strong track record.
- It may be easier to achieve work-life balance outside of academia. However, it is likely you will not escape insecure employment arrangements inherent with 'soft-money' positions. Salaries may not be as competitive, but money cannot buy time!
- If you are curious, give it a shot! At a minimum, you will acquire new knowledge and experience and probably make new friends along the way!

References

Bamberger, M., & Mabry, L. (2019). *RealWorld evaluation: Working under budget, time, data, and political constraints*. Sage Publications.

Chapman, E., Haby, M. M., Toma, T. S., de Bortoli, M. C., Illanes, E., Oliveros, M. J., & Barreto, J. O. M. (2020). Knowledge translation strategies for dissemination with a focus on healthcare recipients: An overview of systematic reviews. *Implementation Science, 15*(1), 14. https://doi.org/10.1186/s13012-020-0974-3

Day, S., Rennie, S., Luo, D., & Tucker, J. D. (2020). Open to the public: Paywalls and the public rationale for open access medical research publishing. *Research Involvement and Engagement, 6*(1), 8. https://doi.org/10.1186/s40900-020-0182-y

Eljiz, K., Greenfield, D., Hogden, A., Taylor, R., Siddiqui, N., Agaliotis, M., & Milosavljevic, M. (2020). Improving knowledge translation for increased engagement and impact in healthcare. *BMJ Open Quality, 9*(3), e000983. https://doi.org/10.1136/bmjoq-2020-000983

Faupel-Badger, J. M., Raue, K., Nelson, D. E., & Tsakraklides, S. (2015). Alumni perspectives on career preparation during a postdoctoral training program: A qualitative study. *CBE – Life Sciences Education, 14*(1), ar1. https://doi.org/10.1187/cbe.14-06-0102

Funderburk, J. S., & Shepardson, R. L. (2017). Real-world program evaluation of integrated behavioral health care: Improving scientific rigor. *Families, Systems & Health, 35*(2), 114–124. https://doi.org/10.1037/fsh0000253

Gold, J., & Mendelsohn, M. (2014). *Better outcomes for public services: Achieving social impact through outcomes-based funding*. Mowat Publication. Retrieved from https://tspace.library.utoronto.ca/handle/1807/99269

Harvey, D., Barker, R., & Tynan, E. (2020). Writing a manuscript for publication: An action research study with allied health practitioners. *Focus on Health Professional Education: A Multi-disciplinary Journal, 21*(2), 1–16.

Jalongo, M. R., Boyer, W., & Ebbeck, M. (2014). Writing for scholarly publication as "tacit knowledge": A qualitative focus group study of doctoral students in education. *Early Childhood Education Journal, 42*(4), 241–250. https://doi.org/10.1007/s10643-013-0624-3

Klocker, N., & Drozdzewski, D. (2012). Commentary: Career progress relative to opportunity: How many papers is a baby's worth'? *Environment and Planning A, 44*(6), 1271–1277.

Larson, R. C., Ghaffarzadegan, N., & Xue, Y. (2014). Too many PhD graduates or too few academic job openings: The basic reproductive number R0 in academia. *Systems Research and Behavioral Science, 31*(6), 745–750. https://doi.org/10.1002/sres.2210

Mason, S., & Merga, M. (2021). Communicating research in academia and beyond: Sources of self-efficacy for early career researchers. *Higher Education Research & Development, 1–14.* https://doi.org/10.1080/07294360.2021.1945545

Mergelsberg, E., Olson, J. L., Jensen, J., Watson, N., & McGough, S. (2021a). Recommendations to improve hospital experiences of people with diabetes in Western Australia: Allowing Self-Management is Key [Manuscript submitted for publication]. Diabetes WA.

Mergelsberg, E., Olson, J. L., Moore, S., Jensen, J., Seivwright, H., & Watson, N. (2021b). Providing evidence from practice: 4.5 years of diabetes self-management education support program evaluation [Manuscript submitted for publication]. Diabetes WA.

Nicholas, D., Watkinson, A., Boukacem-Zeghmouri, C., Rodríguez-Bravo, B., Xu, J., Abrizah, A., Świgoń, M., & Herman, E. (2017). Early career researchers: Scholarly behaviour and the prospect of change. *Learned Publishing, 30*(2), 157–166. https://doi.org/10.1002/leap.1098

Olson, J. L. (2020a). Discussing diabetes: Diabetes and healthy habits. *Diabetes Matters,* 13. Diabetes WA.

Olson, J. L. (2020b). Discussing diabetes: Why keeping on top of your mental health is good for managing diabetes. *Diabetes Matters.* Diabetes WA.

Olson, J. L., Hadjiconstantinou, M., Luff, C., Watts, K., Watson, N., Wagstaff, A., Miller, V. M., Schofield, D., & Calginari, S. (2020). From the UK to Australia: Adapting an online self-management education program to support the management of type 2 diabetes: A tutorial. *JMIR Preprints.* https://doi.org/10.2196/preprints.26339.

Olson, J. L., White, B., Mitchell, H., Halliday, J., Skinner, T., Schofield, D., Sweeting, J., & Watson, N. (2021). The design of an evaluation framework for diabetes self-management education and support programs delivered nationally. *Four Square Preprint.* https://doi.org/10.21203/rs.3.rs-264927/v1.

Olson, J. L., Mergelsberg, E., Jensen, J., Schofield, D., & Watson, N. (in press). COVID-19 concerns, health service utilisation, and social support among Western Australians with diabetes during the pandemic. *Evaluation Journal of Australasia, 21,* 206–225.

Reed, M. (2019). *Writing your impact track record for NHMRC.* Retrieved August 22, 2021, from https://www.fasttrackimpact.com/post/2019/08/03/writing-your-impact-track-record-for-nhmrc

Chapter 19
Asking Why and Saying Yes: How to Make Career Decisions Strategically

Amy Hai Yan Chan

Abstract As researchers, we are often presented with many possibilities and opportunities that could take us down very different paths in our career. This is particularly true for early career researchers, when we are starting to establish our independence and finding our own niche. It is important to be strategic when making career decisions, as a single decision early on can have a big impact on where you end up in the future. In this chapter, I will cover how our careers are shaped by the decisions we make and how to be strategic about our careers, including personal examples of where my decisions have led me throughout my career so far. I will discuss the importance of not losing sight of your 'why' – your reason for doing research, how to weigh up and evaluate your opportunities, why it is worth saying 'yes' more often than 'no' and, above all, that to be strategic is simply *to be kind*.

Keywords Career planning · Research · Career development · Motivation · Decision-making · Opportunity · Strategy · Goal setting · Early career · Long-term goals

Why a Research Career?

When I started my PhD, I did not have a clue what the next few years would look like. I did not know that my degree would be so self-guided, and that for the most part, a PhD research degree is about developing your thinking and your skills and honing your critical thinking, rather than conducting the actual research or engaging in research tasks. As I got more and more immersed into my research, my reasons for wanting to have a research career began to shape up. I started realising that with each finding ('knowledge brick' as my supervisor would call it) emerging from my research, I was adding to a much bigger 'knowledge wall', building on the findings

A. H. Y. Chan (✉)
School of Pharmacy, Faculty of Medical and Health Sciences, The University of Auckland, Auckland, New Zealand

© The Author(s), under exclusive license to Springer Nature Switzerland AG 2022
D. Kwasnicka, A. Y. Lai (eds.), *Survival Guide for Early Career Researchers*, https://doi.org/10.1007/978-3-031-10754-2_19

of others to further the scientific field and ultimately improve humanity in some way. That realisation – which came about two-thirds of the way into my PhD – both humbled and excited me.

That reason – the chance to add to the knowledge wall and in some way to improve people's lives through my work – was, and still is, my primary driver and reason for choosing a research career. But the strength of this reason has waxed and waned over time. When it came towards the end of my PhD, after struggling for seemingly years on the same topic, my reason for doing research was more about the ability to travel and meet people. I could not wait to go on to my first big overseas conference and to book a trip to enjoy the European summer in Barcelona. As I met others involved in research along the way, the rewards I got from meeting like-minded people who were equally as enthusiastic (and lost) as I felt in the research world, who enjoyed a good philosophical discussion about the pros and cons of academic life, became more of a driver than the research itself.

This experience overseas turned out to be one of the key turning points in my life and had a big impact on my next career decision. I was a couple of months out from finishing my PhD with no clear plan of where to go next. I was working in a relatively senior clinical management position at the local hospital, as a result of my decision to remain in clinical training whilst doing my PhD part-time, but with my newfound reason – the desire to connect with others and travel – continuing to work there no longer appealed to me so much, though it did provide a stable income. I wanted to do something that could expand my horizons, challenge me intellectually and satiate my desire to meet new people and explore new cultures and countries. When I heard that one of the key professors in my field of research was coming to our institution for a visit, I decided to drop an email introducing myself and my research. It was what they call a 'cold contact' in job-hunting terms – he had no idea who I was – I had not even thought to connect via a mutual connection or colleague. In hindsight, it might have been better, if I had reached out through a colleague who knew us both, but at the same time, I thought – *what do I have to lose?* The worst outcome would have been a non-response to my email – plus, as you will read in the next section about making the most of your 'doors', this visit was an opportunity – a potential door to be pushed open – so why not?

The decision to meet the visiting professor turned out to be very fruitful. After I had handed in my PhD, I had opportunities to continue to work at the hospital and at the university where I had done my PhD, but when I came back to asking myself about my purpose and values – and my key reason for wanting a research career – it was clear that I needed to explore options outside of my current city and country. The meeting with the professor led to me landing my first official postdoctoral fellowship with the prestigious University College London (UCL) in the UK, some 18 months later. I had not realised at the time just how important that connection would come to be, all of which was driven by my 'why'. This driver was what pushed me to continue applying for jobs overseas, and connect with overseas experts, and even to explore applying to do a masters' degree so I could have the opportunity to live overseas – a potentially 'backwards' step after completing a

PhD. Yet my drive to go overseas was so strong that I explored every option, figuring these connections and experiences would still be valuable, even if it might seem to some that I was going 'backwards' in my career. At the end of the day, my strategy worked well. By focusing on what I really wanted – an experience overseas to meet new people – I was able to achieve what I wanted.

Finding out your motivators can also shape how you find opportunities. Sometimes it can be difficult early in your career to know where you are going in life – what you career path should be and what the ideal job might look like. When you are not certain exactly what your dream job or 5-year plan should be, it helps to go back to your key 'why' in life and visualise what that experience might look like. For example, one of my key reasons for doing research was to help others and to somehow benefit humankind through my work. For me, an academic job was one way to achieve this, but the timelines of this career are often long and drawn out. It is not always clear how your work might benefit society until years down the track. With this in mind, I went to search for opportunities where I might be able to apply my skills to benefit others in a more immediate way.

I had long dreamed of working for an institution like the World Health Organization (WHO) and being able to provide input into global health in some way, but I did not have the connections or the right experience to start. I decided to do a Google search to scope out how I might be able to apply my skills to global health, not really knowing what I might come across. Scrolling through hits on global and health and medicines (in line with my research interests), I came across the Commonwealth Pharmacists' Association, a global health charity with a vision to improve the health and well-being of the commonwealth. I did not know anything about the organisation but thought that there would not be any harm in reaching out to see what would happen. I sent a 'cold call' email to the 'contact us' page, introducing my research experience and background and simply asking whether they would be interested in getting help with some of their work. After a few days I got an email from the Executive Director asking for my CV and then to meet for a coffee.

Soon after, I started volunteering for the organisation, getting involved in health policy and advocacy – areas that I never thought I would have a chance to work in. The experience opened my eyes to the inner workings of global health charities and to different ways to apply my research skills. After a few years, I became an advisor and later the Research Lead, working closely with the International Pharmaceutical Federation (FIP) – another global health organisation representing over 4 million pharmaceutical scientists and professionals and was an observer with the WHO. Through these relationships, I became a Global Lead for the FIP, connecting with members of the WHO. It was all because of that one email many years ago, leading me to one thing after another, closer and closer to what I had dreamt of – to be part of an organisation I had previously thought was impenetrable. All of these opportunities were driven by my key motivator, a drive to make a difference and to be open to seeking opportunities.

Turning Roadblocks into Opportunities

'*When one door closes, another opens*'. I heard this often from people around me, trying to console me as I commiserated over another roadblock in my research path. Roadblocks and setbacks are not unfamiliar to early career researchers. I often reflect and bemusedly wonder why so many of us continue to forge this path. When I try to explain my job to people outside research and academia, describing the myriad of grant applications and papers to write and the rejection rate, it makes me wonder if any other occupations have such high setback rates. With only approximately 1 in 10 grants being funded in each round on average (if we are lucky, depending on the geographic region and funding body) and with many high-impact peer-reviewed journals having a similar acceptance/rejection rate, it seems that the odds of 'success' are sobering. The likelihood of being rejected are much higher than the chances of being successful. If that were the case in any other job, surely one would choose to quit and do something where the chances of success are higher? Take a coffee barista, for example – if they knew that 9 out of 10 customers would be unsatisfied with their coffees, would they continue in that job?

Now this is by no means a way to convince you to put this book down and start searching for 'alternative careers to research' on Google. Rather, when thinking about opportunities and doors opening and closing, I ask, 'Are setbacks and roadblocks really roadblocks, or are they simply a way to guide and re-orientate you to a different direction down the research path?' It boils down to why we are on these research career path, of which both you and I know come down to many reasons: the idea that you know you are giving something back to society, that your ideas are in some way bettering the human race and leaving a legacy or simply because you are an inquisitive and curious soul, and you really want to find that answer to the burning question you have had since you were five (believe it or not, there are some researchers I know who chose a research career for that very reason – hats off to them for being that wee little Einstein from birth!). Of course, there are other more tangible benefits – time flexibility, autonomy, ability to travel, meet people, share ideas and be intellectually challenged. These are all good reasons to choose research as a career.

Reasons are important here, when we talk career paths. 'Knowing your why' (Sinek, 2009, 2019) will help answer the question that I posed before – 'do we need to wait for one door to close to open another'? When it comes to being strategic, my answer is a clear 'no' – and those who know me would know that in most cases my life motto is 'the answer is "yes" unless you can convince me it should be a "no"' (Rhimes, 2015). With that in mind, being strategic in career decisions becomes much simpler. It is not about reading more management consulting books, or reading more guidelines from funders to work out how to frame your research so that it will eventually get funded. Do not get me wrong – those are all important skills and an important part of writing grants – but those skills and approach are not the focus of this chapter.

What I am here to share is about your career path – in fact, one might argue, potentially your life. How you make career decisions and where you end up will no doubt influence your lifestyle and your life choices that you are able to make. When you think of it that way, being strategic is potentially the most important thing in your career. It all comes back to knowing what your motivators are – what pushes your buttons and gets you out of bed each morning? It could be different things for different people – if your passion is simply because you like 'learning and knowing new things', then structure your career choice around a job that can provide you learning opportunities and challenges your thinking regularly. If what is most important to you is stability and certainty in employment, then perhaps a job that offers a permanent role – such as healthcare consultancy or working in industry – may be better suited than fixed-term postdoctoral appointments. Being open to opportunities will help make sure you do not miss chances that align with your motivators when they come up. Every door that you see can, in fact, be opened. It is just up to you whether you go through it.

Let us explore below some of that strategic thinking – why it is important to 'know your why', how to evaluate the different doors that you might see, why you should say 'yes' more often than 'no' and the reason why, if you had to choose one word to guide your life by, it is 'kindness'. With that in mind, those 1 out of 10 chances of success will soon be looking much more like 9 out 10.

Knowing Your 'Why': What Is Your Reason

All of us are on this research pathway for different reasons. I alluded to some before and no doubt there are many others. Your reason can also change during your career, as your life circumstances change. For many, research is a lifelong commitment – not just a temporary job change – and it would be of no surprise that during your career, your life circumstances and your reasons for doing research will change. At the start, the key driver may be because you want to make a change for the world, to do 'good science' and to learn. Or it might simply be because you are not sure where you heading after finishing your undergraduate degree – and staying at university seems like the safest choice (I can admit that was partly the reason for me!).

Evaluating Your 'Doors'

This approach – of always coming back to your 'why' – is something I continue to come back to when pondering my next steps – whether looking at my career as a whole, or when thinking of shorter-term goals. As early career researchers, you may find that you are often asked to be involved in various activities, whether it is teaching, or helping to mentor a student, or collaborating on a proposal. In life, you will often be presented with opportunities that sometimes you might not even notice. We know from behavioural economics that the more options someone is presented with, the greater the cognitive load required to process those options, and the harder it is to make a wise decision (Deck & Jahedi, 2015). It is no different when it comes to career choices.

A good starting point is to begin from a position of 'yes' – however, time is finite and there are times you will need to be strategic with your decisions, weighing up which options are best. In these times, it is helpful to ask 'why am I doing this'? Or as my friend likes to ask 'what's the point'? The key is thinking about 'How does being involved in this activity, align with my motivators, my reasons why I do what I do and why I enjoy what I do (whether it is related to work or not)'? Sometimes the link is not obvious. For example, if your key motivator is to be as productive as possible in your research, then being asked to assist with teaching may not seem to be directly aligned.

However, there might be downstream benefits from saying yes, which may not be immediately obvious. For example, by helping with teaching, you could establish better relationships with faculty, who may later become important research collaborators or reviewers of your work. In some institutions, being involved in teaching is a requirement before you can be promoted to more senior roles. In that regard, when approaching a decision strategically, it would pay to weigh up (a) how it aligns with your 'why', (b) evaluating how it fits in the bigger picture, (c) how much time/resource it is likely to take (can you realistically fit this in, and if so, what are you compromising – and is it worth it?) and, finally, (d) do you want to do it (sometimes it may not be a clearly strategic move but you might want to do it simply because it is fun and enjoyable – a perfectly adequate reason for why!).

It can be hard to decide which door to open when we do not always have the information we need to help us evaluate the opportunities. Additionally, you might not yet know your 'why', or how well the opportunity aligns with your motivators, or perhaps you drivers for 'why' are changing all the time. In the face of such uncertainty, there are four things that I weigh up in my mind which may also be helpful for you:

1. *Is it easy?* If the opportunity feels like an easy one for you to be involved in, then it might be worth giving it a go – for example, if it does not impinge on your commitments or time, then it could be worth checking out.
2. *Does it add something?* Ask yourself – what does this opportunity bring? It does not necessarily have to be beneficial for you or for your career – the opportunity could bring benefits for someone else in your team, or may have positive personal impacts – for example, learning a new skill or meeting new people.
3. *Is it fun?* Sometimes an opportunity is worth doing simply because it is fun and enjoyable for you. If you happen to also gain something from being involved, then it is an even better bonus!
4. *Does it feel right?* There are times in life you just know whether something is right or not; if you have a 'gut' feeling that it does not feel right, or alternatively you feel like you would be missing out on an important opportunity if you said no, then it may be worth exploring your gut feeling further. Ask yourself: why do

you feel the way you do? Is there a reason why it feels so right, or uncomfortable?

When presented with many doors, do not forget that it is perfectly ok to walk past some of them without opening them, and even when looking through open doors, you do not have to walk through them. Remember, every time that you do enter a door, you are losing the chance to walk through another; so, it is important to consider each one carefully, which brings me to the next section – why saying 'yes' more often than 'no' is important.

Why Saying Yes Is Important

I was first approached to write this chapter as one of the editors mentioned to me that she thought I had been strategic in my career decisions to date. She asked me to think of what my number one tip would be in advising other early career researchers in their journey. When I pondered this, the first thing that came to mind was how I generally approach life: why not go for it? At least give it a try and have no regrets, right?

Now, this advice should be taken with a grain of salt. Being a 'yes' person is contrary to many other books that you could read about being strategic with your time. In fact, one might argue that to be strategic means you should be saying 'no' more often and protecting the most precious resource that you have – time. Saying 'yes' all of the time can have detrimental effects on your well-being and sanity, if you find you are running from one commitment to another (believe me, I have also been there – and would not recommend it!). However, all caveat emptor aside – this approach has served me relatively well in life and is the reason why it may seem to others that I have been 'strategic'– simply by adopting a 'yes' attitude, you are more likely to be presented with more opportunities to choose from in life that allow you to align your career better with your 'why'.

Saying 'yes' to most opportunities has helped me to extend my networks and led me to opportunities and jobs that I would not have otherwise had. It can also challenge you to try new things and meet people outside of your immediate comfort zone. When I took up my first postdoctoral position at UCL, I was approached to help organise the early career research day. I did not know anyone in the faculty beyond my own research team. Even though I felt a bit out of my depth with everyone else seemingly having already formed networks and groups from previous events, I said 'yes' and gave it a go. The experience turned out to be much more rewarding than I could have imagined. I got to meet other early career researchers who shared stories of similar issues to what I was facing – with getting funding and fixed-term contracts – and in a new country where I had just arrived, I got to join their social events and form a supportive network of friends. The experience led me to be nominated to be the departmental early career researcher's representative later in my fellowship, which turned out to be an important experience for my promotion later, as I needed to demonstrate examples of leadership. As you can see, one thing led to another, and it is one of those situations where I said 'yes' and just went with the flow, without knowing how important it would be later in my career.

Often the worst enemy of our success is our own mindset; saying 'yes' gives us the chance to grow, to try something new and to expand our horizons. Sometimes you are not sure what you are actually capable of until you give it a go, to fulfil your full potential. Saying 'yes' also gives you a positive 'can-do' attitude. Award-winning creator, producer and writer Shonda Rhimes highlights the same tip in her book 'Year of Yes' (Rhimes, 2015). Saying 'yes' opens new opportunities, invites collaboration and partnership. Empowers and affirms others, creates an environment where it is safe to learn and try new things and importantly means you can have more fun! All of these factors can help to improve job satisfaction and how your colleagues might view you – all positives which can add to your career and growth as a researcher.

Kindness: The One Word that Should Be Guiding Your Life Career

> Unexpected kindness is the most powerful, least costly, and most underrated agent of human change. –Bob Kerrey

Last but not least, the final tip is to remember to be kind and have some fun along the way! To be strategic is often to make the decision that will benefit most, whether it be your colleagues, or your students or yourself. In research, it is often not easy to see where the benefits or gains from your decisions may be until much later, and to that end, traditional tips for being strategic – such as evaluating options to weigh up whether the decision will benefit your career or not – are much less useful compared to a consultancy or corporate setting. The rewards that you may reap are much more likely to be realised years down the track, when you may not even connect that they were related to the decisions you made years ago. We know that at the end of the day, strategy is only meaningful in the context of society and people. By choosing kindness as the default response, and on days that might feel like groundhog day, you know you are having some fun at the same time, then you can rest assured that your decisions are 'strategic', as in that they will lead you down the best path for you at this time.

Research shows us that kindness can be motivating – and importantly being kind to others can make you happier (Curry et al., 2018), and people who are happy at work are 12% more productive than unhappy people (Oswald et al., 2015). Kindness also helps with establishing stronger relationships, which can help you progress more in your career. With that in mind – surely the statistics are clear –to be strategic and successful is ultimately to simply be kind.

Reflecting on the Opportunities

I started this chapter asking whether it is true that when one door closes, another opens. My answer to that is yes and no. The truth is the doors are always there – it is up to us to decide if we want to open more than one door at the same time, and if you do, which one are you going to walk through first, or to close one then open another, and sometimes, that it is ok to keep walking until you get to the door that resonates best with your motivators. Being strategic in your career should be synonymous with fun and kindness, with finding joy through finding your purpose and drivers for your work.

Even though a research career might seem fraught with setbacks at times, in what seems like a competitive world, it is possible to change that 1/10 success rate into a 9/10 if you keep coming back and you stay focussed on your why. Whilst grant and journal acceptance rates may still stay low, by focusing on what matters most to you and redefining what success means to you, it may suddenly be that the grant and publication numbers you were aiming for do not matter as much as the learnings that come with it and the people you meet along the way. By honing in on your key motivators, you may find that you end up choosing grants and journals that better represent your values and your work too, thus changing your acceptance rates. The best researchers I have met are those who have experienced setbacks and who have taken the opportunity to pause, reflect and re-evaluate their options – is the idea still worth pursuing? If so, are there others that I need to connect with to make this happen? Or do I need to rework into something new? The best ideas and innovations often come when we are challenged to think outside the box and to question our current path. None of these are truly 'setbacks' when you look at it like this – they are actually doors, opportunities for you to open and to strategically think: how does this fit in with my why? What would happen if I said 'yes' to other options or ways of doing things? And importantly, how does my decision impact others?

Conclusions and Practical Recommendations

- As an early career researcher, it is easy to feel overwhelmed and confused as to your next career path. Remember choices and opportunities are good things – try looking at where you are at now and seeing where there are untapped opportunities to embark on.
- Know your 'why' – your reason for getting up each day and for doing research should underpin all your decisions.
- When given opportunities, ask yourself whether it feels easy, adds to something for yourself or others, is fun or feels right.
- If feeling unsure, saying 'yes' is a good start when offered opportunities, to see where it might take you – often the worst enemy to our own success and development is our own mindset.

- Saying 'yes' gives you the chance to grow, try something new and expand your horizons. You may not know what you are capable of until you give it a go.
- Do not forget to have fun along the way – on days that may feel particularly gruelling, you know that if you are having some fun at the same time, you can rest assured that you are being 'strategic'.
- Above all, to be strategic is simply *to be kind*. Being kind to others makes you happier and more productive. As Ralph Waldo Emerson said – '*You cannot do a kindness too soon, for you never know how soon it will be too late*'.

References

Curry, O. S., Rowland, L. A., Van Lissa, C. J., Zlotowitz, S., McAlaney, J., Whitehouse, H. J. J., & o. E. S. P. (2018). Happy to help? A systematic review and meta-analysis of the effects of performing acts of kindness on the well-being of the actor. *Journal of Experimental Social Psychology, 76*, 320–329.

Deck, C., & Jahedi, S. (2015). The effect of cognitive load on economic decision making: A survey and new experiments. *European Economic Review, 78*, 97–119. https://doi.org/10.1016/j.euroecorev.2015.05.004

Oswald, A. J., Proto, E., & Sgroi, D. (2015). Happiness and productivity. *Journal of Labor Economics, 33*(4), 789–822.

Rhimes, S. (2015). *Year of yes: How to dance it out, stand in the sun and be your own person*. Simon and Schuster.

Sinek, S. (2009). *Start with why: How great leaders inspire everyone to take action*. Penguin.

Sinek, S. (2019). *Find your why*. Gramedia Pustaka Utama.

Chapter 20
How to Engage the Public in Research

Rebecca Pedruzzi and Anne McKenzie

Abstract As an ECR at Telethon Kids Institute (Telethon Kids) in Western Australia, I wanted to do the best research possible, yet I had little understanding of the importance of consumer involvement or involvement strategies. As Manager of Community Involvement at Telethon Kids, Anne developed and implemented an internationally recognised program to increase community involvement in research. Anne really challenged the status quo in health research across almost two decades of advocacy, training and research. I was fortunate to be guided by Anne through training workshops and via public involvement processes at Telethon Kids. This chapter is a culmination of insights and knowledge gained from both perspectives. To begin we open with two personal stories that emphasise the importance of public involvement in research and demonstrate the challenges faced by those new to the area. We then provide some definitions and benefits of engagement, highlight core principles and ways of working and conclude with practical solutions and support for the integration of involvement activities in research. We hope this guide will make public involvement less daunting and eventually a standard component of your research.

Keywords Public participation · Community participation · Stakeholder participation · Consumer advocacy · Community action

Introduction

From Rebecca I came to Telethon Kids not long after receiving my PhD. My first role was as a Senior Research Officer in Knowledge Translation across the 'Alcohol and Pregnancy' Research Focus Area. In my first week in this role, I was asked to create plain language summaries of research findings for community members in remote Western Australia. Up until this point I had very little knowledge or understanding of consumer and public involvement in research. I never really thought

R. Pedruzzi (✉) · A. McKenzie
Telethon Kids Institute, University of Western Australia, Nedlands, WA, Australia

© The Author(s), under exclusive license to Springer Nature Switzerland AG 2022
D. Kwasnicka, A. Y. Lai (eds.), *Survival Guide for Early Career Researchers*,
https://doi.org/10.1007/978-3-031-10754-2_20

about these skills or that they would be assessed and honed over the coming years. This task– which I assumed would take an hour of my time– was thoroughly critiqued and progressed in consultation with researchers, community members and communication experts who provided extensive review and details about language, design and appropriateness over the next month. I remember feeling baffled about the amount of time and resources dedicated to this task!

Sometime later I was asked to present my research ideas to our project's Community Reference Group for feedback. It quickly became clear that the group was not really engaged with the ideas I was presenting. I realised I had communicated my ideas about research without considering the community or their needs. Whilst I felt embarrassed and somewhat ill-equipped to work in this area, it was a major learning curve! From this point I decided I had to do better by involving consumers in setting the research agenda and priorities. I began to take an interest in how other researchers were involving the public in research and I become better informed via internal processes and training that aimed to support researchers to do involvement activities. Fast forward 2 years and it really clicked when I became a mother and therefore a maternal health consumer myself! Reflecting upon my own experiences I realised that I wanted to have a say in how preventive maternal health programs could enable better outcomes for new mothers and their families.

From Anne As an experienced consumer engagement advocate, when I started at Telethon Kids and The University of Western Australia's School of Population and Global Health (UWA) in 2004, I had little knowledge of research. I had been involved in health and education positions since the birth of my youngest daughter, who was born with a disability. I understood the value of including the community voice in planning/delivery of health services and by extension health research. With genuine will from the leaders of both organisations (Telethon Kids and UWA) to increase community involvement in research, along with my strong community networks, I started from a firm base. Being the only role of its kind in Australia at the time, I got advice from the UK's Support Unit INVOLVE, on establishing an involvement program.

By the end of 2005, Advisory Councils were established at both organisations where I worked, to provide advice on increasing involvement. Council membership was 10–12 community members with an interest in research and a wide range of experiences in chronic conditions, disability, mental health and Aboriginal health. They also contributed to international reviews, major grant applications and strategic plans. Research programs spanning alcohol in pregnancy, cerebral palsy and adverse medicine events in seniors also began to include community involvement activities. Since 2007, I have facilitated 190 training workshops, attended by over 3500 people from across Australia. Topics included the importance of community involvement, funding, terminology and contributing effectively to research. Since 2009, these training workshops have been delivered in universities, institutes and community organisations. In 2019 an online module on Foundations of Community

Involvement was developed. When COVID-19 restricted travel in 2020, the remaining modules transitioned to virtual delivery. In 2020, a national Community Advisory Group for COVID-19 rapid research was established in Australia providing community input into several local, national and international projects. Telethon Kids currently has over 500 community members involved in a wide range of activities across the organisation and is supported by a dedicated community engagement team. I am immensely proud of the achievements that have been made to develop and implement this successful involvement program and I am keen to share them with ECRs who are asking how to involve the public in their research.

Defining Engagement

"In the academic context, engagement is about giving non-academic stakeholders the chance to have a say in what research is done, and how and why. This includes dealing with governments, communities and industry" (Moffat, 2017). Engaging the public in research can take many forms depending on your field. For example, your target audience may be health professionals, private organisations, government bodies or consumers of services or products. Critical to effective engagement is clear involvement in decision-making with or by these groups, e.g. decision-making *with or by* consumers (Ocloo & Matthews, 2016). Engagement goes beyond participation in a research project. Rather than being invited to observe or comment on research, the public is part of the process (McKenzie & Hanley, 2014). Engagement is often overlooked and can become a tokenistic gesture – not due to ill intent but due to time (Martinez et al., 2018) and resource constraints, lack of institutional incentives (Shugart & Racaniello, 2015) or uncertainty of how to do it well (Ocloo et al., 2021). However, it is only through the process of effective engagement that mutual goals can be met with significant benefits for your target group (Ocloo & Matthews, 2016). Effective engagement ensures that research is relevant to the people whose lives you are trying to impact (Rifkin, 2014; World Health Organization, 2017).

Our research is predominantly conducted in the health and medical field. Given the diversity of contexts in which researchers work, we will first provide the following definitions to ensure we are all on the same page.

> **The public** – for this purpose we include everybody! Consumers, communities or people with lived experience of health or other issues.
>
> **Community** – People who share a common interest but not necessarily a common location (Campbell & Jovchelovitch, 2000; McKenzie & Hanley, 2014).

> **Stakeholders** – An individual or group with a key interest in the process and outcomes of a project (Deverka et al., 2012).
>
> **Engagement** – we include terms such as involvement, collaboration, co-design, and co-production.
>
> *A useful way to think about engagement is decision-making with or by the public, rather than 'to', 'about' or 'for' them* (Ocloo & Matthews, 2016).

Why Involve the Public in Research?

Clearly you have consulted this guide because you want to involve the public in your research. If not, you should think about doing so! Every stage of the research cycle from deciding what to research, how to do it, doing it, communicating the results and knowing what to do next benefits from public engagement, and this process is cumulative (McKenzie & Hanley, 2014; National Health and Medical Research Council, 2004). Often researchers start engagement activities when they have results to share but fall short of involvement across the entire research cycle (Boaz et al., 2018; Lawn, 2017). Effective knowledge translation is critical for research impact, and early involvement can assist in better meeting the challenges of translation and impact.

Whilst increasing globally, stakeholder and community engagement is not universally adopted (Spencer et al., 2021). When undertaken, it is often done so for ethical, political and methodological reasons. In Australia, funding bodies (and sometimes research ethics committees) request researchers to demonstrate engagement to ensure research is culturally relevant and practically acceptable with real benefits for the people it aims to serve (National Health and Medical Research Council, 2016). Community engagement enhances the quality and appropriateness of all stages of the research process. Above all, it increases the likelihood of research being relevant, accountable, transparent, issue-driven, supported by the community and translated into policy or practice (George et al., 2015; McKenzie & Hanley, 2014; Spencer et al., 2021). Kylie, a consumer advocate who has worked to improve maternity services received by new mothers, clearly articulates the benefits of engagement activities: "Engaging with members of the community and users of health services is vital to ensure research is targeted towards the demographic needing the services" (K. Ekin, personal communication, 2021).

In our workplace, we have both been involved with a program of research that has championed community involvement in research for almost 20 years. This research has focused on alcohol, pregnancy and foetal alcohol spectrum disorders

(FASD) and has included critical partnerships with advocacy groups, consumers with lived experience, Indigenous Australian communities, health services and non−/government organisations. Priority setting projects informed the research program for a National Centre of Research Excellence and ensured the research performed was issue-driven (Finlay-Jones et al., 2020). Research studies have included community-supported approaches to the prevention of prenatal alcohol exposure (Fitzpatrick et al., 2017b; Symons et al., 2020, 2018), the development of an Australian diagnostic tool for FASD (Bower et al., 2017; Watkins et al., 2013), world leading FASD prevalence studies with vulnerable populations (Bower et al., 2018; Fitzpatrick et al., 2017a) and workforce development initiatives (Passmore et al., 2018, 2020). These initiatives have come about due to a continued commitment and understanding that community engagement is critical for community benefit.

Principles of Stakeholder and Community Engagement

There is no universal definition of engagement; however, there are clear principles and ways of working with partners in the pursuit of common goals. These principles go beyond community participation (Tindana et al., 2007). *"Building authentic partnerships, including mutual respect and active, inclusive participation; power sharing and equity; mutual benefit or finding the 'win-win' possibility"* (Zakus & Lysack, 1998) are critical principles of collaborative research. It is always a two-way process involving interacting and listening for mutual benefit (National Co-ordinating Centre for Public Engagement, 2020). Engagement activities must add value, include diverse groups (Wieland et al., 2021) and use language that is accessible for all people (Baines & Regan de Bere, 2018). Ideally, involvement should begin as early as possible (McKenzie & Hanley, 2014).

For vulnerable populations, these principles are of critical importance. For example, when conducting research with Indigenous populations, a participatory research process is recommended – where community members are active participants at every stage of the research process (Parker et al., 2019). Such guidelines recommend the inclusion of cultural knowledge in research under mutually agreed terms and with the guidance of knowledge holders in the community. Australian funding bodies and Health Research Ethics Committees require community involvement from start to finish for research conducted with Indigenous Australian communities (National Health and Medical Research Council, 2018).

Research needs to be useful and have an impact – consumer involvement can help to ensure this. Consumers have valid knowledge inherent to the expertise of their own experience and their knowledge, time and experience must be remunerated (Dahm et al., 2019). For almost 20 years our workplace has had an expectation that community members are paid an honorarium for any out-of-pocket expenses and time. This is based on an underlying principle that community members should not pay to be involved in research that is funded with public money (McKenzie & Hanley, 2014).

Planning for Engagement

So how do you undertake engagement activities when you are an early career researcher and/or new to the field? McKenzie and Hanley (2014) offer the below core questions to help you throughout the planning process – critical to successful engagement.

1. **Why are you involving community members and what do you want to achieve?**

    Involvement activities must add value and be tied to your objectives. In a recent project conducted by our team (Lemon et al., 2021), we wanted to create and pre-test content for health promotion messages about alcohol use in pregnancy prior to piloting them with community members. We established a review panel which included researchers and workforce supporting families impacted by alcohol. This involvement strategy was performed to ensure the accuracy, appropriateness and relevance of the content to be piloted.

2. **What level of involvement are you aiming for and what stage of the research will involvement occur?**

    There are many ways that the public can be meaningfully involved in research. As a researcher you must be clear about the level of involvement you are seeking and the stage you are seeking it at (Sunderji et al., 2019). It is also important to clarify the roles of community members (McKenzie & Hanley, 2014). Will the public be informed about the research to be undertaken? Or will community members actively lead the research? Both approaches are fine depending on the context. In the project we mentioned in point 1, trained community researchers facilitated focus groups with the public as equal partners in the research – and this was highly appropriate. However, community members leading lab-based studies may not be appropriate (McKenzie & Hanley, 2014). Figure 20.1 can be used as a guide to help define the level of engagement you are seeking. This figure has been adapted from the Public Participation Spectrum which classifies engagement from low (e.g. sharing information about research) to high (e.g. community-led research) across a spectrum (International Association for Public Participation, 2018).

3. **How will you find community members?**

    Scan the environment to determine where you can find community members for engagement activities. Community organisations and peak bodies (e.g. health consumer organisations) are generally good places to start! Advertising can be effective but always consider who you are targeting and their preferred communication methods (e.g. social media, radio, websites). Visual mediums are usually better than written words to connect with people and communicate your research. This might include infographics, videos or even the creation of a space where community members feel supported to have a chat and share common interests (O'Neill, 2018). Some examples from community-based participatory action research include community BBQs (Gauld et al., 2011), film screenings

20 How to Engage the Public in Research

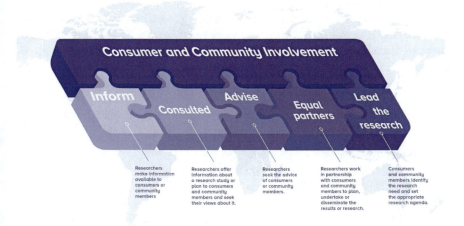

Fig. 20.1 Levels of public involvement. Reproduced from "IAP2 Spectrum of Public Participation 2018 by International Association for Public Participation with permission from Federation of International Association for Public Participation

and collective art projects (Asakura et al., 2020; Ayala & Zaal, 2016). With some populations it may be more appropriate to first connect with grassroots organisations to find and build rapport with your audience. For example, it is common in our field for health professionals to use clinic areas to advertise for vacant involvement positions.

4. **What involvement strategies will you use?**
   Involvement strategies are diverse, and you can be guided by those employed in your field. However, we have described some popular engagement strategies below that may be appropriate to use at different stages of your research.

Reference Groups

A small group of community members who give advice about a specific project. This group may provide advice over the life of the research project or at specific stages, e.g. research planning or knowledge translation (McKenzie & Hanley, 2014). Establishing and consulting reference groups can protect communities and facilitate meaningful research (Quinn, 2004). Members must be remunerated.

Advisory Groups

Although like reference groups, advisory groups tend to provide input across a program of work rather than one specific research project (Consumer and Community Involvement Program, 2020). Advisory groups bring together diverse knowledge and skillsets for public benefit. For example, in a recent research funding application, our advisory group included a consumer representative, the CEO of an advocacy organisation, health services staff responsible for clinical work and strategic planning and two academic staff members. This group assisted in defining the scope of the research and shaping our research questions.

Community Conversations

Several flexible formats exist to host large group dialogue and open conversation around a specific topic (Degeling et al., 2015). World Café methods (The World Cafe, 2021) and town hall meetings (Degeling et al., 2015) provide some examples. The former aims to facilitate open conversation around a specific topic using small group rounds – e.g. four to six people at each table. The environment should be comfortable (like a café!) with a facilitator setting the context. The commentary is captured by a scribe who develops a report from the conversations. Town hall meetings operate using similar aims but tend to include large numbers of the public who deliberate on a specific issue.

Community Researchers and Navigators

Community researchers are people who have been trained to work with researchers. For example, they may assist in the development of study methods, interview community members or co-facilitate focus groups and analyse or interpret results. Community researchers can act like intermediaries (Parker et al., 2019; True et al., 2017). This strategy facilitates practical and valuable outcomes that are important to the community and can be very useful for working with specific groups such as Indigenous peoples or culturally and linguistically diverse (CALD) communities (McKenzie & Hanley, 2014).

Consumer and Community Review

This type of engagement strategy involves consumers or community members providing feedback on research documents such as information sheets, plain language summaries, consent forms and funding applications (McKenzie & Hanley, 2014). If the information contained in these documents cannot be understood by community reviewers, it is likely your research participants will not understand them either! Many funding bodies in Australia require lay summaries of research projects and this is an important skill to develop.

5. **What resources will you need?**

    Once you have considered the above, budget appropriately. Always include expenses for participation activities and honorariums, e.g. remuneration for community reference group members. Budget constraints are one of the leading reasons researchers do not carry out engagement activities (Ocloo et al., 2021). If you are clear about payments at the beginning of the project, you can avoid these pitfalls. Our organisation has processes in place so that researchers can be well-informed, and assisted with budgeting for community engagement. Other organisations may not use formal processes such as this. If not, it is important that you seek out experienced mentors to help you with budgeting tasks.

Conclusions and Practical Recommendations

Public engagement can seem like a burdensome activity – another skill that researchers need to develop as part of an ever-increasing list of requirements. In addition, handing over the reins can be challenging. However, we encourage you to try and integrate engagement activities in your current and future research projects. We promise it will change your research for the better!

If there has ever been a time in your life when you felt vulnerable or wished your voice could be heard by decision-makers, you will easily grasp how lived experience can offer a pragmatic approach and deeper meaning to your research. In my personal experience as an ECR, public engagement is a continual reminder of why we conduct research in the first place. I find this grounding in a field dominated by citation counts, impact factors and competitive research grants.

In conclusion we wish to provide some final points and useful resources so that you can continue to learn about public-oriented research and try it for yourself:

- Speak to people who have lived experience of your research area, or community members united by a common interest. This is an excellent way to begin thinking about the public perspective and the potential impact of your research.
- Seek out internal and external support! There are organisations and processes that exist to support researchers to connect with the public. For example, there may be advocacy organisations in your region that can connect you to members of the public. Many of these are easily found using a quick google search. Some websites and resources that might help you depending on your field include the following:

    International Association for Public Participation
    Cochrane consumer network
    Patient-Centered Outcomes Research Institute
    Canadian Institutes of Health Research
    Australian Health Research Alliance
    National Institute for Health Research

- Remember consumer involvement is now a formal requirement for many research grants schemes. Ensure you are versed in their guidelines.
- Seek out a mentor! The best place to find mentors is within your own organisation with researchers who are already doing involvement – both successfully and not so successfully. There are valuable lessons to be learnt from both groups. At Telethon Kids, a legacy of engagement has shaped ways of working including the way research priorities are generated. As such, there are resources and training available for researchers and the public to access.
- Be flexible and willing to adapt to the needs of your audience – your plan will change, and this is ok!
- Become great at writing plain language summaries of your research. These should clearly define your research aims (e.g. in 80 words or less) and always avoid jargon and acronyms.

References

Asakura, K., Lundy, J., Black, D., & Tierney, C. (2020). Art as a transformative practice: A participatory action research project with trans* youth. *Qualitative Social Work, 19*(5–6), 1061–1077.

Ayala, J., & Zaal, M. (2016). Poetics of justice: Using art as action and analysis in participatory action research. *Networks: An Online Journal for Teacher Research, 18*(1), 2.

Baines, R. L., & Regan de Bere, S. (2018). Optimizing patient and public involvement (PPI): Identifying its "essential" and "desirable" principles using a systematic review and modified Delphi methodology. *Health Expectations, 21*(1), 327–335.

Boaz, A., Hanney, S., Borst, R., O'Shea, A., & Kok, M. (2018). How to engage stakeholders in research: Design principles to support improvement. *Health Research Policy and Systems, 16*(1), 1–9.

Bower, C., Elliott, E. J., Zimmet, M., Doorey, J., Wilkins, A., Russell, V., et al. (2017). Australian guide to the diagnosis of foetal alcohol spectrum disorder: A summary. *Journal of Paediatrics and Child Health, 53*(10), 1021.

Bower, C., Watkins, R. E., Mutch, R. C., Marriott, R., Freeman, J., Kippin, N. R., et al. (2018). Fetal alcohol spectrum disorder and youth justice: A prevalence study among young people sentenced to detention in Western Australia. *BMJ Open, 8*(2), e019605.

Campbell, C., & Jovchelovitch, S. (2000). Health, community and development: Towards a social psychology of participation. *Journal of Community & Applied Social Psychology, 10*(4), 255–270.

Consumer and Community Involvement Program. (2020). *Types of consumer and community involvement*. Retrieved from https://cciprogram.org/researcher-services/types-of-community-involvement/

Dahm, M. R., Brown, A., Martin, D., Williams, M., Osborne, B., Basseal, J., et al. (2019). Interaction and innovation: Practical strategies for inclusive consumer-driven research in health services. *BMJ Open, 9*(12), e031555.

Degeling, C., Carter, S. M., & Rychetnik, L. (2015). Which public and why deliberate? – A scoping review of public deliberation in public health and health policy research. *Social Science & Medicine, 131*, 114–121.

Deverka, P. A., Lavallee, D. C., Desai, P. J., Esmail, L. C., Ramsey, S. D., Veenstra, D. L., & Tunis, S. R. (2012). Stakeholder participation in comparative effectiveness research: Defining a framework for effective engagement. *Journal of Comparative Effectiveness Research, 1*(2), 181–194.

Finlay-Jones, A., Symons, M., Tsang, W., Mullan, R., Jones, H., & McKenzie, A. (2020). Community priority setting for fetal alcohol spectrum disorder research in Australia. *International Journal of Population Data Science, 5*(3), 1359.

Fitzpatrick, J. P., Latimer, J., Olson, H. C., Carter, M., Oscar, J., Lucas, B. R., et al. (2017a). Prevalence and profile of neurodevelopment and fetal alcohol spectrum disorder (FASD) amongst Australian aboriginal children living in remote communities. *Research in Developmental Disabilities, 65*, 114–126.

Fitzpatrick, J. P., Oscar, J., Carter, M., Elliott, E. J., Latimer, J., Wright, E., & Boulton, J. (2017b). The Marulu strategy 2008–2012: Overcoming fetal alcohol spectrum disorder (FASD) in the Fitzroy Valley. *Australian and New Zealand Journal of Public Health, 41*(5), 467–473.

Gauld, S., Smith, S., & Kendall, M. B. (2011). Using participatory action research in community-based rehabilitation for people with acquired brain injury: From service provision to partnership with aboriginal communities. *Disability and Rehabilitation, 33*(19–20), 1901–1911.

George, A. S., Mehra, V., Scott, K., & Sriram, V. (2015). Community participation in health systems research: A systematic review assessing the state of research, the nature of interventions involved and the features of engagement with communities. *PLoS One, 10*(10), e0141091.

International Association for Public Participation. (2018). *IAP2 spectrum of public participation*.

Lawn, S. (2017). What researchers think of involving consumers in health research. *Australian Journal of Primary Health, 22*(6), 483–490.

Lemon, D., Swan-Castine, J., Connor, E., van Dooren, F., Pauli, J., Boffa, J., et al. (2021). Vision, future, cycle and effect: A community life course approach to prevent prenatal alcohol exposure in Central Australia. *Health Promotion Journal of Australia*. https://doi.org/10.1002/hpja.547

Martinez, L. S., Carolan, K., O'Donnell, A., Diaz, Y., & Freeman, E. R. (2018). Community engagement in patient-centered outcomes research: Benefits, barriers, and measurement. *Journal of Clinical and Translational Science, 2*(6), 371–376.

McKenzie, A., & Hanley, R. (2014). *Planning for consumer and community participation in health and medical research: A practical guide for health and medical researchers.* The University of Western Australia.

Moffat, I. (2017). *Pilot study on why academics should engage with others in the community.* Retrieved from https://theconversation.com/pilot-study-on-why-academics-should-engage-with-others-in-the-community-76707

National Co-ordinating Centre for Public Engagement. (2020). *What is public engagement?* Retrieved from https://www.publicengagement.ac.uk/about-engagement/what-public-engagement

National Health and Medical Research Council. (2004). *A model framework for consumer and community participation in health and medical research.* https://hic.org.au/wp-content/uploads/2019/10/HIC-NHMRC-framework-consumer-participation-research.pdf

National Health and Medical Research Council. (2016). *Statement on consumer and community involvement in health and medical research.*

National Health and Medical Research Council. (2018). *Ethical conduct in research with aboriginal and torres strait islander peoples and communities: Guidelines for researchers and stakeholders.* file:///C:/Users/rpedruzzi/Downloads/Indigenous-ethical-guidelines.pdf

O'Neill, M. (2018). Walking, well-being and community: Racialized mothers building cultural citizenship using participatory arts and participatory action research. *Ethnic and Racial Studies, 41*(1), 73–97.

Ocloo, J., & Matthews, R. (2016). From tokenism to empowerment: Progressing patient and public involvement in healthcare improvement. *BMJ Quality & Safety, 25*(8), 626–632.

Ocloo, J., Garfield, S., Franklin, B. D., & Dawson, S. (2021). Exploring the theory, barriers and enablers for patient and public involvement across health, social care and patient safety: A systematic review of reviews. *Health Research Policy and Systems, 19*(1), 1–21.

Parker, M., Pearson, C., Donald, C., & Fisher, C. B. (2019). Beyond the Belmont principles: A community-based approach to developing an indigenous ethics model and curriculum for training health researchers working with American Indian and Alaska native communities. *American Journal of Community Psychology, 64*(1–2), 9–20.

Passmore, H. M., Mutch, R. C., Burns, S., Watkins, R., Carapetis, J., Hall, G., & Bower, C. (2018). Fetal alcohol Spectrum disorder (FASD): Knowledge, attitudes, experiences and practices of the Western Australian youth custodial workforce. *International Journal of Law and Psychiatry, 59*, 44–52.

Passmore, H. M., Mutch, R. C., Watkins, R., Burns, S., Hall, G., Urquhart, J., Carapetis, J., & Bower, C. (2020). Reframe the behaviour: Evaluation of a training intervention to increase capacity in managing detained youth with fetal alcohol spectrum disorder and neurodevelopmental impairments. *Psychiatry, Psychology and Law*, 1–26.

Quinn, S. C. (2004). Ethics in public health research: protecting human subjects: the role of community advisory boards. *American journal of public health, 94*(6), 918–922. https://doi.org/10.2105/ajph.94.6.918

Rifkin, S. B. (2014). Examining the links between community participation and health outcomes: A review of the literature. *Health Policy and Planning, 29*(suppl_2), ii98–ii106.

Shugart, E. C., & Racaniello, V. R. (2015). Scientists: Engage the public! *In* (Vol. 6, pp. e01989–e01915). American Society for Microbiology.

Spencer, J., Gilmore, B., Lodenstein, E., & Portela, A. (2021). A mapping and synthesis of tools for stakeholder and community engagement in quality improvement initiatives for reproductive, maternal, newborn, child and adolescent health. *Health Expectations, 24*, 744–756.

Sunderji, N., Nicholas Angl, E., Polaha, J., & Gao, C. (2019). Why and how to use patient-oriented research to promote translational research. *Families, Systems & Health, 37*, 1–9.

Symons, M., Pedruzzi, R. A., Bruce, K., & Milne, E. (2018). A systematic review of prevention interventions to reduce prenatal alcohol exposure and fetal alcohol spectrum disorder in indigenous communities. *BMC Public Health, 18*(1), 1–18.

Symons, M., Carter, M., Oscar, J., Pearson, G., Bruce, K., Newett, K., & Fitzpatrick, J. P. (2020). A reduction in reported alcohol use in pregnancy in Australian aboriginal communities: A prevention campaign showing promise. *Australian and New Zealand Journal of Public Health, 44*(4), 284–290.

The World Cafe. (2021). *World cafe method*. Retrieved from http://www.theworldcafe.com/key-concepts-resources/world-cafe-method/

Tindana, P. O., Singh, J. A., Tracy, C. S., Upshur, R. E. G., Daar, A. S., Singer, P. A., et al. (2007). Grand challenges in global health: Community engagement in research in developing countries. *PLoS Medicine, 4*(9), e273.

True, G., Alexander, L. B., & Fisher, C. B. (2017). Supporting the role of community members employed as research staff: Perspectives of community researchers working in addiction research. *Social Science & Medicine, 187*, 67–75.

Watkins, R. E., Elliott, E. J., Wilkins, A., Mutch, R. C., Fitzpatrick, J. P., Payne, J. M., et al. (2013). Recommendations from a consensus development workshop on the diagnosis of fetal alcohol spectrum disorders in Australia. *BMC Pediatrics, 13*(1), 1–10.

Wieland, M. L., Njeru, J. W., Alahdab, F., Doubeni, C. A., & Sia, I. G. (2021). *Community-engaged approaches for minority recruitment into clinical research: A scoping review of the literature.* Paper presented at the Mayo Clinic Proceedings.

World Health Organization. (2017). *WHO community engagement framework for quality, people-centred and resilient health services*. Retrieved from Geneva.

Zakus, J. D. L., & Lysack, C. L. (1998). Revisiting community participation. *Health Policy and Planning, 13*(1), 1–12.

Chapter 21
Thinking Like an Implementation Scientist and Applying Your Research in Practice

Andrea K. Graham

Abstract This chapter aims to equip early career researchers with an understanding of implementation science to enhance their capacity to successfully translate their research into practice. Implementation science is the study of methods to facilitate the integration of evidence-based practices into routine practice to improve health services. In this chapter, facets of implementation science are reviewed, namely, how implementation science differs from efficacy and effectiveness research, identifying implementation research questions, building and sustaining research-practice partnerships, testing implementation strategies and monitoring adaptations, measuring implementation outcomes, and sustaining an intervention in practice. Personal examples are provided to exemplify these points. The chapter closes with lessons learned and recommendations for best practices for future early career researchers who are pursuing efforts to apply their research in practice. Recommendations include building equitable collaborations with practice partners; being systematic in applying frameworks, specifying strategies and mechanism, tracking adaptations, and measuring outcomes; embracing flexibility and the likely need for adaptation; and humbly challenging existing paradigms to create impactful change.

Keywords Implementation science · Research-practice partnerships · Intervention · Implementation strategies · Monitoring · Adaptations · Implementation outcomes

Introduction

During graduate school, I had my first opportunity to spearhead a project applying research into practice. My graduate advisor in St. Louis, Missouri, and her collaborator in Palo Alto, California, had conducted several large clinical trials testing

A. K. Graham (✉)
Center for Behavioral Intervention Technologies, Department of Medical Social Sciences, Northwestern University Feinberg School of Medicine, Chicago, IL, USA

© The Author(s), under exclusive license to Springer Nature Switzerland AG 2022
D. Kwasnicka, A. Y. Lai (eds.), *Survival Guide for Early Career Researchers*, https://doi.org/10.1007/978-3-031-10754-2_21

different digital interventions to prevent eating disorders in college-age women. Each digital intervention focused on a different subpopulation of individuals at risk for eating disorders: specifically, a universal prevention program focused on individuals at low risk, a selective prevention program focused on individuals at high risk, and an indicated prevention program focused on individuals at very high risk for eating disorders. Independent trials testing these interventions had shown their efficacy in reducing key symptoms or risk factors implicated in the onset of eating disorders. We also had successfully developed an online screening tool that could be used to identify individuals at varying levels of risk for eating disorders or with a possible eating disorder.

This accumulating evidence got us thinking about the potential to combine these interventions into one platform. We could use our online screen to identify a person's risk profile, from which we could direct them to a program best suited to their needs; individuals with a possible eating disorder would receive a referral to seek further care. Because up until now these interventions had been tested independently of one another, a platform approach would enable managing eating disorders with these different programs across the entire college campus population.

From there, we needed a college who was willing to partner with us to test this platform with their student population. We began meeting with leadership at our two respective universities about the possibility of piloting this platform with students on the two campuses. We met with a broad array of stakeholders about the project, including leaders of student affairs, residential life, and campus health and wellness. Because eating disorders affect not only students' health, but also their coursework and engagement on campus, in addition to their peers, it was important to engage stakeholders across these different facets of university leadership. We needed to ensure the appropriate decision-makers were on board to successfully implement our platform across the campus.

The stakeholders saw the value in our idea and were interested in partnering with us to pilot test this opportunity. Interestingly, the two universities decided to implement the platform in two different ways. At one university, all incoming first-year students would be made aware of the screen through direct emails to all first-year students, along with presentations in the residence halls. At the other university, the screen would be available to anyone on campus (e.g., through presentations, flyers), but not through campus-wide direct emails.

The project successfully launched, and our research team collected data on both implementation outcomes and clinical outcomes. We assessed penetration (the number of students who completed the screen relative to the number of students to whom the screen was made available) as well as results from screening (the number of students who screened as low risk, high risk, or with an eating disorder warranting clinical intervention). Qualitative feedback from students and leadership indicated the platform and implementation were acceptable.

We published the results of this pilot project (Jones et al., 2014) and shared the findings in several presentations to campus leaders and student groups at our universities. Additionally, the relationships and learnings led to the submission of several grant applications, including the team's receipt of two large grants from the United States' National Institutes of Health.

Since this pilot project, I have deepened my understanding of the field of implementation science, through didactic trainings, mentoring relationships, engagement with relevant professional societies, and collaborations on research projects in "real-world" practice settings. I am pleased to share with you what I have learned in this chapter, to enhance your capacity to successfully translate your research into practice through future implementation or applied translational research efforts.

What Is Implementation Science?

Implementation science has been defined as "the scientific study of methods to promote the systematic uptake of research findings and other evidence-based practices into routine practice, and, hence, to improve the quality and effectiveness of health services" (Eccles & Mittman, 2006; page 1). In effect, it is the study of how to help people or places (e.g., organizations) go about *doing* an evidence-based practice. A practice could be one of many things, such as an intervention, policy, procedure, or tool (Lane-Fall et al., 2019). For ease of reference, this chapter will primarily refer to interventions as the practice of focus.

Implementation research is distinct from efficacy and effectiveness research (Curran, 2020; Lane-Fall et al., 2019). Leaders in implementation science have used simple heuristics to describe implementation science and differentiate it from effectiveness research, which are summarized here. Imagine you are studying a digital intervention (an "app") that helps with stress management. The stress management intervention is "the thing" you are focusing on. If you are conducting research to learn if "the thing" *works* to improve stress levels, that is efficacy or effectiveness research. Efficacy research is testing if the intervention works in a research setting, and effectiveness research is testing if the intervention works in a real-world setting. By contrast, if you are conducting research to learn how best to help other people and places *do* "the thing," that is implementation research.

Within implementation science, there are numerous theories and frameworks that can help a researcher understand, organize, and evaluate the implementation of interventions (e.g., Tabak et al., 2012). There also are many different approaches that researchers can use to help people and places do "the thing" in practice; these are called implementation strategies (Powell et al., 2015; Proctor et al., 2013), or more simply, "the stuff we do." Finally, the outcomes of implementation research focus on how well or how much people and places do "the thing."

A relevant example, at the time of writing this chapter, of implementation science in action was the implementation of interventions to address the COVID-19 global pandemic. The onset of the pandemic forced the world to shut down to prevent the spread of disease, which had an unprecedented impact on nearly every aspect of people's day-to-day functioning. Early scientific discoveries showed that wearing a mask could substantially lower people's risk of infection and prevent spread. Therefore, wearing a mask was an evidence-based intervention ("the thing") that people could implement to stay healthy. To help people "do the thing," different implementation strategies were enacted such as requiring masks when entering indoor spaces. Measures of how well mask implementation was working included monitoring if people were wearing masks correctly (fidelity) and assessing the proportion of people wearing masks in various settings (penetration); the distal clinical outcome entailed monitoring rates of infection spread. To improve these outcomes, additional implementation strategies were enacted, like creating visual aids of correct mask wearing and offering free masks as people enter indoor spaces. The arrival of the COVID-19 vaccine saw a similar pattern: once the vaccine (another "thing") was available, numerous implementation strategies were enacted, monitored, and iterated on to promote vaccination.

This example from the COVID-19 pandemic reminds us that having evidence-based interventions available does not mean they will automatically uptake into day-to-day practice. Systematic attention is often needed to ensure successful implementation occurs. With this understanding of what implementation research is, let us now turn to discussing different facets of implementation research, starting with ways to identify an implementation research question.

Filling in Gaps: Identifying an Implementation Research Question

The first step in any research process is knowing if you have a research question that is suitable for study. As was described in the previous section, implementation research "starts" when there are data showing that an intervention is efficacious, and the question now is how to get the intervention to more people. For example, in your line of work, you might imagine asking yourself, "Wow, I have some exciting findings, and I think there are significant implications for helping other people. I want to get my findings out there so that more people in the world can benefit from them. What is the best way for me to do that?" Stated another way, in getting started with translational research, it can help to think about where there are gaps in your and your field's understanding of how to go about making an intervention or an evidence-based practice accessible and available to those who would benefit from it.

Let us go back to the example of the digital intervention for stress management. Suppose you want to implement this app in a network of primary care clinics, and you are wondering how best to get consumers to make the decision to adopt (i.e., initiate, or download) the app. You might be asking yourself the following questions, all of which fall within implementation research:

- Who is the right person in the organization (e.g., nurse, primary care physician, psychologist) to introduce consumers to the app so that consumers decide to download it onto their phones?

- What training is necessary for staff in the organization to have about stress management and the stress management app so they can talk to consumers and help them decide to download it?
- When during a visit to the organization should the app be introduced to consumers (e.g., while in the waiting room, during the session with a provider, after the session, so they are most likely to decide to download it?
- Where in the building should information materials about the app be located so consumers can learn about and most easily download it?

These questions are useful for framing your research study and help the researcher to think about the types of implementation strategies that could be used to help an organization successfully implement the intervention to achieve adoption.

Various research designs can be used to study implementation (Brown et al., 2017). One new group of study designs are known as effectiveness-implementation hybrid designs (Curran et al., 2012; Landes et al., 2019). These designs are relevant for instances when it may be useful to test an intervention for both its effectiveness (that the intervention works in practice) and its implementation (how best to help others do the intervention in practice). Rather than following the standard approach of conducting different trials sequentially to answer these questions, which can take many years, the hybrid designs are being used to assess both effectiveness and implementation concurrently. There are three types of hybrid designs, which are differentiated by whether the trial's primary focus is on effectiveness outcomes (hybrid type 1), implementation outcomes (hybrid type 3), or both (hybrid type 2).

Building and Sustaining Research-Practice Partnerships

Because implementation research focuses on understanding how to help other people and places do an intervention, this work hinges on collaborative work with a practice partner. Therefore, one of the most important components of conducting this work is building and sustaining partnerships. Yet while many organizations may be interested in implementing an intervention, not all organizations want or have the capacity to partner for research. There are several reasons why this may be the case.

For one, people are busy. Organizations have workflows and day-to-day activities that they need to maintain to function, and it may be challenging for an organization to commit to partnering in a research project since it likely involves adding additional activities for an organization to perform. Indeed, as a researcher, it is important to acknowledge the added burden of engaging in research (e.g., attending meetings about the project, contributing to data collection such as through stakeholder interviews or sharing data from consumers) and to recognize that organizations may not have capacity to devote staff time away from regular work activities for these purposes. Although some research projects may provide compensation to the organization for the research activities to help alleviate some of that burden, doing so also could reduce real-world generalizability for how delivering the intervention could be sustained in practice.

Two, there are multiple stakeholders within an organization, and stakeholders may differ in their perceptions of whether or how much of a priority it is to implement an intervention. For example, hospital executives may be excited about adopting your app for stress management, but the behavioral health clinicians may feel concerned about the burden of offering a digital service within their clinic when the rest of their work uses face-to-face delivery. Because of this, it can be essential to establish buy-in and consensus across multiple key stakeholders in an organization, including beyond only those who make decisions about whether to partner in the project. Additionally, organizational priorities can shift over time, meaning that as other changes in an organization may occur, an organization's interest or capacity may diminish to sustain the partnership and/or the intervention's implementation in their practice. Finally, staff turnover within organizations can be common, which is another reason that multilevel buy-in is important.

Three, some organizations may not want to partner in research due to historical injustices that they have experienced when they have previously engaged in research (Harrington et al., 2019). Past relationships with researchers, from your own or related institutions, may have left an organization no better or even worse off than before, without anything to show for their investment in the research. Instead, researchers need to be aware of and acknowledge the historical injustices that may have occurred and be attentive to how they will engage differently and in a meaningful, collaborative manner.

Across all of these potential barriers, it is imperative to engage organizations as partners in this work. Research methodologies exist that promote this type of shared partnership and decision-making, such as community-based participatory research and user-centered design (also sometimes called human-centered design). Rather than approaching the project by saying, "Here's what I want to do," an effective partnership engages the organization in understanding what they want or need with an intervention and research collaboration. Researchers should ask themselves: how will this project benefit the organization and/or the people they serve? How will this project create lasting change that improves something about the organization?

It also is important to collaborate with your partner(s) in considering, from the start, whether the intervention you are implementing is something that can be sustained in the long term, after the project ends. Thinking back to the example of an app for stress management, if you are studying different ways to deliver this intervention in primary care clinics, the organization may have to pay to use the digital program after the project ends, which may not be appealing or feasible for them. By contrast, studying different strategies for training clinicians to deliver evidence-based psychotherapy for stress management has the potential to help the organization after the study ends, because those clinicians now are equipped to deliver the therapy.

Lastly, from the researcher perspective, not all organizations who are interested in implementing an intervention may be viable partners for implementation research. Organizational readiness for change through implementing a new "thing" can be an important indicator for the future success of an implementation project. Assessing organizational readiness may be helpful (e.g., Shea et al., 2014). It also could be the case that an organization is not a good fit for an implementation research project, such as if the organization is too small. Because implementation outcomes assess how well people or places do an intervention, the people or places are the units of analysis; this means randomization occurs at the level of organizational staff/leaders or the organization itself. For example, in your study testing implementation strategies for referring consumers to your stress management app, you may decide to randomly assign the different referral strategies to different clinicians within a clinic or to different clinics within the network. Therefore, to detect meaningful differences in outcomes between the referral strategies, there must be a sufficient number of units (i.e., clinicians or clinics) for randomization. What this means is, to adequately test your research question, you may need to partner with an organization that is large enough to have enough individuals to be participants or you may need to engage several organizations in the project.

Implementing an Intervention: Testing Implementation Strategies and Monitoring Adaptations

When preparing to translate your research to practice, it is important to specify the implementation strategies you will use to implement the intervention (Proctor et al., 2013). Implementation strategies have been referred to as the "how to" component of creating change in a practice. There are numerous implementation strategies that can be applied during the implementation process (e.g., Graham et al., 2020; Powell et al., 2015). The selection of implementation strategies should be based on theories of how that strategy will lead to changes in an implementation outcome(s) (Lewis et al., 2018). Specifying and testing models by which a strategy is hypothesized to lead to changes in proximal and distal outcomes are critical for helping the field understand the mechanisms by which implementation strategies lead to changes in outcomes.

During the process of implementation, it is common for interventions or implementation strategies to be modified to fit the implementation context. While such adaptations may be helpful to ensure that implementation is successful, it is important to document these changes to understand the impact of those changes on the clinical and implementation outcomes as well as to inform future implementation efforts (Miller et al., 2021; Stirman et al., 2013).

Measuring Success: Implementation Outcomes

The outcomes of implementation research focus on how much or how well people or places perform the intervention in practice; these outcomes have been operationalized into eight variables. Detailed definitions of these outcomes have been published (Hermes et al., 2019; Proctor et al., 2011), and brief summaries are provided here.

Acceptability is the perception by relevant stakeholders that an intervention is satisfactory or useful. *Adoption* is the intention or initial decision to use an intervention, or the actual initiation of an intervention. *Appropriateness* is the perception by stakeholders that the intervention is a good fit for the organization, meaning it aligns with the organization's goals or workflows and has relevance to the given context. *Cost* is how much it costs to implement the intervention. *Feasibility* is how possible it is to implement an intervention in the organization; it is the extent to which an intervention can be successfully used in that context. *Fidelity* is how closely the intervention is delivered relative to how it was originally designed and intended to be delivered. *Penetration*, sometimes referred to as reach, is the number of individuals who use an intervention relative to how many individuals are eligible to use the intervention; it is a measure of how well an intervention has been integrated into an organization. Finally, *sustainability* is the degree to which an intervention continues to be delivered in routine practice; in implementation research, this could refer to how well an intervention is maintained in practice once outside support (e.g., from researchers) is removed.

Implementation outcomes differ from patient and service outcomes, which focus on effectiveness, equity, safety, satisfaction, and symptomatology (Proctor et al., 2011). As noted earlier, the effectiveness-implementation hybrid trial designs enable researchers to measure both implementation and effectiveness outcomes.

Sustaining an Intervention in Practice

Earlier in the chapter, there was a call for researchers and their collaborators to consider, from the start, how an intervention that is being implemented will be sustained in practice. This callout is because sustainment is an essential but often neglected component of implementation research (Johnson et al., 2019). Sustainment is the phase of implementation in which an evidence-based practice is delivered as part of usual practice after implementation ends, ideally (within reason) in perpetuity. At this phase of an implementation research project, research supports are removed, and an organization implements the intervention on their own.

Despite the fact that sustainability is a key outcome of an implementation project, it often fails. This can happen for several reasons. For one, the involvement of the research team often enables having access to more human support/labor and resources than would be available under usual circumstances. This means that once the research team leaves, the organization may not have sufficient capacity to deliver the intervention on their own and sustainment may fail. Additionally, the implementation strategies that are successfully deployed to support implementation may not be ones that an organization could realistically and reasonably sustain on their own. For example, if an implementation strategy to deliver an intervention entails hiring new staff, an organization may not be able to support these positions in the long term without outside (e.g., research) funds for deployment. If implementation involves creating new workflow processes for delivering the intervention, the processes may be misaligned to the organization's other workflows, resulting in disruption and potential failure.

To prevent such failures, it is essential that implementation researchers consider sustainability from the very start of the implementation process and iteratively adapt the intervention so it can continue to align to the local context as part of an evolving ecosystem (Chambers et al., 2013). Progress toward sustainability can be benefitted by researchers and organizations talking openly about and reviewing critically how the procedures that are being employed fit within the larger implementation context and then iterating on solutions as needed to ensure continued delivery.

Conclusions: Lessons Learned and Recommendations for Best Practices

This chapter started with a story of a successful implementation project. I will close with one that has left me with regret and will share the resulting lessons learned and recommendations for future research that it spurred. I was in my latter years of graduate school, and some colleagues and I had developed an online intervention for high school students that aimed to prevent eating disorders and promote healthy behaviors for weight management. We then wanted to test it in practice. We established a partnership with a local high school who was interested in offering the intervention. The project successfully launched, and several students in the health classes agreed to participate. They received access to the online program and completed surveys to assess changes in their eating and activity behaviors. The intervention produced favorable results, which were published shortly thereafter.

Because data collection ended, regretfully, the collaboration ended there, too. But, it should not have. When we learned the results of the analyses, we should have returned to the school to share the findings. When we learned the school did not have the resources to sustain the intervention, we should have worked with the stakeholders to identify alternate plans for expanding their health curriculum. These activities are some of the hallmarks of a collaborative partnership, and our team did not engage with the partner beyond the research study to ensure ongoing value to the school.

Going forward, I remind myself of the "should haves" from this project as I embark on new collaborations to apply research in practice. The lessons I learned have helped me reflect on best practice recommendations for early career scientists pursuing translational research, which I share below.

First, be excited and impactful. Translational work aims to address a problem by bringing research findings into practice to benefit people or places in need. As scientists, we are driven to solve problems! As you get started on efforts to translate your research into practice, think about who can benefit from what you know, how they can benefit, and why. Think also about equity and inclusion and the steps you need to take to ensure the translation of your research can offer benefit to all people or places in need. This can help you scope where and how to focus your efforts while also considering the broader potential impact of your work.

Second, be collaborative. Partner with your practice partners. Equitable collaborations are those that occur over the duration of the implementation process, from before the project begins through after the project is done; equitable collaborations respect the experiences and expertise that each party brings to the table. Although good partnerships can be time-consuming to cultivate, the investment is imperative. Relatedly, embrace multidisciplinary collaborations. My career trajectory has been greatly influenced by mentors and colleagues in fields outside my own, especially as it relates to implementation research. Indeed, the field of implementation science draws on many other disciplines to expand its reach and impact, such as behavioral economics, human-computer interaction, psychology, and medicine (e.g., Beidas et al., 2021; Lyon & Koerner, 2016; Tabak et al., 2012). Openness to approaches outside our own are necessary for accelerating our science.

It also helps to leverage existing collaborations and resources to facilitate progress. As an early career investigator, it may be challenging to establish your own networks for research-practice partnerships. I have found it invaluable to work with more senior colleagues on their large-scale implementation projects to gain experience with these processes. Doing so also can open avenues to carve out your own niche project that may be part of a broader program of research.

Third, be systematic. Like any good research project, translational research benefits from systematic approaches to bringing research findings into routine practice. This includes using frameworks, specifying strategies and their mechanisms, tracking adaptations, and measuring outcomes. Documenting the specifics of your work will help advance the field.

Fourth, be flexible. Doing research in the "real world" comes with real-world challenges. Translational research is purposefully less tightly controlled than laboratory-based studies. As you progress through the process of implementation, you may need to adapt your plans along the way. It can be helpful to maintain a flexible mindset that embraces these challenges as opportunities for learning.

Finally, be bold. The field of implementation science emerged from challenging the long-held fallacy that "if we build it [an evidence-based intervention], they will come." With too many interventions failing to be used in practice, researchers realized that systematic attention was needed for studying how to implement interventions. Our fresh perspectives as early career scientists may make us well positioned to challenge paradigms and question existing practices while humbly acknowledging that there is much we do not know and still need to learn. It is such bold thinking that will enable our scientific discoveries to be most accessible to and impactful for those who would benefit from them.

References

Beidas, R. S., Buttenheim, A. M., & Mandell, D. S. (2021). Transforming mental health care delivery through implementation science and behavioral economics. *JAMA Psychiatry*. https://doi.org/10.1001/jamapsychiatry.2021.1120

Brown, C. H., Curran, G., Palinkas, L. A., Aarons, G. A., Wells, K. B., Jones, L., Collins, L. M., Duan, N., Mittman, B. S., Wallace, A., Tabak, R. G., Ducharme, L., Chambers, D. A., Neta, G., Wiley, T., Landsverk, J., Cheung, K., & Cruden, G. (2017). An overview of research and evaluation designs for dissemination and implementation. *Annual Review of Public Health, 38*, 1–22. https://doi.org/10.1146/annurev-publhealth-031816-044215

Chambers, D. A., Glasgow, R. E., & Stange, K. C. (2013). The dynamic sustainability framework: Addressing the paradox of sustainment amid ongoing change. *Implementation Science, 8*, 117. https://doi.org/10.1186/1748-5908-8-117

Curran, G. M. (2020). Implementation science made too simple: A teaching tool. *Implementation Science Communications, 1*, 27. https://doi.org/10.1186/s43058-020-00001-z

Curran, G. M., Bauer, M., Mittman, B., Pyne, J. M., & Stetler, C. (2012). Effectiveness-implementation hybrid designs: Combining elements of clinical effectiveness and implementation research to enhance public health impact. *Medical Care, 50*(3), 217–226. https://doi.org/10.1097/MLR.0b013e3182408812

Eccles, M. P., & Mittman, B. S. (2006). Welcome to implementation science. *Implementation Science, 1*(1), 1. https://doi.org/10.1186/1748-5908-1-1

Graham, A. K., Lattie, E. G., Powell, B. J., Lyon, A. R., Smith, J. D., Schueller, S. M., Stadnick, N. A., Brown, C. H., & Mohr, D. C. (2020). Implementation strategies for digital mental health interventions in health care settings. *The American Psychologist, 75*(8), 1080–1092. https://doi.org/10.1037/amp0000686

Harrington, C., Erete, S., & Piper, A. M. (2019). Deconstructing community-based collaborative design: Towards more equitable participatory design engagements. *Proc. ACM Hum.-Comput. Interact., 3*(CSCW), Article 216. https://doi.org/10.1145/3359318.

Hermes, E. D., Lyon, A. R., Schueller, S. M., & Glass, J. E. (2019). Measuring the implementation of behavioral intervention technologies: Recharacterization of established outcomes. *Journal of Medical Internet Research, 21*(1), e11752. https://doi.org/10.2196/11752

Johnson, A. M., Moore, J. E., Chambers, D. A., Rup, J., Dinyarian, C., & Straus, S. E. (2019). How do researchers conceptualize and plan for the sustainability of their NIH R01 implementation projects? *Implementation Science, 14*(1), 50. https://doi.org/10.1186/s13012-019-0895-1

Jones, M., Kass, A. E., Trockel, M., Glass, A. I., Wilfley, D. E., & Taylor, C. B. (2014). A population-wide screening and tailored intervention platform for eating disorders on college campuses: The healthy body image program. *Journal of American College Health, 62*(5), 351–356. https://doi.org/10.1080/07448481.2014.901330

Landes, S. J., McBain, S. A., & Curran, G. M. (2019). An introduction to effectiveness-implementation hybrid designs. *Psychiatry Research, 280*, 112513. https://doi.org/10.1016/j.psychres.2019.112513

Lane-Fall, M. B., Curran, G. M., & Beidas, R. S. (2019). Scoping implementation science for the beginner: Locating yourself on the "subway line" of translational research. *BMC Medical Research Methodology, 19*(1), 133. https://doi.org/10.1186/s12874-019-0783-z

Lewis, C. C., Klasnja, P., Powell, B. J., Lyon, A. R., Tuzzio, L., Jones, S., Walsh-Bailey, C., & Weiner, B. (2018). From classification to causality: Advancing understanding of mechanisms of change in implementation science [perspective]. *Frontiers in Public Health, 6*(136). https://doi.org/10.3389/fpubh.2018.00136

Lyon, A. R., & Koerner, K. (2016). User-centered design for psychosocial intervention development and implementation. *Clin Psychol (New York), 23*(2), 180–200. https://doi.org/10.1111/cpsp.12154

Miller, C. J., Barnett, M. L., Baumann, A. A., Gutner, C. A., & Wiltsey-Stirman, S. (2021). The FRAME-IS: A framework for documenting modifications to implementation strategies in healthcare. *Implementation Science, 16*(1), 36. https://doi.org/10.1186/s13012-021-01105-3

Powell, B. J., Waltz, T. J., Chinman, M. J., Damschroder, L. J., Smith, J. L., Matthieu, M. M., Proctor, E. K., & Kirchner, J. E. (2015). A refined compilation of implementation strategies: Results from the expert recommendations for implementing change (ERIC) project. *Implementation Science, 10*, 21. https://doi.org/10.1186/s13012-015-0209-1

Proctor, E. K., Powell, B. J., & McMillen, J. C. (2013). Implementation strategies: Recommendations for specifying and reporting. *Implementation Science, 8*, 139. https://doi.org/10.1186/1748-5908-8-139

Proctor, E. K., Silmere, H., Raghavan, R., Hovmand, P., Aarons, G., Bunger, A., Griffey, R., & Hensley, M. (2011). Outcomes for implementation research: Conceptual distinctions, measurement challenges, and research agenda. *Administration and Policy in Mental Health, 38*(2), 65–76. https://doi.org/10.1007/s10488-010-0319-7

Shea, C. M., Jacobs, S. R., Esserman, D. A., Bruce, K., & Weiner, B. J. (2014). Organizational readiness for implementing change: A psychometric assessment of a new measure. *Implementation Science, 9*(1), 7. https://doi.org/10.1186/1748-5908-9-7

Stirman, S. W., Miller, C. J., Toder, K., & Calloway, A. (2013). Development of a framework and coding system for modifications and adaptations of evidence-based interventions. *Implementation Science, 8*, 65. https://doi.org/10.1186/1748-5908-8-65

Tabak, R. G., Khoong, E. C., Chambers, D. A., & Brownson, R. C. (2012). Bridging research and practice: Models for dissemination and implementation research [research support, N.I.H., extramural research support, U.S. Gov't, P.H.S. review]. *American Journal of Preventive Medicine, 43*(3), 337–350.

Chapter 22
Final Thoughts: A Fulfilling Scholarly Career

Dominika Kwasnicka and Alden Yuanhong Lai

Abstract As Early Career Researchers (ECRs), we face many competing demands in our work that require distinct skillsets to effectively be involved in research, acquiring funding, teaching, mentoring, service, professional development or any of the other numerous demands placed on us. We may encounter imposter syndrome. We may want to work towards better work-life balance. We may find ourselves suddenly thrusted into the limelight to talk about our research with the media. This book is foremost an acknowledgement of the challenges that ECRs face, and we have therefore sought to put together a compendium of hacks that you can use to deal with those challenges. In this chapter, we share main themes that have emerged throughout this book: self-discovery, building your support team, having a career strategy and having an impact. These key issues were highlighted by our contributing authors as some of the key drivers to their career success.

Keywords Fulfilling career · Career strategy · Self-discovery · Impact · Social support

Self-Discovery

A starting point for many successful ECRs is understanding themselves as a person. While many of us may have an elevator pitch ready on 'who we are' and 'what we do', we refer to such self-discovery here as a deeper understanding of ourselves and

---

D. Kwasnicka (✉)
SWPS University of Social Sciences and Humanities, Wrocław, Poland

NHMRC CRE in Digital Technology to Transform Chronic Disease Outcomes, Melbourne, VIC, Australia

School of Population and Global Health, University of Melbourne, Melbourne, VIC, Australia

A. Y. Lai
School of Global Public Health and Stern School of Business, New York University, New York, NY, USA

our work. For example, some ECRs may, having spent many years getting a doctoral degree, question if research is really the 'right' career for them. Some of us may, after securing a highly sought-after position at a university, question if they really belong there as compared to the industry or not-for-profit sectors. ECRs can thrive in many career settings but a fundamental step begins with understanding your individual motivations, needs, preferences and life circumstances. Most importantly, people evolve, circumstances change, and life can be unpredictable so you may find the need to rethink your career path and choices.

Several chapters in this book point towards the importance of self-discovery. Alden wrote about assessing one's scholarly identity in Chap. 2, Lauren described the need to reflect on your values to understand what optimal 'work-life balance' looks like in Chap. 3, Mike and Kelsey asserted that your scientific ideas are more likely to become contagious when they are meaningful to you ('do it for the love!') in Chap. 16, and Amy emphasised the need to know your 'why' when making career decisions in Chap. 19. Our peers' wisdom highlights the importance of self-discovery as a process that ECRs should engage in. Finding your answers to some of these self-discovery questions may take weeks, months or even years. You may need the help from others around you (e.g., family, friends, colleagues) in your self-discovery journey. Ultimately, taking time to clarify your 'why' can ensure you have a career that is fulfilling to you.

Building Your Support Team

Another theme throughout this book is the importance of developing and relying on a good support team. To succeed, you need to surround yourself with people who are able to support you and guide you through the twists, turns and curveballs throughout your career. The fact that you are reading this book is a great starting point. In Chap. 6, Laura discussed how to seek mentorship and sponsorship, i.e., people who have power and influence, and are willing to use it on your behalf to promote you. If your workplace does not have anyone who could mentor you, reach out beyond your institution or organization. Anne, in Chap. 7, talked about managing your supervisors to ensure that they are on your side, doing what you need them to do for your projects and research endeavours to be successful. Throughout the book the authors have emphasized that you cannot do it alone: that you need to have your teammates, your coach (supervisor/mentor) and your cheerleading squad (colleagues, friends, family, other academics you can relate to) in order to have a successful career in research.

Elaine, in Chap. 8, talked about networking and collaborating and doing so strategically and (most importantly!) enjoyably. If it happens that things go pear-shaped in your research project (international pandemic or something like that), it is good to have a supportive network to fall onto. It is also crucial to keep in mind that openness, managing expectations, and enjoyment help you develop and foster these supportive networks and will help you keep them going.

In Chap. 12, Sarah also emphasised that when you are writing about your work, it is important to communicate with your supervisor and mentor. Kim (Chap. 13) gave us a good lesson on providing peer feedback – he outlined how to do it in a meaningful and supportive way. You need to keep in mind that people who review your work can benefit from your suggestions but you can also do some harm when providing feedback that is not easy to follow, constructive or relevant.

In several chapters, the authors also pointed you towards specific societies, groups and university infrastructure that you can harness to improve your work. For instance, in Chap. 15, Nikki mentioned how press offices can support you in contacting relevant news outlets, ensuring you present your research effectively and meaningfully to a variety of audiences. We want you to remember that you are never alone, and there are always people around who can help you build a fruitful career and enjoy yourself throughout the process. We have found that even colleagues we have never met before were willing to meet with us as we navigated external funding applications and career changes. Usually you only need to ask, and the worst someone can say is 'no' (but we bet they will try to help in some way).

Having a Strategy

Throughout this book, the authors wrote about having a strategy, i.e., making plans and meaningful decisions that will affect you, your projects and career not only now but in many years from now. Setting yourself up for success is part of this strategy and developing relevant skills is key to thriving in academia. Michael Porter at the Harvard Business School aptly says, *'The essence of strategy is choosing what not to do'*. We love this quote and feel it is a good summary of recommendations of many of our authors. Throughout the book they talked about being selective in terms of what you contribute your time to, what career options you take on, and who you surround yourself with. That is, what you choose *not* to do can be just as important in shaping your career as what you choose to do.

Part of the career strategy can be also recognising what our key strengths are and building on them. Most authors emphasized that you do not need to know it all and do it all yourself – the modern research world emphasises collaborative work over solitary projects. We learn from watching others do their work but we also learn from other sources – the Internet, online tutorials, and international collaborators. They can all be complementing sources of knowledge and wisdom that we have access to. Flexibility and adapting to new challenges are also integral to strategy-setting. Remember, you do not have to stay in academia to be a successful researcher; industry, not-for-profit and other organisations also need us (and Chaps. 17 and 18 covered that). In general, career strategy includes planning what your key aims are and what key decisions and actions can bring you closer to them while cultivating the necessary skills to support you along the way.

We highlighted several skills that we consider crucial for ECRs working in various settings. Apart from the key skills that are commonly emphasised to us throughout our careers such as project management (Chap. 7), networking (Chap. 8) and effective writing (Chap. 12), our authors also covered the skills and trends that are relatively new in terms of impactful ECR training. Emma has explained to us how to develop and adapt Open Science in our work (Chap. 9), suggesting that we all should try to gradually incorporate different Open Science practices to accelerate our careers. Olga demonstrated to us how to be agile in the ever-changing research world (Chap. 10). When we are early in our careers, that may be the best time to experiment, learn and develop skills, and find what our niche is. Most of our contributors suggested that self-development and investing (protected) time in self-development and learning new skills, techniques, and research methods will pay off in the long-term.

Having an Impact

The final theme that we want to highlight here is 'having a real impact'. Oftentimes, our performance as a researcher is evaluated based on our publications, citation metrics and grants, especially when we are based in an academic institution. As a result, many of us may have been conditioned to focus on publications as our primary goal, while knowledge translation, science communication and implementation remain in the background. However, having read the insights from Silja on presenting about your work (Chap. 14), Nikki on engaging with the press and media (Chap. 15), Mike and Kelsey on making your science go viral (Chap. 16) and Rebecca and Anne on engaging the public with our work (Chap. 18), we suspect that a focus on knowledge translation, communication and stakeholder engagement as the end goal, instead of publications, may be a recipe for career success for ECRs.

Concentrating on the impact of our work forces us to focus on research topics that are relevant and meaningful right from the beginning. This is especially relevant when you hope for your research to be applied in real-world settings and, more generally, to improve the society we live in. It shifts our mindset from asking 'How many articles can I write, and which journals can I publish them in?' to 'What do I need to articulate to my stakeholders for them to use my research findings to enact change?' At a time when our performance as researchers is evaluated for scientific impact *in addition* to output, the latter mindset ensures that knowledge translation and stakeholder engagement do not remain an afterthought. It trains ECRs to be more strategic in their research activities, which puts them in better positions for promotion and future opportunities. When you ask yourself 'why are you doing it?'

22 Final Thoughts: A Fulfilling Scholarly Career

and 'what is really important to you?', it will probably remind you that you are set to contribute to new discoveries and to change people's lives. Your work will centre on real-life impact, while journal impact factors[1] and your h-index[2] will only be guideposts of your scholarly progress.

Summary

Imagine yourself at a conference, having a beer or a coffee with one of your peers whose work you admire. You may ask them: 'How did you do so well in your early research career?' In this book, your peers answered this question and provided examples from the psychological, sociological and management sciences along with their own stories and experiences. They provided relevant resources and references that you can look up to expand what you learned on each topic. This book is relevant whether you are considering a career in research, if you are already a PhD student, postdoctoral fellow or otherwise developing your career in the early stages. Building a successful research career requires many 'soft' skills, including management, communication, strategic thinking and resilience. These skills are not usually taught through formal university coursework and some of us may not have access to mentors who can appropriately guide us. This book, written *by* peers *for* peers, highlighted potential challenges you may face, included personal narratives and provided guidance for you to deal with those challenges. We hope you liked it!

---

[1] The impact factor (IF) or journal impact factor (JIF) of an academic journal is a sciento-metric index calculated by Clarivate that reflects the yearly mean number of citations of articles published in the last two years in a given journal, as indexed by Clarivate's Web of Science. We do not recommend that you **solely** use this metric to decide on the quality of the journal and instead consider other metrics and content.

[2] The h-index is an author-level metric that measures both the productivity and citation impact of the publications, initially used for an individual scientist. We do not recommend that you use this metric to compare different scientists. We suggest that you look at the real-life impact that they had.

Index

A
Academia, 2–4, 8–10, 16, 28, 31, 32, 42, 54–61, 71, 87, 89–98, 100, 101, 103, 114, 120, 125–127, 144, 145, 151, 152, 169, 171, 180, 195–203, 208, 214–216, 222, 255
Academic writing, 6, 7, 134–136
Adaptations, 9, 120, 209, 247, 250
Applied research, 8, 199, 200
Audience, 5–8, 17, 71, 91, 92, 94, 96, 100, 110, 126, 134, 136, 138, 139, 155–158, 160–167, 173, 175, 176, 180, 185, 188, 191, 195, 212, 231, 235, 237, 255

B
Behaviour change, 29, 104, 112, 115, 156, 197, 211
Being agile, 4, 5, 109–116, 210
Blogs, 6, 76, 135, 136, 180, 185–187, 191

C
Career development, 64, 65, 91, 152
Career path, 8, 9, 19, 28, 34, 57, 197, 207–216, 221–223, 227, 254
Career planning, 151
Career strategy, 4, 9, 10, 69, 71, 255
Collaboration, 5, 8, 9, 16, 20, 34, 57, 89–97, 99, 101, 103, 105, 136, 137, 157, 165, 166, 170, 198, 199, 201, 202, 226, 232, 243, 246, 249, 250

Communication, 4, 6, 9, 18, 60, 85, 88, 97, 136, 137, 139, 140, 151, 157, 158, 161–163, 180, 189, 190, 200, 209, 211, 212, 230, 232, 234, 256, 257
Community participation, 233, 236
Competencies, 4, 5, 31, 145, 209
Constructive feedback, 111, 145, 148–149, 151, 152
Consumer advocacy, 233
COVID 19, 5, 110–112, 114, 115, 119–121, 124–126, 128, 170, 175, 189, 213, 231, 243, 244
Critical thinking, 6, 143–152, 198, 201, 219
Criticism, 6, 145, 148–152
Curiosity, 5, 42, 114–116, 197

D
Decision-making, 3, 22, 34, 36, 80, 81, 111, 211, 231, 232, 246
Diffusion of Innovation, 113

E
Early career, 15, 28, 59, 77, 126, 127, 146, 225, 250
Early career researchers (ECRs), 2–9, 13–17, 19–23, 27–39, 42–49, 55, 59, 83, 86, 87, 91, 93–97, 100, 103–105, 110–115, 120, 121, 128, 134–138, 145–152, 164–166, 197–199, 201, 203, 212–215, 222, 223, 225, 227, 231, 234, 237, 253, 254, 256

© The Editor(s) (if applicable) and The Author(s), under exclusive license to Springer Nature Switzerland AG 2022
D. Kwasnicka, A. Y. Lai (eds.), *Survival Guide for Early Career Researchers*,
https://doi.org/10.1007/978-3-031-10754-2

Effective writing, 6, 134, 135, 137–140, 256
Engagement, 9, 148–151, 158–163, 165, 190, 199, 203, 210, 230–237, 242, 243, 256
Evaluation, 8, 14, 16, 19, 20, 158, 162, 207–216

F

Feedback, 6, 22, 60, 66, 83, 84, 93, 97, 111, 114–116, 123, 124, 136, 139, 143–152, 166, 175, 183, 230, 236, 242, 255
Flow, 33, 126, 139, 160, 166, 186, 196, 226
Fulfilling career, 253–257
Funding, 2–5, 8, 14, 16, 19–21, 24, 65, 90, 91, 95, 103, 113, 119–129, 157, 162, 166, 171, 208, 210, 211, 213–216, 225, 230, 235, 236, 255
Funding bodies, 8, 101, 209, 211, 213, 215, 222, 232, 233, 236

G

Goal setting, 60, 112, 115
Grant proposals, 6, 123–125, 128, 129, 135
Grants, 5, 6, 9, 14, 20–22, 31–36, 83, 84, 90, 91, 93, 100, 105, 119–129, 134–137, 139, 140, 213, 214, 216, 222, 227, 230, 237, 243, 256

H

Health services, 8, 9, 196, 199, 207–216, 230, 232, 233, 235, 243

I

Impact, 3–6, 8, 10, 18, 19, 33, 64, 65, 70, 71, 81, 87, 89–98, 100, 101, 103, 109–116, 122, 125, 126, 129, 144, 149, 152, 156–159, 161, 163, 170–172, 175, 179–191, 200, 208, 211, 213, 215, 216, 220, 224, 227, 231–233, 237, 243, 247, 250, 256, 257
Implementation outcomes, 9, 242, 245, 247, 248
Implementation science, 9, 243, 244, 250
Implementation strategies, 9, 243–245, 247, 249
Industry, 2, 7–9, 14, 15, 19, 22, 24, 38, 65, 68, 77, 121, 122, 125, 140, 151, 157, 164, 165, 199–202, 208, 214, 215, 223, 231, 254, 255
Innovation, 8, 64, 111, 146, 201, 202, 227
Institutional environment, 2, 13–15, 18, 20, 23, 24

Intellectual humility, 114
Interpersonal resonance, 7, 156–158, 160, 163, 164, 166
Intervention, 9, 100, 110, 144, 197, 198, 201, 242–250
Interviews, 7, 66, 82, 90, 114, 126, 138, 149, 169, 172, 174–176, 236, 245

J

Journal articles, 20, 104, 135

K

Knowledge translation, 9, 211, 212, 216, 229, 232, 235, 256

L

Leadership, 4, 18, 22, 23, 64, 65, 69, 71, 96, 162, 209, 216, 225, 242
Living review, 110–113, 115

M

Managing people, 82–86
Managing process, 4, 80–82
Media, 6, 7, 22, 113, 116, 137, 139, 170–176, 256
Media training, 173, 176
Mental health, 4, 28, 31, 33, 39, 42, 43, 87, 88, 91, 230
Mentoring, 2, 20–22, 24, 30, 91, 95, 96, 137, 151, 158, 161, 211, 243
Mentorship, 21, 22, 24, 68, 69, 94, 151, 161, 208–210, 214, 215, 254
Mind-body connection, 7, 156, 158–160, 166
Monitoring, 82, 244, 247
Motivation, 16, 43, 56, 70, 79, 134, 181, 254

N

Networking, 4, 5, 17, 31, 54, 89–98, 124, 161, 213, 254, 256
Not for profit, 8, 9, 196, 207–216, 254, 255

O

Open Access publishing, 5, 105
Open Data, 105
Open Materials, 102
Open peer review, 104, 113
Open science, 5, 7, 85, 92, 100–106, 110, 111, 113, 183, 191, 212, 256
Open-Source Software, 102

Index

Opportunity, 3, 6–9, 15, 23, 35, 42, 48, 56–58, 60, 61, 65–68, 70, 71, 90–98, 104, 112, 114–116, 121, 122, 124, 126, 136, 151, 157, 160, 161, 164–166, 170, 171, 174, 181, 196–198, 200–202, 208, 209, 211–216, 220–227, 241, 242, 250, 256

P

Peer review, 6, 100, 115, 116, 135, 140, 143–152, 213
Planning, 4, 31, 46, 58–60, 77, 79, 80, 85, 87, 103, 112, 114, 115, 209, 210, 230, 234, 235, 255
Pre prints, 5, 110, 111
Preregistration, 5, 101, 103, 104, 106
Presenting, 6, 7, 146, 155–167, 179, 180, 198, 230, 256
Press, 6, 7, 22, 23, 171, 185, 212, 255, 256
Professional development, 2, 15, 18, 23, 24, 30, 69, 71, 96, 161
Project management, 4, 60, 61, 75–77, 81, 82, 85, 87, 256
Public participation, 234, 235, 237
Public speaking, 157, 164
Publication, 19, 61, 84, 100, 101, 103, 110, 111, 137, 138, 144, 145, 149, 171, 183, 191, 208, 212, 213, 216, 227, 256, 257

R

Recovery experiences, 43, 45–49
Recovery from work, 31, 38, 42–49
Registered Reports, 102
Rejection, 5–7, 90, 98, 120, 135, 144–145, 149, 150, 152, 159, 222
Reports, 22, 103, 135, 136, 138–140, 151, 164, 180, 197, 198, 203, 209, 214, 215, 236
Research, 2–10, 14–24, 29–31, 44, 46, 54–61, 65, 68, 75–87, 89–96, 99–106, 109–115, 119–129, 133–135, 137, 138, 140, 146, 148–152, 156–159, 161–166, 170–172, 174, 179–191, 195–203, 207–216, 219–227, 229–237, 241–250, 254–257
Research Dissemination, 6–8
Research practice partnerships, 245–247, 250
Research skills, 4, 5, 111, 198, 221

S

Scholarly identity, 2, 3, 13–15, 17, 18, 20, 21, 23, 24, 254
Science communication, 7, 70, 190, 191, 256
Science dissemination, 6
Self discovery, 253, 254
Service, 2, 3, 8, 18, 19, 22–24, 54–61, 100, 125, 202, 208, 210, 211, 213, 214, 231, 232, 246, 248
Skills acquisition, 112–113
Sleep, 30, 33, 42, 46–49, 139
Social media, 6, 96, 97, 109, 115, 183–187, 191, 234
Social networks, 33, 97
Social support, 33, 46, 91, 148, 151
Start-ups, 8, 14, 196, 202
Strategy, 3, 4, 6, 9, 28, 29, 34, 38, 54, 57–61, 65, 81, 84, 86, 103, 120, 134, 135, 138, 188, 221, 226, 234–236, 246, 247, 250, 255, 256
Systematic reviews, 91, 100, 135

T

Teaching, 2, 3, 5, 14, 16, 18–24, 28, 30, 54–61, 76, 80, 101, 124, 165, 210, 223, 224
Time management, 4, 33, 34, 36, 60, 69, 77, 137
Transferable skills, 87

W

White papers, 6, 136, 137
Work–life balance, 215, 216, 254
Work–life balance inventory, 38, 39
Writing habits, 137
Writing skills, 91

Printed in the United States
by Baker & Taylor Publisher Services